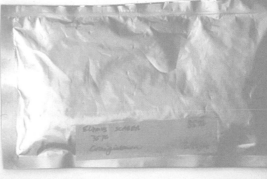

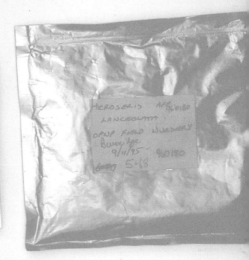
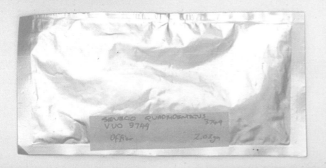

AUS TRALIAN PAVILION 2018

AUSTRALIAN INSTITUTE
OF ARCHITECTS
AUSTRALIAN PAVILION
BIENNALE ARCHITETTURA
2018

CREATIVE DIRECTORS
Baracco+Wright Architects
in collaboration with Linda Tegg

VERNISSAGE
24-25 May 2018

EXHIBITION
26 May-25 November 2018

AUSTRALIAN INSTITUTE
OF ARCHITECTS
AUSTRALIAN PAVILION
COMMISSIONER
Janet Holmes à Court AC

PUBLISHED BY
ACTAR PUBLISHERS
440 Park Avenue South, 17th fl.
New York, NY 10016, USA
www.actar.com
www.urbannext.net

CO-PUBLISHER
Australian Institute of Architects
Level 1, 41 Exhibition Street
Melbourne Victoria, 3000
Australia

WEBSITE
architecture.com.au/
venicebiennale

EDITORS
Mauro Baracco and
Louise Wright

ESSAYS
Giovanni Aloi
Mauro Baracco
David Freudenberger
Carroll Go-Sam
Susie Kumar
Paul Memmott
Catherine Murphy
Tim O'Loan
Caroline Picard
Chris Sawyer
Lance van Maanen
Jonathan Ware
Louise Wright

SUBEDITOR
Catherine Murphy

GRAPHIC DESIGN
Studio Round

AUSTRALIAN INSTITUTE
OF ARCHITECTS
VENICE BIENNALE COMMITTEE
Jill Garner (Chair)
Luca Belgiorno-Nettis
Clare Cousins
Janet Holmes à Court AC
Helen Lochhead
Ken Maher
Rachel Neeson

AUSTRALIAN INSTITUTE
OF ARCHITECTS
PROJECT MANAGER
Miranda Grace

ISBN
978-1-948765-00-8
PCN number: 2018935353
A CIP catalogue record for this
book is available from Library
of Congress, Washington,
D.C., USA

PRINTING
DAI Singapore

DISTRIBUTION
Actar D, Inc.

New York
440 Park Avenue South, 17th Floor
New York, NY 10016, USA
+1 2129662207
salesnewyork@actar-d.com

Barcelona
Roca i Batlle 2
08023 Barcelona, SP
+34 933 282 183
eurosales@actar-d.com

CULTURAL WARNING
Aboriginal and Torres Strait
Islander people are warned
photographs in this book may
contain images of deceased
persons which may cause sadness
or distress.

(Back cover)
Photograph, Linda Tegg.

(Endpaper)
Packets of seed used to make
Grasslands Repair.
Photograph, Linda Tegg.

(Endpaper)
Acacia melanoxylon,
growing for *Grasslands Repair*.
Photograph, Linda Tegg.

REPAIR

AUS
TRA
LF
2018

Architecture actively
engaging with the repair
of the places it is part of

Edited by Mauro Baracco
and Louise Wright

Australian Institute of Architects
Australian Pavilion
Biennale Architettura 2018

Creative Directors
Baracco+Wright Architects
in collaboration with Linda Tegg

**Australian
Institute of
Architects**

CONTENTS

ESSAYS

FROM THE AUSTRALIAN INSTITUTE OF ARCHITECTS
AUSTRALIAN PAVILION COMMISSIONER
Janet Holmes à Court AC

What a privilege to have been invited once again to act as Commissioner for Australia for the 16th International Architecture Exhibition of La Biennale di Venezia. I sincerely thank the Australian Institute of Architects for this opportunity. As usual, it has been both interesting and exciting working with the Australian Institute of Architects Venice Biennale Committee, so ably led by Victorian Government Architect Jill Garner, to sift through numerous applications and choose creative directors to represent Australia in the stunning pavilion in the Giardini in Venice in 2018.

To watch as the ideas of the Creative Team crystallised, has been immensely satisfying. Louise Wright, Mauro Baracco (Baracco+Wright Architects) in collaboration with artist Linda Tegg, represent Australia at the 2018 Venice Biennale.

They were most fortunate in that the overall theme chosen by this year's international curators, Shelley McNamara and Yvonne Farrell, was announced far earlier than in previous years, and so was known to them when preparing their application. That theme is *Freespace*, and I believe Louise, Mauro and Linda have responded to it sensitively and superbly.

In the 230 years since the colonisation of Australia, enormous damage has been done to this continent – or to paraphrase Tim Winton, 'our island home'.(1) The land which our Indigenous people had nurtured for over 70,000 years has lost 40 per cent of its forests and woodlands; more than half the wetlands have been destroyed, thirty mammals, native to this country, have become extinct – feral predators have been implicated in twenty-eight of these extinctions. The felling of billions of trees to make room for farming has caused salinisation of an estimated 30 per cent of the land area, making farming difficult, if not impossible. Miners, farmers, timber millers, developers and town planners have all played a role in this degradation. Architects have not been innocent.

Repair is needed right now in Australia, and this is the theme the exhibition in our Australian Pavilion is investigating. I congratulate the Creative Directors in illustrating so insightfully how they, and many other architects, are working across disciplines with ecologists, landscape architects, horticulturalists and others to commence the repair we so desperately need.

(1) Winton, T 2015, *Island Home: A Landscape Memoir*,
      Penguin, Melbourne, Victoria, Australia.

FROM THE AUSTRALIAN INSTITUTE OF ARCHITECTS VENICE BIENNALE COMMITTEE CHAIR
Jill Garner

I was thrilled to be an architectural tourist in Venice when Australia's new pavilion proudly hosted its first Biennale Architettura in 2016 – the immersive experience of *The Pool*. To see Venice (with its own mythologies of architecture and place) threaded with contemporary architectural encounters from all over the world was exhilarating. It is not just the Giardini's pavilions (wonderful architectural moments that represent decades of design response) that are layered with current architectural thinking – the city's galleries, its warehouses, even the hidden spaces within its palazzos, are filled with provocative exhibitions. Important issues are on display and shared, and the city's streets and cafes play host to discussions imbued with an architectural theme.

Australia's exhibition for 2018 is *Repair*, curated by Louise Wright, Mauro Baracco (Baracco+Wright Architects) in collaboration with Linda Tegg. *Repair* was inspired by a provocation from this year's overarching theme *Freespace* which prompted the Australian Creative Directors to consider the relationships architecture effects and how it impacts, or is impacted by, nature, advocating a role for architecture that catalyses or actively repairs the place it impacts.

Repair will fill the Australian Pavilion with an exhibit that immerses architecture in a landscape of threatened grass species – reminding us what is at stake. There are many people to thank for their input to the project. I am indebted to the Australian Institute of Architects for its leadership and coordination, the Australian Institute of Architects Venice Biennale Committee for their considered participation, the architecture and building community, governments and partners for their generous support. It has been a delight to work with Janet Holmes à Court AC in her role as Australian Pavilion Venice Biennale Commissioner.

Above all, I would like to thank and congratulate the creative team – Louise, Mauro and Linda – for their vision, passion, and commitment and for embracing the challenge of being in the international spotlight with an important and timely message.

The Australian Institute of Architects is proud to once again host the Australian Pavilion at the 16th International Architecture Exhibition of La Biennale di Venezia. Perhaps more than at any previous Biennale, the Australian Pavilion exhibition, *Repair*, goes to the heart of our goal – to make the world a better place through architecture. Curated by Creative Directors Mauro Baracco and Louise Wright (Baracco+Wright Architects) in collaboration with artist Linda Tegg, *Repair* talks to the impact of architecture on the environment. Through a unique live and immersive experience, it explores an emerging approach to architectural thinking that examines how architecture can play a role in repairing the places it is part of from a uniquely Australian perspective.

As the Creative Directors have highlighted, Australian architects practise in one of the most diverse and ecologically sensitive landscapes in the world. As an island, not flush with water but surrounded by it, what is our capacity to cope with a big population given our natural resources? *Repair* will highlight the critical role architects have in the design, planning and engineering of our continent for future generations. This is a conversation the Institute is delighted to facilitate and one which we look forward to leading beyond the duration of Biennale Architettura 2018.

Importantly, the Australian Pavilion provides an unrivalled platform for showcasing Australian architecture as a globally competitive industry and one of exceptional innovation. It offers an unparalleled opportunity to promote our architects on the world stage while at the same time offering them the chance to network and collaborate.

The Institute is deeply engaged in the development, promotion and delivery of the installation in the Australian Pavilion. The very nature of this project is a collaboration; an exchange of ideas and sharing of information. The appointment of the Creative Directors, their extended team and the personnel surrounding the Australian Pavilion installation could not be achieved without such a collaborative approach.

We are pleased this Architecture Biennale is able to offer educational opportunities as an extension of the exhibition, as well as hands-on experience by working at the Australian Pavilion. Our exhibition offers the chance to engage not only with the architectural profession, including Institute members, but also students, emerging architects and the wider community. This engagement extends across the entire built environment profession. Through diverse conversation, exposure and participation networks are built on an international stage. Such development promotes greater collaboration between local and international architects and built environment specialists.

The Australian Pavilion provides a platform for discussion that provokes questions, ideas, and potential works.

The Institute also engages thirty volunteers who are architecture students and graduates. These volunteers have the opportunity to work for three to four weeks at a time in the Australian Pavilion alongside the Creative Directors and their extended team. This unique experience enables skills, experience and networks to be enhanced.

By engaging with various organisations, associations and architecture professionals, this collaborative exhibition will showcase one theme through a variety of touch points. The installation will evoke sensory as well as traditional engagement. *Repair* will spark conversation which will directly create the exchange of ideas and in turn knowledge sharing.

Our intention with this Australian Pavilion exhibition is to increase our level of engagement with the wider community, from the perspective of participation, information access and inclusion. We will achieve this through the engagement of both a local and international public relations agency to expose the project to the widest possible audience, in Australia and abroad. By leveraging the opportunity the Architecture Biennale affords, we will enhance appreciation of the value our profession has in the communities and cities in which we work and which we help shape for the future.

INTRODUCTION
Mauro Baracco and Louise Wright

Freespace + Repair

Responding to the theme *Freespace*(1) at the 16th International Architecture Exhibition of La Biennale di Venezia, *Repair* at the Australian Pavilion aims to expand the point of view from the object of architecture, to the way it operates in its context. In so doing, we are advocating a role for architecture that catalyses or actively engages with the repair of the places it is part of: the soil, hydrology, habitat, connections, microorganisms, vegetation and so on. This type of repair is central to enacting other types of repair: urban health, social, economic and cultural among others.

The aim to present architecture from a different point of view was behind the decision to collaborate with artist Linda Tegg, whose practice often presents us with a different way of looking. Together, we have created three 'works': *Grasslands Repair*,(2) a living installation of over sixty species of Western Plains Grassland plants – the most threatened plant community in Australia – that aims to disrupt the point of view to reveal the (symbolic) landscapes that we destroy; *Skylight*, a life-sustaining lighting installation consisting of LED lights that hovers over *Grasslands Repair* as an artificial 'skylight'; and videos of selected Australian built and unbuilt projects in *Ground* – directed and made by Tegg with David Fox – that present architecture that respond to ideas of repair.

To assist us in exploring this theme for the Australian Pavilion, a broad team – described below – was assembled, who have contributed in widening the investigation of the notion of 'repair' through reflections on architecture, landscape architecture, urban design and ecology from unconventional positions to the theme 'repair'.

The ambition of *Freespace* is above all about generosity, thoughtfulness and a desire to engage. The curators, Shelley McNamara and Yvonne Farrell, describe examples where architects go a step further than they might have to create a moment, to engage with a place, to register light. To us the act of repair is the extra act embodied by *Freespace*. In this way, and the curators state, they are interested in "going beyond the visual"(3) to dwell upon the relationships architecture can make, frame and reveal between ourselves, where we live, how we live, and with nature.

Freespace is, at the same time, about the affirmation of the role of architecture, what it has to offer and what it is capable of. *Repair* addresses Farrell and McNamara's call "to stimulate discussion on core architectural values"(4) and to validate the "relevance of architecture on this dynamic planet".(5)

The curators have asked Biennale participants to "encourage reviewing ways of thinking, new ways of seeing the world, of inventing solutions where architecture provides for the well being and dignity of each citizen of this fragile planet".(6) In response, *Repair* exhibits architectural provocations alongside an installation of thousands of undervalued and threatened plant species from Western Plains Victorian Grasslands (south-east Australia),(7) revealing what is at stake when we occupy land, and reframing how we see and value our environment and architecture's role, and therefore, how we might make it.

Repair

Repair: "restore (something damaged, faulty, or worn) to a good condition".(8)

What can 'repair' mean to us, given the extensive state of disrepair of the environment in Australia and inability to reverse history and complex ecological change processes? Where is the role for architecture?(9)

Repair, as described above, is not defined as restoring to an original or pre-existing condition, but rather to a 'good' one. What might it look like to 'make good' our soil, hydrology, landscape systems across small and large scales within, around and outside the built environment, and to address the health of endemic species in urbanised and semi-urbanised environments?

Our aim and provocation is that through a primary approach of the repair of the natural environment, human physical and mental health, social, economic and cultural health will in turn be repaired through the care required to do so, and the connection to and presence of nature in our everyday lives. While most of our focus has been on achieving repair outcomes through addressing the natural environment, we have also been interested in an expanded idea of cultural, social or economic repair; examples of this include the reuse of old buildings, the remediation of industrial land and the presence of indigenous culture in our cities. We have chosen to include some examples of such repair as this approach perhaps offers a more accessible and achievable way for architects to engage with repair.

At the centre of the theme *Repair* at the Australian Pavilion is the fact that architecture takes up land and effects the natural environment.(10) A statement so obvious it should go without saying – and yet in order to consider the consequences and potentials of architecture in relation to repair, we need to focus on this very elemental fact.

Since we have been making buildings and cities in Australia it has mostly been to separate – to divorce – us from our position (as human beings) in the natural environment. Since we have been practising western agriculture it has been at the expense of the indigenous ecosystem. The consequences of the disregard of natural systems are now being felt and there is a shift in thinking among built environment disciplines towards repairing the natural environment as a meaningful and enduring framework for urban form – an expansion of the natural environment in a sort of reverse order of urban sprawl.

We are faced with the need to repair (and that might mean adapt) beyond and within the (mostly) built environment of our cities. Distinctions between 'city' and 'country' are now blurred, and we understand that our decisions have an impact at both micro and macro scales. The problem of repairing is discussed in this catalogue/book between the seemingly disconnected micro and macro in Australia: between the large scale landscape reparation required of land, waterways and oceans and the smaller scale, say at the building and 'site' scale, needed to repair more immediate contexts. This connection at scale is rarely articulated and certainly is rarely part of architectural dialogue or ambition; we have sought to let these often distinct discussions run in parallel, occasionally crossing, as ultimately we think the argument is made for the role of the very small in the very large, and the need to act no matter how small or ambitious.

The process of preparing this exhibition has unearthed a lot of uncertainty in our team about how to act, and at various points a kind of paralysis set in as we are keenly aware that others have been active in this field for a long time, and to consider a contributory role for architecture is full of complexity. What has emerged is that we are at a moment in time where we know we cannot go backwards, where we accept an idea of a novel ecology (more on this later), but where we are grappling with the nuance required in an Australian context and that ultimately we need to engage with the concept of repair.

As such, we have conviction that repair as an approach to architectural thinking is set to become a critical strategy of architectural culture.(11) It is particularly relevant to Australian architects who work cheek-by-jowl in one of the most diverse and ecologically sensitive landscapes in the world, but often have limited tools or capacity to act. Our cities are interspersed and bordered by remnant vegetation and often connected to large natural systems, as well as built over the traditional cultural landscapes of our First Nations peoples.(12)

We (the Creative Directors) have often struggled with our relationship as architects in the use of land. This is no small act. For some time, we have been thinking about this in our office, teaching and research activities. We do not have any definitive solutions. Our hunch is that it requires transdisciplinary methods, a coming together across disciplinary boundaries, and a widening of the architectural knowledge base to a front-end, detailed understanding of a site across multiple scales, where the very small scale action has a role in the larger scale, and a facilitation of repair of the environment through the many decisions we make. It also requires leadership in planning and governance so that barriers to repair such as the incompatibility of legal boundaries with natural ones, and the questioning of whether we should even be building in a particular place can be addressed.

The land management profession, landscape architects and urban ecologists among others are actively working on repairing the natural environment, yet architects are rarely present in this discussion and activity. We keep wondering what the role for architecture might be. In fact, this catalogue/book, is full of questions.

To separate professions (as we have listed above) is indicative of one of the problems in how we make the built (and how we make the 'natural') environment in Australia. We mark out and act in our disciplinary 'territory' with fervour. It seems this is most strongly felt between architects and landscape architects, a distinction many other countries do not spend too much energy on. This sets up barriers to meaningful collaboration which will be required if architecture wants to evolve to be a part of acts of repair; landscape architects have been working in this area and are more advanced in their understanding of the problems. If architects are not able to change their processes to include landscape modes and knowledge bases, we risk what architects often do (to many disciplines), which is to assume a quasi-landscape architect role without real engagement.

When we first proposed the theme *Repair*, we were not sure how many architects in Australia were engaging with these ideas. The process of choosing projects for exhibition involved an open invitation for submissions and the response revealed that a lot of people are thinking carefully about diverse types of repair. Australian architects, landscape architects, urban designers, planners and policy makers are deeply embedded in addressing very complex, diverse and unique issues facing our built and natural environment, which all contribute in one way or another to the types of repair we have listed. At the same time, reviewing them raised a lot of questions around whether or not repair was being effected, especially that of the natural environment and especially whether or not the architecture had much to do with it.

Over the six months or so leading up to the production of this catalogue/book our position has shifted, as you would hope when you have a lot of people weighing in. It has become more nuanced and we hope the different voices in this catalogue/book reflect this. *Repair* is a theme of possibilities, suggestions and above all provocation.

Creative Team

David Freudenberger, Paul Memmott, Tim O'Loan, Catherine Murphy, Chris Sawyer, Lance van Maanen and Jonathan Ware have joined us and contributed closely to the conceptual framing and discussion through their expertise in architecture, landscape architecture, urban design, ecology and Indigenous culture to provide a broad filter to the gaps, possibilities and issues. In addition to these, Giovanni Aloi and Caroline Picard have been invited to discuss Linda Tegg's approach, and Carroll Go-Sam to share her insights on Indigenous architecture involved with the repairing practices. Susie Kumar has provided balanced and gracious insight. David Fox has worked quietly and solidly with

Tegg to collaborate on the video *Ground*. Many others have provided generous and invaluable assistance.(13)

This Catalogue/Book

This catalogue/book is more than just a cataloguing of the exhibition. It is a chance to capture the country's theme providing a legacy that can stand somewhat alone beyond the dense Biennale experience and the limitations of exhibition.

We have used the catalogue/book in this way, unpacking the theme *Repair* through the diverse lens of our team and invited authors. In our contribution we provide an overview of the challenges and possibilities to repair (the natural and urban environment), focussing in particular to the relationship between open vegetated and built space. In addition to this essay, through an additional text with Linda Tegg, we explain the conceptual underpinnings of our collaborative installations; Paul Memmott explores ways by which contemporary Australian architects (including Indigenous ones) are attempting to achieve cultural repair employing an ethnographic historical narrative technique centred on the south-east Australian grassland; Dyirbal(14) researcher Carroll Go-Sam explores case studies of Australian architecture (for and by Indigenous) that combine forms of both environmental and cultural sustainability; David Freudenberger sets the scene of large scale environmental repair; Chris Sawyer and Susie Kumar reflect on the issues facing them in their profession as landscape architects, providing an insight to the issues architects can engage with; Tim O'Loan discusses repair of our urban environments as the logical next phase in Australian cities and the need for a shared lexicon; Giovanni Aloi connects Tegg's work with a capacity to recover alternative gazes that can lead to a substantial rethinking of our relationship with the living, and Caroline Picard brings this practice to life in an interview with Tegg; Lance van Maanen and Jonathan Ware conduct an enquiry into what repair as an approach to architecture might mean for the future of how we practise; and Catherine Murphy reveals the background and making of *Repair* at the Pavilion. Contextualising these discussions, the exhibited projects are indeed catalogued and present approaches to repair.

How built and open space designers can repair will be an exciting and critical development of architecture not yet fully imagined.

(1) The title *Freespace*, assigned by the general curators Yvonne Farrell and Shelley McNamara (Grafton Architects, Dublin) to the 16th International Architecture Exhibition of La Biennale di Venezia, also refers back to the notion of "free space" as used by Cedric Price (and others) to describe a condition of the project Fun Palace (1959-1961) – it implies an anti-architect approach to space that privileges the user and flexibility. See Mathews, S 2007, *From Agit-Prop to Free Space: The Architecture of Cedric Price*, Black Dog Publishing, London, UK.

(2) *Grasslands Repair*, includes the word "repair" to distinguish it from *Grasslands*, a work by Tegg in 2014. See Linda Tegg 2014, *Grasslands*.

(3) Farrell, Y & McNamara, S 2017, '16th International Architecture Exhibition, Biennale Architettura 2018, Freespace', *La Biennale di Venezia*, viewed 15 June 2017, <www.labiennale.org/en/architecture/2018/16th-international-architecture-exhibition>.

(4) Ibid.

(5) Ibid.

(6) Ibid.

(7) The state of Victoria (capital city: Melbourne) is located in the south-east corner of Australia.

(8) English Oxford Living Dictionaries n.d., *repair*, English Oxford Living Dictionaries, viewed 9 April 2017, <https://en.oxforddictionaries.com/definition/repair>.

(9) The projects are architectural as well as by combined teams of landscape architects and architects. The main aim of the exhibition was to provoke the role of architecture, acknowledging that the landscape architecture profession has been addressing notions of repair for a long time.

(10) "Natural environment means all living and non-living things that are natural." See Wikipedia n.d., *Natural environment*, Wikipedia, viewed 15 January 2018, <https://simple.wikipedia.org/wiki/Natural_environment>.

(11) We invited two young architects, Jonathan Ware and Lance van Maanen to be part of the Creative Team to gain their perspective on what will be a dominating aspect of their careers – see their contribution in this catalogue/book in the form of a conversation with other young practitioners.

(12) "Aboriginal people on the continent now known as 'Australia' are not the 'First Australians', they are made up of peoples from the First Nations that all have their own specific names, and in many instances, speak/spoke their own specific language. Therefore as a group they are the First Nations peoples or Original peoples", also called Indigenous Australians and Aboriginals and Torres Strait Islanders. See Sovereign Union - First Nations Asserting Sovereignty n.d., *The difference between the 'First Australians' and the 'First Nations'*, Sovereign Union - First Nations Asserting Sovereignty, viewed 28 January 2018, <http://nationalunitygovernment.org/content/difference-between-first-australians-and-first-nations>.

(13) Individual biographies of the Creative Directors and the collaborative team can be found at the end of this catalogue/book.

(14) The Dyirbal are an Indigenous Australian people living in Queensland. See Wikipedia n.d., *Dyirbal people*, Wikipedia, viewed 27 January 2018, <https://en.wikipedia.org/wiki/Dyirbal_people>.

(Overpage) *Ground*. Photograph, Linda Tegg. View from Melbourne's northern grasslands towards the city.

ESSAYS

REPAIR:
THE MICRO/MACRO
CONTINUUM

MAURO BARACCO
AND LOUISE WRIGHT

Grassland in flower (*Stackhousia*) and urban waste,
Altona, Melbourne.
Photograph, Louise Wright.

Australia is one of the most biologically diverse countries on the planet. It is home to more than one million species of plants and animals, many of which are found nowhere else in the world, and less than half have been described scientifically. About 85% of flowering plants, 84% of mammals, more than 45% of birds, and 89% of inshore, freshwater fish are unique to Australia. Destructive feral populations have long established in Australia, with at least eighteen exotic mammals including cats and foxes responsible for the decline and extinction of several native animals. As well, at least 2,700 non-native plants have established populations in Australia; of these, 68% are considered a problem for natural ecosystems.(1) And the most serious problem for the marine pollution is caused by land-based activities – soil erosion, fertiliser use, intensive animal production, sewage and other urban industrial discharges.(2)

Urban development/bushland, Nerang, Queensland.
Imagery ©2018 CNES / Airbus, DigitalGlobe,
Map data ©2018 Google.

In south-west Victoria, less than 1%(3) of the largest grassland, the natural temperate grassland of the volcanic plains of the Western District, remains, having been destroyed through agriculture and urbanisation. It was this statistic, this 1%, that prompted us to propose an exhibition consisting of this plant community at the Australian Pavilion for the Biennale Architettura 2018.

One could argue that architecture as a profession has little to do with these destructive practices, which have been widespread since 1788. Suggesting that architects can contribute to the repair of the natural environment is akin to trying to shut the stable door after the horse has bolted. Figures released in October 2017 showed a 33% rise in land clearing in the state of Queensland to almost 400,000 hectares in 2015-16 (that is equivalent to 9,238 Melbourne Cricket Ground fields or 2/3 the annual rate of deforestation in the Brazilian Amazon); of this 35% of clearing was remnant bushland.(4)

As these figures suggest, and a critical issue that the theme of repair has to engage with, is that Australian environment suffers from too much long-term change and damage to meaningfully or effectively repair it to some arbitrary pre-European settlement time. Yet, the alternative of not engaging in the face of this hopelessness is even less helpful. In this catalogue/book, we have tried to capture some of the complexities of this challenge; the questions, the nuances, the limitations while also expanding on examples of engagement of architects in these challenges through the discussion of the *Repair* projects.

Challenges

Challenges abound: how can we address issues around repair in the often short timeframes of architecture? How do we approach building in certain landscapes where we probably shouldn't be building? What type of repair is realistically possible within the constraints of some projects? How can we act within the limitations of a lack of control of governance or planning direction?

In response to these questions, *Repair* centres around the micro/macro relationships and the role of the small in the large. There are two broad but connected scales of action of repair that we are advocating architects can engage with: one is the larger scale of the environment, much of which is degraded through agricultural practices, industry, mining and urbanisation; the other is the scale of the building and its more immediate site. The decisions architects make can contribute to and facilitate repair at both scales.

So what do we mean by repair? It is inconceivable to return to landscape conditions as these were prior to colonisation. In his essay, Paul Memmott takes us to this landscape and his description renders this impossibility clearly.(5) However, we can conserve remaining remnant landscapes (from removal at least) and instigate Indigenous management practices. We can also regenerate, rehabilitate and revegetate. Such approaches acknowledge that ecosystems are not static: regenerative development brings new life, for example after a fire; rehabilitated land repairs a disturbance such as pollution; and revegetation is about 'putting back' a vegetation that has been removed. Often these are combined. Ultimately they will be regenerative(6) and always 'new' and even sometimes artificial.

The notion of a 'new nature',(7) a sort of hybrid environment of natural and man made infrastructure favouring some species but also creating environmental problems for others, debunks the concept (that architecture very often embraces) that nature is somehow the 'other'. It is widely acknowledged that new ecosystems have evolved, including in urban environments, and humans are involved in all of this. This careful argument (sustained by Low among others) has been very often adapted however to dismiss aims of regeneration, rehabilitation and revegetation as somehow 'romantic' practices in favour of an inescapable 'new nature'.

It would be problematic to zealously accept a 'new nature', especially one that has humans at the centre, without pausing to check what we are displacing, which is different in each unique place. Overall, in this age of the Anthropocene,(8) a decentering of the human requires a shift in perspective to consider architecture beyond human use – as suggested by *Freespace,* the earth is also our client.(9)

Grassland surrounded by industrial development at Ngarri-djarrang, Melbourne. Photograph, Linda Tegg.

Architects in Australia will inevitably work on projects on or next to remnant bushland,(10) even those who work mainly in urban areas. They are also likely to work on a piece of land that is polluted, as well as one that effects a waterway either directly through runoff or through the altering of its hydrology – but, what do architects really know about this micro/macro relationship they are involved in? In addition, they will always be working on top of the land of the First Nations peoples – how do we do this in a culturally respectful way?

How to act

When we look at the projects selected and submitted for *Repair*, the overarching quality is in how the 'site' is treated and the way the built elements underpin or facilitate that treatment. This is where architecture's role is evident in the intention to repair. Mainly, it is to do with the location of the building on the actual site (the 'legal' title boundary) and the understanding of this site within the larger context beyond its boundaries, both 'natural' and built. Influential considerations of the locating of the building are arrived at through an understanding of the larger context, be it a floodplain, wildlife corridor, street, along a sacred path, among others. All these conditions exist in our urban, peri-urban and rural built environments. Consideration of such contexts influences the design of the building: its shape and interplay with vegetated space, if it seals the

ground or not, its level of engagement or 'offering' to the public realm, whether it joins or isolates open space, how it works with stormwater and overland flow, and so on. These seemingly basic determinations are not necessarily about a highly technical approach to repair, although some projects do display a sophisticated understanding of ecosystems, phytoremediation and water filtration (in more landscape architecture-based projects), and the application of building science to energy performance, for example. These fundamental decisions are at the core of a built environment's framework and the way a building can be meaningful in that framework to enable its repair, which also sometimes means that the building is not directly repairing, but is enabling other disciplines to act less impeded. In this way, every architectural and landscape project can make a difference.

Perhaps this approach of rethinking a 'site' beyond its 'legal' boundary and importance of physical connectivity in the natural environment is a revisited 'contextualism',(11) where the building takes its cues from its surroundings. If it is, we suggest it is with a whole new perspective on intention and possibilities, a new way of looking at the context not necessarily on and probably beyond architecture's usual terms.

Connecting the small and large

An important aim in repair-based strategies of landscape management is that of connectivity. Interestingly, this is also an important concept in urban design. This requires a shift of perspective in the design approach – a relevant re-adjustment in conceiving architecture from an object within space to the way 'it' relates and operates in its context.

As an example, the biodiversity of small (sometimes remnant), isolated fragments of bushland, interspersed and surrounding our urbanised areas, is often not considered of value. A re-evaluation of these important pockets of land might consider these as providing a framework for the meaningful regeneration of land in urban environments.(12)

The opportunity here is to ameliorate the effect of urban processes on the wider natural environment.

Discussing this correlation, scientists and academics Mark McDonnell and Kelly Holland suggest that the preservation, restoration and ecologically sound management of urban biodiversity are crucial to the maintenance of local and regional biodiversity (now commonly referred to as Urban Ecology):

"The preservation of a diversity of indigenous plants and animals in cities and towns contributes to the quality of life of city dwellers. In addition to providing valuable ecosystem services, such as cleaning the air, ameliorating climate and reducing impacts of potential pests and pathogens, and so on, biodiversity satisfies the human need to have contact with other organisms...

Typically, the preservation of biodiversity in urban environments requires the preservation of open space and remnant plant communities, but gardens, roadside and riparian strips can also provide valuable habitat for indigenous organisms... Loss of native habitat can be minimised during urban planning by reducing low-density sprawl and maintaining green spaces and habitat corridors...The 'matrix' in urban areas can also be enhanced to provide additional habitat and linkages between remnants for a wider variety of species in parks, dead trees and understorey vegetation." (13)

Tree Sprawl cover, envisioning vegetated corridors along Merri Creek and into urban development in Melbourne.

Amy K Hahs further describes the meaningful role of biodiversity in urban environments:

"Biodiversity helps shape our natural and cultural heritage and give us a sense of place and identity. It is important for modifying environmental conditions related to urbanisation. It helps provide us with sustainable and resilient ecosystems, and it is also incredibly important for human health and well-being – for the people who live, work and visit our cities...We can design our cities to manage biodiversity in such a way where we don't lose as much as we would in the face of non-action." (14)

Issues identified by the Urban Design Task Force in 1994 (15) pointed to the lack of connectivity within our urban environments, albeit from the perspective of built space. In his editorial for the November 2017 issue of *Landscape Architecture Australia,* Ricky Ricardo cites John Mant (the urban planner appointed as convener of the Taskforce): "Everything is controlled, but very little is designed. Each design problem is treated as an island in a huge sea, with no relation to its neighbour." (16) This sentiment will be very familiar to Australian designers of the built environment.

What one realises is that fragmented in-between space is, actually the natural environment, in a continuum of open space, which one could generally consider as the ground, from the concreted urban through to remnant vegetation and physical systems of hydrology (among other dynamic systems). To begin projects with the consideration of being and acting and defining this continuum would be a reversal of how we mostly conceive buildings; where we start – and very often end too – with the object in 'space'. This is where a role for architecture in repairing can develop.

Almost a decade ago we investigated the possible connectivity of space of the natural environment within the inner-north urban area of Melbourne through a series of design studios called *Tree Sprawl* at RMIT University, (17) using the Merri Creek, Wurundjeri-willam land, (an ongoing since 1976 rehabilitated 40 kilometre creek vegetated corridor that connects outer Melbourne to its centre and

Bald Hill, a dormant volcanic formation with grassland in the foreground seen from the north, an area planned for housing development, Beveridge, Melbourne. Photograph, Brian Bainbridge.

abuts many varying built environments from suburban, industrial, recreational and inner conglomerate) as a starting point for opportunities within the urbanised environment to expand the reaches of this vegetated corridor.

With a variety of programs of urban densification in mind (from residential, community services and urban farming) the approach was to minimise the occupation of land by not using any uncleared or vacant land and conserving it from the built environment, or rehabilitating it to increase the amount and integration of vegetated open space that connected back to the creek corridor. (18) This included the consolidating of existing developed areas where possible through altering and rationalising access, changing ground materials, and removing some buildings, while densifying others in parts of the urban fabric that were already infrastructured. Contiguity and densification of overlaying activities were instrumental to the pruning of urban territories and the possibility of releasing them from their pervasive built spreads. Larger-scale visions focussed on the ecological significance of open spaces in the extensive urban territory and their relevant contribution as links to natural systems. The aims were mutually beneficial to natural systems and the urban environment.

Melanie Dodd, when writing about our practice's project Garden House,[19] described this approach as

"...interested in the way that the infrastructure of towns and cities can be more mindful of (their) environments, ecosystems and local landscapes. In fact, the practice wants to redefine architecture through this process – or rather restate its relevance. The architects want to experiment and devise architectural typologies that, for example, could allow water to move through them, or that could permit the joining up of vegetated space across property boundaries and open up a deeper acknowledgement of a site's geography, geology and hydrology..." and,

"...a quietly progressive architectural urbanism that places indigenous vegetation and ecosystems at its heart... a strategic approach to how the city can be retrofitted or adjusted through techniques that can accommodate densification of otherwise difficult urban sites – flood plains, creeks and futility easements, for example...These regimes could be scaled up to effect urban regeneration (and densification – authors' note) at the scale of the city and the environment. This sensitivity for moving back and forward between 1:1 and 1:1000 scale infrastructures of the city (or our role in them – authors' note) is a foil to the conventionally detached bird's-eye view..."[20]

Very small, 1:1

It is through the lens of the Garden House project that we began thinking about the idea of repair for the Biennale Architettura 2018. Symptomatically, the project of this house goes to the question of the building on a site. This sort-of house offers little more enclosure than a tent-like structure: a raised deck, which allows the natural ground to pass under mostly unsealed, is covered by a transparent 'shed' and surrounded by an interior garden space that takes the place of the perimeter veranda. The regeneration of the indigenous vegetation present on the site, connection to the vegetation adjoining the site and the way ephemeral water systems moved across the site were central in the siting and formal resolution of the project; a reversal in approach to traditional development. This work is not an exemplar for most development, being quite experimental in its living conditions, but its underlying concerns are broadly applicable.

One important outcome this project raised, at the scale of 1:1, was contradictory to the belief that only very large areas of land can meaningfully contribute to biodiversity, or address what has been displaced, reinforcing the lack of value attributed to small remnant or regenerated landscapes, and the role that architecture can play in supporting their repair. Without doubt, the detrimental effects of land use could be found in every corner of Australia, even where somewhat intact landscapes are still available to us – however, not much is known about how these have been affected by various management practices, and how 'intact' they really are. For instance, could one say that the hundreds (possibly thousands) of Greenhood Orchids (*Pterostylis nutans*) that were 'regenerated' through weeding and avoided in the situating of the house, and enabled to survive and flourish on the small piece of land of the Garden House,

Ground. Video still, Linda Tegg.
Baracco+Wright Architects, Garden House, Westernport, Victoria.

are insignificant? Scientifically and on a large scale perhaps they are. But, we did not feel ready to destroy them (forever) because the story of the orchids is greater than just their presence: they are evidence of the presence of *Mycorrhiza* (required at the germination stage) and often a symbiotic relationship with certain tree; *Mycorrhiza fungi* is a crucial foundation for healthy soils and have recently been credited with the network used by trees to communicate with each other.(21) If there had been continued mowing and fertilization of the (non-native) grass on the site when it was purchased, a hasty positioning of
the house, potential changes to the hydrology of the site such as water penetration/overland flow/microclimate, and symbiotic tree removal, among other actions,
then these orchids would have disappeared over time.

As an alternative to their destruction, very simple approaches were adopted to work more empathetically with the natural environment of this site and its wider context, that is a combination of Heath and Open Grassy Woodland(22) that can be seasonally dry and very wet, set within a larger system of ephemeral creeks and overland flow paths draining to a large bay. The choice of location of the 8 x 8 metre structure came about after observation and research of the site's vegetation and hydrology in an area where no vegetation regenerated because of some previous fill. Other areas responded quickly to weed removal; raising the floor by almost 1 metre to allow the natural ground plane to pass under and having a structure that required minimal footings and a perimeter enclosure that can be opened (large sliding doors) meant that the overland water flow can pass through the building (which was the place of an ephemeral creek). A lack of 'cutting' the ground plane also assists the hydrology of the site. The site has been flooded once since construction with little obstruction. Flooding plays an important role in the life-cycle of many ecosystems (as does fire). The abundance of natural light has meant that some rhizomatic species (mainly tea tree) have regenerated inside the actual indoor perimeter garden: a building that supports life.

This description of the site repair reads more like a landscape architecture project, or even more like a vegetation regeneration project. While the regeneration of the vegetation could have occurred without the architecture, its presence ironically supports repair through stewardship that may not have otherwise come about. What it does though, beyond stewardship, is to allow the intent to repair to 'push back' on important decisions about siting, treatment of the ground, the floor plane and materiality that can effectively open the door to a physical role of architecture in repairing. In this project the site repair does not stop at the exterior wall, and it is this type of thinking that we propose as one important direction for architecture.

As a result of our applied understandings of these processes, we feel confident in putting forward at least two elements critical to the involvement of architecture in the repair of the natural environment at a micro and macro scale: a shift in process of how buildings are conceived and primary attention to the ground plane in decision making. The shift in process we propose is to commence a design by also including the study of micro and macro conditions of natural systems and to identify opportunities and strategies for repair and allow these to influence the formal decisions. This requires that architects widen their knowledge base to include the knowledge domains of

Baracco+Wright Architects, Outside/Inside, Garden House, Westernport, Victoria.
Photograph, Louise Wright.

(Overpage) Nodding Greenhood Orchid (*Pterostylis nutans*).
Photograph, Robert Wyatt.

disciplines of landscape architecture, urban design, urban ecology and land management. Rather than architects becoming all things, these disciplines can excitingly meet, converge and influence each other at their physical thresholds.

Attention to the ground involves: avoidance of clearing remnant vegetation; reuse of existing buildings; primary decision making/advocacy/agency on whether or not buildings should ethically be situated in certain environments at all due to the incompatibility of their presence and occupation with the health of that ecosystem; building form that allows for dynamic natural systems to evolve (for example floods, sand dunes) such as through a small or elevated footprint that creates minimal impact on the ground plane avoiding to 'cut' or seal the soil; positioning of the building/built elements to allow for connection of open space to that around it and beyond; long term strategies that might even include architecture that can be moved or removed; allowing water to move across the site potentially filtered through vegetation; stopping sediment runoff; enough and proportionally correct open space for canopy trees (and linking canopy trees); and the reinstatement of natural systems wherever possible such as wetlands, indigenous vegetation and creeks.

We imagine an architecture and thus an urban fabric where the site is thought through at the micro and macro scale and does not stop at the property boundary or building envelope. The exhibited projects provoke this approach with diverse forms of repair.

(1) See following definitions of the terms 'ecosystem' and 'ecology': "ecosystem - a biological community of interacting organisms and their physical environment", English Oxford Living Dictionaries n.d., *ecosystem*, English Oxford Living Dictionaries, viewed 6 June 2017, <https://en.oxforddictionaries.com/definition/ecosystem>; "ecology and ecosystem describe the relationship between biotic and abiotic factors in an environmental system. Ecology is the study of ecosystems", Quora n.d., *What is the difference between ecosystem and ecology?*, Quora, viewed 14 January 2018, <https://www.quora.com/What-is-the-difference-between-ecosystem-and-ecology>.

(2) See Australian Government n.d., *Our natural environment*, Australian Government, viewed 2 January 2018, <http://www.australia.gov.au/about-australia/our-country/our-natural-environment>.

(3) See Greening Australia n.d., *Great Southern Landscapes: Victorian Volcanic Plains*, Greening Australia, viewed 20 January 2017, <greeningaustralia.org.au/project/Victorian-volcanic-plains>.

(4) See Robertson, J 2017, ' 'Alarming' rise in Queensland tree clearing as 400,000 hectares stripped ', *The Guardian*, 5 October, viewed 18 October 2017, <https://www.theguardian.com/environment/2017/oct/05/alarming-rise-in-queensland-tree-clearing-as-400000-hectares-stripped>.

(5) See essay by Paul Memmott in this catalogue/book.

(6) See Gilbert, J 2018, 'Call of the Reed Warbler: A manifesto for regeneration', *Landscape Australia*, 19 January, viewed 26 January 2018, <https://landscapeaustralia.com/articles/call-of-the-reed-warbler-charles-massys-call-to-action/>, a review of Massy, C 2017, *Call of the Reed Warbler: A New Agriculture - a New Earth*, University of Queensland Press, St Lucia, Queensland, Australia, where Gilbert writes: "Charles Massy too has provided us with a call to action - a manifesto that both reinforces the necessity to understand this country on its own terms and the disturbing extent to which so much remains unknown. The tools for this understanding lie, for Massy, in an approach to practice - an approach that must of necessity itself be regenerative."

(7) See Low, T 2002, *The New Nature: Winners and Losers in Wild Australia*, Viking Books, Melbourne, Victoria, Australia. This book, and other following analogous theoretical positions, discuss the inclusive character of the natural environment, consisting of a mix of indigenous and exotic species as well as human actions, arguing that nature is found in humanised environments, always capable of adapting to whatever humans do.

(8) The Anthropocene, a notion popularised by the atmospheric chemist and author Paul Crutzen, is described as "human dominance of biological, chemical and geological processes on Earth". See Schwägerl, C 2011, 'Living in the Anthropocene: Toward a New Global Ethos', *Yale Environment 360*, 24 January, viewed 10 January 2018, <http://e360.yale.edu/features/living_in_the_anthropocene_toward_a_new_global_ethos>.

(9) Farrell, Y & McNamara, S 2017, '16th International Architecture Exhibition, Biennale Architettura 2018, Freespace', *La Biennale di Venezia*, viewed 15 June 2017, <http://www.labiennale.org/en/architecture/2018/16th-international-architecture-exhibition>.

(10) Remnant vegetation is native vegetation that has not previously been cleared or grazed since European settlement. It is however in a sort of paralysed state, at a point in time when Indigenous Australians were for the most part forcibly removed and could not continue their land management. For tens of thousands of years, the lives and sense of cultural identity of Indigenous Australians were inextricably linked to the land, its forms, flora and fauna.

(11) "Contextualism, or contextual architecture, is a principle of design in which the structure is designed in response to its specific urban and natural environment. In an architectural sense, context can be defined as giving meaning to the various parts of a building through reference to its wider surroundings", Designing Buildings Wiki n.d., *Contextualism*, Designing Buildings Wiki, viewed 28 January 2018, <https://www.designingbuildings.co.uk/wiki/Contextualism>.

(12) In Victoria, Australia, several local Councils map such remnant vegetation. Their value, as well as that of other vegetation in urban environments is entering a new phase of re-evaluation through the science of Urban Ecology, a recognition that urban densification and the physical and mental health of urban inhabitants rely on amenity - largely provided through open and vegetated space. For a detailed and scientific review of Urban Ecology see the two following articles: Ossola, A, Hahs, AK & Livesley SJ 2015, 'Habitat complexity influences fine scale hydrological processes and the incidence of stormwater runoff in managed urban ecosystems', *Journal of Environmental Management*, vol. 159, 15 August, pp. 1-10, viewed 20 November 2017, ScienceDirect, <https://www.sciencedirect.com/science/article/pii/S030147971530058X?via%3Dihub>; Threlfall, CG, Mata, L, Mackie JA, Hahs AK, Stork, NE, Williams NSG & Livesley, SJ 2017, 'Increasing biodiversity in urban green spaces through simple vegetation interventions', *Journal of Applied Ecology*, vol. 54, no. 6, pp. 1874-1883, viewed 20 November 2017, Wiley Online Library, <http://onlinelibrary.wiley.com/doi/10.1111/1365-2664.12876/full?platform=hootsuite>.

(13) McDonnell, M & Holland, K 2008, 'Biodiversity', in PW Newton (ed.), *Transitions: Pathways Towards Sustainable Urban Developments in Australia*, CSIRO Publishing, Collingwood, Victoria, Australia.

(14) Hahs, AK 2017, 'Soft cities: Making room for nature in our urban future', *Foreground*, 20 April 2017, viewed 20 November 2017, <https://www.foreground.com.au/environment/biodiversity-in-our-urban-future/>. Amy K Hahs has been working as a staff of the Australia Research Centre for Urban Ecology, the University of Melbourne; the authors would like to acknowledge the ground breaking work undertaken by the Research Centre, and that, unfortunately, notwithstanding that at the exact moment this research is most needed, due to a lack of sustainable funding, ARCUE ceased operations on 31 December 2016.

(15) See Prime Minister's Urban Design Taskforce 1994, *Urban Design in Australia: Report*, Commonwealth of Australia, Australian Government Publishing Service, Canberra, ACT, Australia, viewed 19 February 2018, <https://urbandesign.org.au/content/uploads/2015/08/PMs_Taskforce_on_UD_1994.pdf>.

(16) Ricardo, RR 2017, 'Editorial: Tracking Australian Urban Design', *Landscape Architecture Australia*, no. 156, November, p. 6.

(17) See Baracco, M (ed.) 2011, *Tree Sprawl*, School of Architecture and Design, RMIT University, Melbourne, Victoria, Australia. This study is the precursor of the research project Grassland Common: Linking Ecology and Architecture undertaken at RMIT University in 2015, as a collaboration between the School of Architecture and Urban Design (d___Lab - Centre for Design Practice Research) and the School of Global Urban and Social Studies (Centre for Urban Research); a description of this project is included in this catalogue/book.

(18) As observed by ecologist and Merri Creek Management Committee Manager Luisa Macmillan, "the problems created by an overabundance of untreated stormwater from urban areas require an ambitious 'water sensitive retrofitting' of the entire urban landscape." See Macmillan, L 2011, 'Merri Creek', in M Baracco (ed.) 2011, op. cit.

(19) A description of this project is included in this catalogue/book.

(20) Dodd, M 2015, 'Garden House', *Architecture Australia*, vol. 104, no. 5, September/October, pp. 66-71.

(21) See Wohlleben, P 2016, *The Hidden Life of Trees: What They Feel, How They Communicate - Discoveries from a Secret World*, Blanc Inc., Carlton, Victoria, Australia.

(22) Another characteristic of many of Australia's ecosystems is that due to their high diversity, plant communities and soil types can change metre by metre, making decisions about where to put things very meaningful.

A DAMAGED LAND
DESERVING REPAIR

DAVID
FREUDENBERGER

Australia is a distinctive continent of unusual creatures, ancient plants and diverse environments. It's a land shaped by 65 million years of isolation from any other continent. It's a vast land of deserts fringed by coastal forests, from the tropical north to the cool and wet forests of Tasmania. It's an ancient land worn flat by erosion and seldom disturbed by mountain uplifts or volcanic eruptions. It's the land of 140 species of pouch bearing marsupials, 700 eucalyptus trees and a 1,000 species of nitrogen fixing acacias shrubs and trees, all toughened by regular periods of drought and fire.(1) It's a land so infertile that termites consume more vegetation than kangaroos do. It's a land of subtle beauty with the lowest population density of people of any continent other than Antarctica.

But sadly, Australia's lands and waterways are in great need of repair. Two hundred years of industrial agriculture, urbanisation and wonton introduction of weedy plants and feral animals has devastated much of this ancient land. Australia has some of the most intact deserts and tropical savannahs in the world, but its woodlands and grasslands have been cleared for agriculture down to the last 10%. This vast continent has been over-run with 3,000 introduced plants and eighty-three invasive animals including rabbits, foxes and cats. Habitat loss from land clearing and these introduced wild species, along with the spread of cattle, sheep and goats across 60% of the continent, are the major contributors to the greatest number of twentieth century mammal extinctions – twenty-six – anywhere in the world. Plants have fared no better, thirty-six species are extinct, plus a staggering 700 Australian plants are now teetering on the brink of extinction.(2)

Of particular concern is the cool climate grasslands and grassy woodlands of south eastern Australia where the majority of Australians live. These productive ecosystems supported Aboriginal Australians for tens of thousands of years. An active and intimate management of these grasslands nurtured the great diversity of plants and animals that provided food and cultural identity to these first Australians. As detailed elsewhere in this book, Aboriginal people harvested a vast array of plant foods and abundant

wildlife in addition to using native plants for fibre, shelter and fuel. The purposeful use of fire was a critical element in facilitating hunting and sustaining a patchy diversity of plants and wildlife habitats.

This enduring coexistence of people and native biodiversity was severely and rapidly disrupted with the arrival of European colonisers throughout the nineteenth century. The fertile grasslands and grassy open woodlands were ready made pastures for settlers' sheep, goats and cattle. The colonial economy rapidly developed on the sheep's woolly back. Like all other temperate grasslands around the world, the plough and sowing of cereal grains soon followed, ripping open soils for the first time in human history. The purposeful obliteration of these beautiful ecosystems has continued to the present time, but has created Australia's fruit and bread bowl that supports domestic and export markets worth over $50 billion of value annually.

The great financial wealth generated from Australia's temperate grasslands and woodlands has come at a great cultural price. The displacement of Aboriginal nations from their grasslands and woodlands is nearly complete. The intimate relationships, knowledge and land nurturing practices are nearly completely severed. Unlike northern Australia, there are only tiny pockets of temperate grasslands that have remained under continuous stewardship of First Nations peoples.

With cultural loss comes biodiversity loss. Yam daisies (*Microseris lanceolate*) and native lilies (*Arthropodium* species) were once so abundant in grasslands as to be a staple for Aboriginal diets. They are now exceedingly rare; occasionally found along roadsides, railway easements and old cemeteries free of livestock grazing. Less than 0.1% some kinds of grassy woodlands remain with an intact ground cover of native grasses and hundreds of species of wildflowers. Orchids (for example, *Caladenia* species) are particularly sensitive to agricultural disturbances; nineteen are listed nationally as critically endangered.(3)

Many grassy woodland wildlife species have been devastated as well. The small marsupials have suffered the most. The Toolache Wallaby, Eastern Hare Wallaby and Pig-faced Bandicoot are extinct. The Rufous, Brush-tailed and Southern Brown Bandicoot have been banished to tiny remnant populations just hanging on. Formally widespread grassland birds including the Plains-wanderer and Bush Stone-curlew are now locally extinct. Only the large Grey Kangaroo has survived in abundance across most of southern Australia that still have patches of eucalypt woodlands.

A country of healing

In contrast, for many people, Australia's land, culture and economy has provided great solace and opportunities. Much of colonial Australia was settled by prisoners shipped out from England who were often freed to create functional families and productive livelihoods. Australia's multicultural society has been created over the past century by over a hundred nationalities who have successfully sought escape from wars, tyranny and poverty. Australia is the only continent-country that has never experienced the wide spread devastation of industrialised war. Only Darwin (then a town and harbour) was bombed during the Second World War.

Unfortunately there is a deep contradiction in modern Australian history. The deep healing and great prosperity experienced by so many immigrant Australians came at the cost of nearly complete Aboriginal land dispossession. It was not until 1992 that the Australian High Court finally rejected the colonial and post-colonial notion that Australia was an empty land (*terra nullius*) free for the taking. The 1993 Native Title Act now recognises that some Aboriginal and Torres Strait Islander peoples have rights to, and interests in, certain land because of their traditional laws and customs. Recognition of Native Title is one important part of the process of reconciliation that is slowly occurring across Australia's land, waters and cultures.

At about the same time as the recognition of Native Title, there was a growing recognition that Australia's brutally damaged land and waters needed healing. In 1989, as part of the Australian Prime Minister's Statement on the Environment, the One Billion Trees Program was announced along with the a national Landcare Decade program to assist farmers and community groups to repair degraded land. Subsequent national and state-based land repair programs continue, involving thousands of farmers and hundreds of thousands of volunteers in rural and urban communities.

Deep roots

The largely unseen challenge of land repair is to nurture an abundance of deep roots back into the soil. Keep this in mind; for every kilogram of plant biomass above ground, there is a kilogram below ground. Industrial agriculture has created vast landscapes devoid of deep roots that sustains life many metres into the soil and many metres above.

Industrialised farmlands have just a thin veneer of shallow rooted annual crops that at best get roots down through one metre of soil and only for a month or two during spring, before drying up and dying. Pastures grazed by sheep and cows are seldom any better. A continuously grazed pasture is often just a few centimetres in height, thus there is only a few centimetres of root. Our food producing systems are perilously thin. Shallow rooted farming systems require a continuous input of fertiliser to maintain plant nutrients in the top few centimetres of soil. Much fertiliser is lost as it moves deeper into the soil, well past shallow rooted crops and pastures.

Only deep rooted native grasses, trees and shrubs remain green and alive during the inevitable Australian drought. Photograph, David Freudenberger.

Shallow rooted crops and pastures can only access soil water in the first dozen or so centimetres. When the inevitable dry time returns, farmland fields dry up and die. Yet Australia's native grasslands and woodlands remain green and alive. The deep roots of native grasses access soil nutrients and water long after most crops and pastures have withered.

It always rains during drought, but not much. This living mass of deep perennial roots and leaves is alive to the passing showers of rain that typify dry times. Living roots keeps the soil alive. Dead soil is water repellent. Living soil is water absorbent. Rainfall infiltrates the soil through millions of microscopic bio-pores created by a vast array of soil organisms; from large worms to the tiniest insects. They are kept alive by the mass of living roots and carbon giving life provided by dead leaves found in great quantities in every healthy grassy woodland.

(1) See Harlan, B 2015, 'Digging Deep Reveals
     the Intricate World of Roots',
     National Geographic, 15 October, viewed 26
     November 2017, <https://www.nationalgeographic.
     com/photography/proof/2015/10/15/digging-deep-
     reveals-the-intricate-world-of-roots/>.

(2) See Carolyn Young, <http://www.carolynyoung.com.
     au/>.

(3) See Hicks, LE & King, RJH 2007, 'Confronting
     Environmental Collapse: Visual Culture, Art
     Education, and Environmental Responsibility',
     Studies in Art Education, vol. 48, no. 4, pp.
     332-335.

(4) See Batchen, G 1992, 'Terrible Prospects', in A
     Shiell & A Stephen (eds), *The Lie of the Land*,
     National Centre for Australian Studies,
     Monash University, Clayton, Victoria, Australia,
     pp. 46-48; Bonyhady, T 2004, 'Woodchipping the
     Spirit of Tasmania', *Art Monthly Australia*,
     no. 173, September.

(5) See Duxbury, L 2010, 'A Change in the Climate:
     New Interpretations and Perceptions of Climate
     Change through Artistic Interventions and
     Representations', *Weather, Climate and Society*,
     no. 2, p. 294; Lakoff, G 2010, 'Why It Matters
     How We Frame the Environment', *Environmental
     Communication: A Journal of Nature
     and Culture* 4, no. 1.

(6) Duxbury, L 2010, op. cit.

(7) Hicks, LE & King, RJH 2007, op. cit.

My image *Grassy woodland: a comparison of groundcover plant roots*, is the result of a collaboration between myself and Dr. David Freudenberger. Inspired by Jim Richardson's photographs of prairie grasses in the USA,(1) David wanted to visually show the significance of native grass root biomass in Australian grassy woodlands through comparison with other groundcover forb species. Dominating this photograph is the fibrous roots of the kangaroo grass (*Themada australis*), which was grown without grazing pressure and carefully dug up to minimise disturbance to its roots, although the clay clinging to the fine roots caused us some loss. Placed along a horizontal line that suggests the ground interface are: native flowering forbs, a grazed-down grass, fungi and organic detritus all collected from the same grassy woodland ecosystem.

The still-life form, in which the plant is extracted from its ecosystem and photographed on a black background, enables the viewer to appreciate the morphology and comparative scale of individual plant species which are often visually hidden in landscape photographs. I first developed this photographic style while making the *Grassy Woodlands* series(2) to show the changes in vegetation composition and structure when grassy woodlands are increasingly turned to agricultural uses. The *Grassy Woodlands* series was the result of collaboration, but this time with ecologists and farmers endeavouring to manage the land sustainably. Ecologists are struggling to communicate their knowledge on endangered grassy woodlands. Collaborations between artists and scientists enable the sharing of ecological knowledge, through visual art, to new audiences.

In my art practice, I aim to build connections between culture and nature. By representing the environment in art, we invest it with meaning and cultural relevance.(3) Australian wilderness photographers have made salient the sublime vistas and sweeping panoramas of Tasmanian ecosystems that the Australian public has come to understand as 'untouched' or 'pristine' and therefore worth conserving.(4) In the making of high quality photographs of 'unspectacular' grassy woodlands my aim was to not only raise the public's awareness of these endangered ecosystems, but also to extend the public's perception of what is an aesthetic and necessary ecosystem. Affective engagement, which art can provide, is integral to creating meaningful communication between humans.(5) When looking at a work of art, the viewer is invited to engage in their own reflections, and recall their own experiences to evaluate and interpret the work in a process of critical thinking.(6) Learning to repair the land is, "a cultural challenge to our very sense of who we are and what we should aspire to become", and artists are needed to help people to critically, "... re-think, re-imagine the human place in nature."(7)

(Overpage) Carolyn Young, *Grassy woodland: a comparison of groundcover plant roots*. Deep-rooted perennial grass tussocks support a wonderful array of above and below-ground life. Photograph, © Carolyn Young, 2017.

Regenerative farming

The past three decades of farmer and community led land repair is slowly returning a diversity of deep roots into Australia's ancient soils. Most of these deep roots are from planting of native woodland trees and shrubs along the edges of traditionally cultivated and grazed fields. Away from these plantings, the field is a dead zone during hot and dry summer months. These needlessly dead fields reflect the ten thousand year history of farming that too often leaves a legacy of destruction, death and societal collapse. (4) Farming is founded on the ancient tradition of land clearing and annual cultivation of the soil. This is farming by obliteration.

A few Australian farmers are challenging this destructive tradition. They are planting their wheat and oat crops into native grasslands, rather than first ploughing up and destroying the deep roots and living diversity of grasslands. They are fundamentally reinventing how we grow our daily bread. They are farming with biodiversity, not against it. They are inventing 'no-kill' farming systems that regenerate (repair) soil and grasslands, rather than destroy. They are planting their cool season crops into summer active native grasslands with dozen of plant species with masses of deep and fibrous roots. Their precious soil is never left bare of vegetation. It is perennially alive and responsive to passing showers of rain. Their farmland is continuously productive. The day their wheat or oats is harvested, is the day they bring in their sheep and cattle to graze a luscious and nutritious native pasture that has grown up beneath the crop. There is seldom any need for imported fertiliser. Their deep rooted grasses capture and recycle plant nutrients found deep within the soil. A diversity of nitrogen fixing grassland herbs and microbes provide the balance. A truly radical root-based way of farming without harming.

A regenerative way of farming. Oats ready to be harvested from a perennially alive grassland that is no longer cultivated. The soil is never bare of vegetation. Photograph, David Freudenberger.

Repair of the soul

Most of the land care farmers and community members I have met over the past thirty years plant trees and nurture grasses and wildflowers because it feels and looks good. Land repair is a salve for the soul. The leading regenerative farmers of Australia abandoned destructive practices in response to personal crises of confidence. (5) Their confidence was deeply shattered by devastating drought, destructive wildfire and financial strife. An antidote to destruction and death was needed. They found it nurturing deeply rooted and diverse native vegetation.

Fire is a regular feature of Australian grasslands, woodlands and forests. They recover quickly and diversely. These trees are all still alive; green leaves sprout from the trunks and branches. Photograph, David Freudenberger.

Australia's national capital, Canberra, is part of the healing that comes from land repair. On 18 January 2003, a mega fire-storm literally roared out of the nearby forested mountains and smashed into the suburban fringes of Canberra. Five hundred homes were destroyed, four people died. Canberra's drinking water supply was imperilled. The city's main water supply catchment had been incinerated. Post-fire rain storms washed polluting ash and sediments into the reservoirs. Fortunately, the upper water catchment that has been protected by native eucalyptus trees, shrubs and grassy ground cover for millions of years quickly recovered on its own. These forests have evolved with intensive fire. In contrast, the exotic pine plantation planted around the nearest water reservoir remained blackened and dead. In response, a remarkable restoration took place. A traumatised citizenry came together and healed themselves through repairing the land. Over the next ten years, 15,000 Canberrans, young and old, volunteered their time (47,000 hours) to plant 300,000 woodland seedlings (tree, shrubs, wildflowers and grasses) across 500 hectares of the most badly effected land. The water in this reservoir is clean again.

Native wildlife is returning. The human and natural community is now much more resilient and prepared for the next wildfire that will inevitably come back down from the mountains on some hot and windy day.

The past is not a blue print

Canberra's repaired water catchment and the regenerative farmlands of Australia are not the same as what once was. The native grasslands and woodlands of southern Australia are forever changed. Australia is no longer populated with a million or so Aboriginal people present before European colonisation. Australia now supports 24 million people with abundant food and fibre. Cows and sheep will no doubt continue to graze upon this ancient land for centuries to come. The vast majority of the 3,000 plants and eighty-three animals introduced to Australia will likely persist for centuries. Pristine wilderness is now mythology, globalised biota and changed climate is the reality. Our farms, cities and towns are unlikely to return to sweeping plains of purely native grasses and woodlands.

Rather a new nature for a new geological epoch, the Anthropocene, is emerging. The past is an important guide, but not a recipe of what might be possible and desirable. Our limited knowledge of past ecosystems clearly guides us to nurture natural and built places that are based on deep roots and deep foundations. Three decades of Australian land care, reconciliation and research demonstrates that coexistence is possible. We now know that diverse on-farm plantings of native trees and shrubs support a glorious

15,000 citizens of Canberra came out on weekends to repair their water supply catchment damaged by seventy years of exotic pine plantations, then fire that burnt it all. Photograph, David Freudenberger.

diversity of colourful native birds and cryptic reptiles.(6) We now better appreciate that reconciliation with the first Aboriginal settlers of Australia enriches Australia's new culture and deeply informs sympathetic land stewardship. We now know that given sufficient effort and ingenuity we can bring endangered species back from extinction. We now have the technical knowledge to restore species-rich grasslands.(7) The Australian Pavilion at this Biennale showcases innovative ways to sensitively integrate built spaces into natural and cultural landscapes.

Scale matters

The challenge is to scale up; to increase land repair activities to a continental scale rather than a demonstration scale. All Australians need to be involved in learning to live more lightly and care more deeply. Australia is highly urbanised; 70% of us live in major cities. Thus most of us impact on the land through our lifestyles; on what we consume and on the nature of our community relationships. We mostly demand inexpensive food subsidised by soil degradation, rather than food that is carefully nurtured from deep-rooted farming systems that integrate habitats for native plants and animals.

Land repair is a process that takes centuries, not just decades. This is farmland being restored to woodland for wildlife habitat and carbon bio-sequestration in south western Australia, L-R 2008, 2010, 2012, 2012, 2013, 2017. Photographs, David Freudenberger.

Land repair needs to move from the innovative margins of Australia's public and private investment to the mainstream if scale is to be achieved. Australia is particularly good at investing in built infrastructure, public and private. We have cities with world class clean water delivery systems and efficient waste removal and resource recovery. Our stock of housing and employment spaces are in excellent condition and built to very high standards. What is missing is a commensurate level of investment in green infrastructure that underpins human well-being. The current investment in deep rooted vegetation to deliver a broad range of valuable ecosystem service, particularly clean water, soil regeneration and climate moderation (for example, cooling) is insufficient to adequately address the legacy of land destruction.

But starting small is OK. We now know that even a few square metres of native grasses and wildflowers in our cities, suburbs and towns can provide viable habitat for many native wildlife species. A plains wander bird needs many hundreds of hectares of high quality native grasslands, but native butterflies, bees, and small lizards can live for generations within a few hundred square metres. Urban green spaces do not have to be just high maintenance turf lawns requiring irrigation and fertiliser. Restored grassland meadows full of hundreds of species of plants and animals should also be part of the mix of open spaces weaving through our built landscapes. This is slowly happening as landscape architects, horticulturalists, plant nurseries and home gardeners embrace an ever-expanding diversity of native plants commercially available for use. These are being increasingly used to restore wetlands for natural purification of storm water to restoring grassy woodlands for shade, air pollution reduction, wildlife habitat and the spaces for all ages of people to explore and discover.

Repair is a process – not a destination

Land and social repair takes generations which can span hundreds of years for many Australian eucalypt trees. The trees being planted today will not provide habitat (homes) for hundreds of wildlife species for at least a hundred years. It takes that long for a eucalypt tree to get old enough and damaged enough to start forming hollows (cavities) in large branches and the tree trunk. These hollows provide resting and nest sites needed by all Australia's colourful parrots, tree living marsupials like possums, a myriad of insects, bats and even some ducks.[8]

We need to learn to more fully embrace death because it supports life. Too often in our cities we cut down old dead trees seeing them as ugly and dangerous. Rather they need to be carefully conserved and appreciated as they provide shelter to native animals for many decades even when they eventually fall. Embracing death includes recycling of organic waste material back in the soil of farms and cities.

The science, art and practice of land repair is a very new human endeavour. We are very good at land destruction, we have refined it over 10,000 years of clearing for agriculture. In contrast, land repair is a dynamic process that requires learning, and learning often requires failures. This requires courageous humility. An essential component of the land repair journey is to carefully listen to past experience, try (experiment) and sensitively learn from successes and failures. There is much to learn.

Land repair is a deeply hopeful process. I have personally planted over a thousand trees and shrubs over the past thirty years. My community of volunteers and I have done so, not just for our own gratification (it is satisfying work), but also for the benefits of those yet to be born. Building homes, schools and hospitals supports services for better lives now and well into the future. So does nurturing greenery to surround us with colour, coolness, scent and sound of the many creatures finding homes amongst plants, particularly native ones.

Unlike built spaces, green spaces can be self-repairing. Given the right conditions, trees, grasses and flowers set seed, die, but then are reborn as vigorous seedlings. Land repair can reinstate a renewal process that can last for millennia.

Values are invisible

Values are in our heads and hearts. We display them though our actions. Architecture is a tangible expression of individual and societal values. Financial wealth is invisible, so the rich and proud show it off by commissioning mansions of oversized dimensions and encumbered by paraphernalia. We need built spaces that reflect values needed for surviving the Anthropocene: social and environmental gratitude and care for all of life. Edifices to ego consume far too many resources for our crowded Earth. A much greater abundance of sensitively built spaces are needed that embrace nature, inspire creativity, facilitate social engagement, as well as provide comfort and healing.

Commendation

The living display of Australian grasses and wildflowers at the Australian Pavilion at the 2018 Biennale is thus deeply symbolic and reflective. It reflects new thinking and a new ethos of caring for people and the nature that supports us all. It is symbolic of the new journey so many Australian farmers and passionate community members have started. A journey to create communities and built spaces with deeper connections to the land, and a land with deeper roots supporting a diversity of nature, regenerative agricultural enterprises, and caring relationships, urban and rural. I commend you to reflect on this symbolism of hope and humanity.

(1)   Morton, S, Sheppard, A & Lonsdale, M (eds) 2014,
      Biodiversity: Science and Solutions for Australia,
      CSIRO Publishing, Collingwood, Victoria, Australia.
(2)   Ibid.
(3)   Australian Government 2006, *White Box - Yellow Box -
      Blakely's Red Gum Grassy Woodlands and Derived Native Grasslands*
      listing advice and conservation advice, viewed 12 December 2017,
      <http://www.environment.gov.au/system/files/pages/dcad3aa6-2230-
      44cb-9a2f-5e1dca33db6b/files/box-gum.pdf>.
(4)   Montgomery, DR 2008, *Dirt: The Erosion of Civilisations*,
      University of California Press, Berkeley, USA.
(5)   See Massy, C 2017, *Call of the Reed Warbler:
      A New Agriculture - a New Earth*, University of Queensland Press,
      St Lucia, Queensland, Australia.
(6)   Lindenmayer, D, Michael, D, Crane, M, Okada, S, Florance, D,
      Barton, P & Ikin, K 2016, *Wildlife Conservation in Farm Landscapes*,
      CSIRO Publishing, Clayton South, Victoria, Australia.
(7)   Gibson-Roy, P & Delpratt, J 2015, 'The restoration of native
      grasslands', in N Williams, A Marshall & JW Morgan (eds),
      *Land of Sweeping Plains: managing and restoring the native
      grasslands of south-eastern Australia*, CSIRO Publishing,
      Clayton South, Victoria, Australia, pp. 331-398.
(8)   Gibbons, P and Lindenmayer, D 2002, *Tree Hollows and Wildlife
      Conservation in Australia*, CSIRO Publishing, Collingwood,
      Victoria, Australia.

MITIGATE, REPAIR, ADAPT OR EVOLVE? SOME THOUGHTS ON REPAIR

CHRIS SAWYER AND SUSIE KUMAR

Repair is kindness

In our work as landscape architects we are often confronted with the dilemma that climate change poses in Australia – the undeniable drying and heating of the country is rendering some, if not many, ecosystems vulnerable, unstable and potentially unsustainable in the coming century as species types and compositions fail to evolve or adapt quickly enough to meet this new climate. Understanding what is valuable to retain, important to modify or in need of repair have become challenging questions when climate change compresses a geological timeframe of millennia into centuries or decades.

Repair is not a new idea, but one we have increasingly forgotten about in our information rich and disposable world. One approach to repair is beautifully illustrated by the collection of annotated photographs taken by the landscape architect Edna Walling documenting the construction of her house in the Otways during the 1940s. Walling is best remembered for her beautiful gardens, but perhaps her greatest legacy is as a strong and fearless advocate for the indigenous Australian landscape. The images contain her annotated observations about the site and the process of constructing her house and reveal a genuine tenderness and respect for the landscape in which the building sits. Interestingly, the photographs are primarily of the landscape, with the building sitting off centre, slightly blurred or just out of frame. While the photographs document the construction of the building, ultimately it is the topography, the plants, the fauna and the soils which informed her decision making. Seventy years on, Walling's photographs are a lovely reminder of the importance of taking the time to observe and understand how a site works.

Writing these words have also been an act of repair for us. Many conversations and disagreements later, we have come to realise that it is too easy to dwell on the negative and that enacting repair requires a kindness and hopefulness that is often absent from practice.

It is also clear that agreeing on what repair is and how to achieve it is often very difficult – it seems that everyone has different expectations, tools, timeframes and languages to discuss repair.

Rather than critique the projects of others, we have decided the best way to discuss repair is through the lens of our own work. We present these thoughts not necessarily as examples of successful repair, but rather as a method through which to better understand complex and contradictory ideas about the country we live in and the landscapes we inhabit. Ultimately our purpose is to make repair very much a part of everyday practice.

Small urban repair

What is it about small, degraded, isolated and often forgotten landscapes that spark our interest? We seem to end up working on many such sites scattered across the city and suburban fringe. They are often located on highly damaged or disturbed sites that have undergone extensive modification and reuse. In many cases the pre-settlement landscape has been largely erased and what does remain is a palimpsest of prior occupations. Making sense of these landscapes is often very challenging.

Despite this disturbance, these sites do contain functioning natural systems. By natural systems, we are referring to the broader natural and biological processes that continue to operate within every environment and are always present within the city. On every site, these processes continue to exert themselves through the forces of rainfall, hydrology, temperature, air movement and microclimate. These processes are dramatically modified by the local urban condition, as well as global human induced climate change. While we can plot what is there physically on the site (via surveys, flora and fauna studies, geotechnical reports and the like), understanding how the underlying natural systems perform may not always be obvious or easy, as these systems are interrelated in complex ways, highly sensitive to change and usually operate at scales larger that the individual site.

Over time, we have learnt to never take these natural systems for granted or to underestimate their value. While many remnant ecologies are difficult to see, we remind ourselves that in Melbourne we are very lucky to live in one of the world's most biologically diverse cities supporting a vary array of species, many of which are threatened. (1) Up to twenty endangered plants and animals remain present within the city despite the seemingly hostile urban environment. (2) This reinforces the importance of conservation within the city and challenges the notion that valuable ecologies only occur within less disturbed, non urban environments.

It also reminds us that there are responsibilities that extend beyond the provision of social infrastructure for people when working on these sites. While other design disciplines focus more exclusively on solving human problems, landscape architecture generally has a broader field of vision and an opportunity to focus on issues other than ourselves. Perhaps this is the reason we are drawn to these forgotten and overlooked sites, the 'freespace' within the city. It is not so much the absence of people that interests us but rather the freedom from intense programmatic and functional requirements that can overburden a project and site.

In 2012 we designed a boardwalk through the Seaford Foreshore Reserve along Port Phillip Bay. Due to increasing visitation, the existing track to the beach was becoming highly eroded, causing damage to the landscape, a barrier to the movement of animals and a threat to the structural integrity of the primary dune. While the boardwalk itself is for people, the underlying purpose is environmental repair and focussed on building greater strength and resilience into the dune which will be battered by more frequent storms and higher sea levels over the coming years.

Using natural systems to repair the landscape is a very compelling strategy to us. A starting point is the geography of dune formation and the manner in which wind blown sand is captured by vegetation and deposited where it needs to be, a nuclei leading to an incremental increase in the dune over time. While we think of the dune landscape as quite fragile, it is also true that these dunes have been in place for many thousands of years; dune formation is a very slow process. The fragility of the dune environment today is a result of the degree of disturbance outpacing the incremental rate of sand accretion. The dilemma we now face is whether we have sufficient time to wait for natural systems to repair themselves or whether we need to give these systems a helping hand.

At Seaford the discussion focussed on whether the dune should be strengthened by natural or mechanical means. On the one hand, mechanical methods (such as the use of large earth moving equipment) offer the ability to recreate a dune rapidly yet impose significant disturbances and ongoing costs to the landscape. Natural accumulation on the other hand offers less disturbance to the landscape but may take too long to provide any meaningful strength against ongoing disturbances and sea level rise, perfectly highlighting the dilemma of repair we often face.

In the end, we focussed on dune protection through the careful alignment of the boardwalk to avoid damage to the existing vegetation, as well as to minimise the funnelling of winds which can lead to dune blowouts. The raised wings of the boardwalk act as dune protection fencing, capturing wind blown sand at the base of the fence and hopefully leading to an increase in the size of the dune over time. The irony of repair in this case is that the social success is measured by the provision of all-abilities beach access unencumbered by sand drift, whereas the environmental success is measured by the eventual burying of the

L-R "No! We didn't want a garden here...the golden dust everlasting (*Helichrysum semipapposum*) came up between the paving…"; "One of our friends"; "Showing the galley window, woolsack and steps up to car park"; "The edge of the paved terrace came to the top of the retaining wall, the goat track runs down between the iron barks", Edna Walling, ca. 1947, *The Happiest Days, East Point*. Source, Edna Walling Collection, State Library of Victoria.

Mitigate, Repair, Adapt or Evolve? Some Thoughts on Repair

Site Office, McCulloch Avenue Boardwalk, Seaford, Melbourne.
Photograph, Lisbeth Grosmann, Site Office Collection.

Site Office, McCulloch Avenue Boardwalk, Seaford, Melbourne.
Photograph, Lisbeth Grosmann, Site Office Collection.

boardwalk by sand, highlighting the misalignment of social and environmental repair objectives on many projects. Perhaps in another twenty-five years, we will be asked to design a new boardwalk on the interred remains of the old.

While repair strategies often focus on the visible elements of the site (such as the dune), we are also interested in the connections to the broader landscape that may be out of sight and thus out of mind. One of the characteristics of repair is that you are often designing for things that you may never see. In the case of the boardwalk, the fauna assessment revealed several species of ground-dwelling animals (including the Blotched Blue-tongued Lizard, Swamp Rat, Tree Dragon, White's Skink, and Weasel Skink) which could be impacted by the construction through potential fragmentation of habitat and barriers to movement.

Moonee Ponds Creek (30 October 2015), Melbourne.
Photograph, Site Office.

To assist we included two 'critter crossings' with the aim of providing crucial vegetation cover for ground dwelling creatures, thereby encouraging passage underneath the boardwalk. In these locations, steel grating was installed to allow light penetration for the establishment of planting below. While our hope was for the blue tongues, skinks and swamp rats to avail themselves of this opportunity, a few months after construction of the boardwalk was completed an inspection was made of the crossings. Unfortunately the only footprints appeared to be those of cats.

Not to be discouraged, the lessons of Seaford have taught us to be open minded and inventive about the possibilities for repair. While we may have designed a successful crossing for cats and foxes, the project forced us to consider things on site that we may otherwise not have seen. If working on these sites has taught us anything, it is that successes and failures are not always what they seem.

Large urban repair

One of the problems we face is how to reconcile the scale of natural systems with the spatial limitations of each site; strategies for repair often appear modest or insignificant in their inability to resolve complex environmental issues, especially when small scale interventions may be entirely reliant on broader strategies to achieve success. An opportunity posed by fragmented urban sites is understanding how these fragments fit within a larger whole. While not to diminish the value of what can be achieved on a small site (acting local is precisely what gives repair agency), the more we practise the more we realise that opportunities to enact repair are enhanced by working at larger scales that cross physical and municipal boundaries. Consequently, we have become more interested in the potential for repair across larger urban sites where the scale of the site is more consistent with the operation of the underlying natural systems.

Over the last three years we have been working with the local community, councils and government agencies on strategies to improve the health of the Moonee Ponds Creek in Melbourne. The creek is largely an urban waterway within the urban growth boundary of the city and as a result it suffers from the litany of problems experienced by urban waterways all over the world – poor water quality, peak flooding, pollution and bureaucratic neglect. The creek is best known as a concrete drain, having been progressively channelised by the Board of Works (MMBW)(3) over the last century.

What has been surprising is the scarcity of information analysing the ecological performance of the creek, despite it being an integral component of the city. Ironically, one of the most helpful documents has been the MMBW's own history of the creek written in the early 1980s describing with great pride and detail the conversion of the creek into an engineered trapezoidal concrete drainage channel. While much is known about its hydraulic performance, very little is known about its ecological performance. Much time is spent piecing together fragments of information to form a more complete picture, highlighting one of the challenges of repair – you often don't know what you are repairing.

This problem was apparent when analysing the existing and emergent ecologies that are not necessarily indigenous to the area, but perform important ecological functions, including the provision of habitat, bank stabilisation, slowing of flood water and water filtration. These ecologies differ substantially to their pre-settlement counterparts (which often form the benchmarks for revegetation) and usually include non-indigenous species that are better adapted to urban landscapes heavily modified by humans. Time, energy and expense is often expended removing these emergent ecologies based on a conservation paradigm that views such 'weed' ecologies as wrong. Yet there is a growing recognition that these 'feral' plant communities often work harder, are more resilient and are better adapted to the disturbances of a tough urban environment than many indigenous ecologies.

A good example are the large stands of Common Reed (*Phragmites australis*) which now dominate many non-channelised portions of the creek. Although *Phragmites* does prevent a diversity of other riparian and aquatic plants from establishing by forming dense monocultures, it nonetheless is an excellent colonising plant that quickly finds a foothold in damaged and disturbed landscapes and performs very useful roles in removing nutrients, preventing erosion and providing habitat. It is, in other words, a very good plant for repair. Much more research is required to understand the value of these emergent ecologies which challenge our ideas about the 'correct' state of nature, as well as the necessary timeframes for repair.

The emergence of urban ecology has helped clarify these discussions by placing humans front and centre of every ecosystem, focussing on the crucial role that natural systems, biodiversity and contact with living things plays in our health and by extension the health of the city. It challenges the diverse array of 'nature deficit disorders' we now face, such as a lack of empathy with the natural world, vitamin D deficiencies, morbid obesity due to insufficient exercise and lack of exposure to microbes that bolster the immune system. Urban ecology reminds us the city is composed of relationships between living things; in other words, it understands the city as an ecology rather than a series of singular objects. As a result, it encourages us to consider all components holistically rather than as fragments, challenging the twentieth century, mono-functional city which has been designed as a monoculture of infrastructure where each component of the city is largely considered in isolation. When we view the city as an ecosystem, we become much more interested in the relationship and interaction between components, and much less likely to take a fragmented, isolated view.

Our work on the Moonee Ponds Creek has shown us that there are no simple answers to these complex questions.

Moonee Ponds Creek (30 October 2015), Melbourne. Photograph, Site Office.

Large scale urban repair will only be possible through the overlap and collaboration between multiple projects and strategies. While our project began with the simple objective 'remove the concrete', we have come to recognise that singular design gestures offer little in isolation unless these fragments are considered as part of the whole. Ultimately, this way of understanding the city organically as vectors and flows rather than concretely as objects recognises the fundamental limits of natural systems, the interrelationships

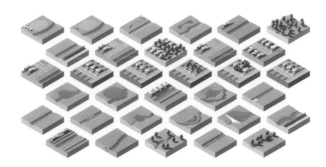

Site Office, Moonee Ponds Creek, Water Investigation Tools, masterplan graphic. Image, Site Office.

(Overpage) Neville HP Cayley, *Vanellus miles: Masked Lapwing bird*. Watercolour of Masked Lapwing birds, *Vanellus miles*, 1892. Source, Museums Victoria/Artist: Neville HP Cayley.

between all components of the city and, by extension, the necessary compromises that need to be made. While infinitely more complex and at far greater risk of failure, it does suggests that the most important role for designers in coming years will be working on the strategic governance of cities where our ability to identify relationships between elements is most useful.

Two final observations about the Moonee Ponds Creek before we move on. The first is the importance of having friends in the right places. While these projects are large and complex by nature, they are often only made possible by the hard work and generosity of local Friends groups who display an enormous appetite for repair over many years. These people are the real visionaries for repair, often recognising the opportunities years before bureaucrats or designers pick up their pens. In the case of the creek, it was these people who called a halt to the channelisation program thirty years ago, a timely reminder that repair begins in your backyard. The second observation is hopeful – one afternoon we discovered a tree growing opportunistically out of the concrete channel, a compelling sign of urban nature re-exerting itself within the most forbidding environments.

Large rural repair

While most of our time is spent working within the city, it is outside the city where the vast bulk of damaged and disturbed landscapes are located and consequently where

Mitigate, Repair, Adapt or Evolve? Some Thoughts on Repair

43

the greatest opportunities for repair lie. This includes the large swathe of rural landscapes shaped by primary production, stretching from intensive agricultural food production, plantation forestry, large monocultures of grain, livestock grazing, intensive mining and mineral extraction. Each of these landscapes is defined by a cavalcade of ecological problems, yet because they exist beyond the edge of the city, they typically sit outside of people's minds. Unhelpful binary oppositions such as city and country are no longer relevant when the impact of the city now extends to every landscape across the country. These damaged landscapes are a consequence of where and how we choose to live.

Since 2016, we have been working on Woowookarung, a 640 hectare regional park located on the outskirts of Ballarat. Consolidated from numerous government owned land parcels, the newly created park represents a patchwork of intact yet heavily disturbed forest blocks, intersected by regenerating former timber plantation blocks. The intact forest blocks consist of what many people would call 'bush', that vague descriptor often applied to those landscapes that are neither city nor rural and clearly contain gum trees.

While the forest does contain important ecologies, it has also been heavily disturbed, including during the Gold Rush(4) when the forest was heavily logged as a source of

Moonee Ponds Creek, Union Street (19 May 2008), Melbourne.
Photograph, Friends of the Moonee Ponds Creek.

timber for the goldfields. While the lack of gold spared the landscape much of the destructive mining activities that levelled entire hillsides nearby, the traces of gold mining activity are obvious, including earthworks, dams, water races, diggings and mullock heaps. Perhaps most notable is the lack of big old trees within the park as a result of consistent firewood collection over the years.

By the 1950s the government had established timber plantations within the forest, which continued until 2012 when the last plantations were removed due to dwindling yields on the poor soil and the land handed back to government. The hand back followed standard forestry practices and included the removal of all remaining trees, the

ripping and inversion of the soil profile with large mechanical equipment to remove tree roots, followed by aerial seeding. Photographs reveal the extent of devastation to the land and the resulting patchwork of intact and cleared forest.

Understanding the most effective methods to regenerate the former plantation blocks and reunite them with the remaining mature, yet disturbed forest fragments, has been a significant challenge at Woowookarung. There has been much focus on whether the existing ecological communities

Woowookarung Park, aerial, (28 February 2014), Victoria.
Photograph, Micky Rootes.

within the park are representative of what existed on the site prior to white settlement, and whether these ecologies are both appropriate and sustainable heading into an uncertain future. As was the case with Moonee Ponds Creek, decision making at Woowookarung has been hampered by the lack of information, analysis and understanding of the natural systems and ecologies found on site and how they may work.

While everyone has been pondering the best strategy to reunite the forest fragments, the landscape has been quietly going about its business and regenerating. In the six years since the plantations were removed, the forest has been steadily growing back, another great example of the capacity for damaged landscapes to heal themselves. Even when we do nothing something happens. Comparative photographs taken by the local field naturalists from known reference points within the park have plotted the progression of this growth. We also undertook comparative analysis using historical aerial photography to plot the evolution of the forest structure over the last eighty years. Once again, the capacity of the forest to regrow after damage has been astounding.

What is growing back at Woowookarung is not necessarily representative of what was once there and raises the vexing question as to whether we choose to intervene within this natural process or alternatively allow nature to run its course. The regenerating forest now consists of many different plants, some which are not indigenous to the original forest and others which are declared weeds, including significant infestations of gorse and broom which pose an ongoing threat to the ecologies in the adjacent intact forest blocks. Similarly in the time since the plantations were felled, larger groups of kangaroos have come to the park to enjoy a variety of ground story plants not found within the intact forest. Once the forest regrows, these kangaroos will move elsewhere.

Evidence of such rapid change questions whether such ecologies should remain locked in a steady state condition defined by inflexible ecological benchmarks, or alternatively allowed to evolve according to the prevailing conditions. The revelation that many pre-settlement ecological communities upon which so much repair and conservation is benchmarked, is the result of long term human intervention, offers a transformative moment in how we perceive the Australian landscape and how we choose to act within it. The fact that our First Nations peoples worked in symbiosis with natural systems for millennia, carefully shaping a lifestyle and landscape, is a timely reminder that such stewardship is both possible and necessary.

How we develop a contemporary relationship with country that recognises the realities of the modern world, population growth and the carrying capacity of a large yet fragile Australian landscape is a significant challenge. Useful clues to what this relationship to country might be are provided by Charles Massy, a farmer, whose recent book *Call of the Reed Warbler*[5] outlines regenerative agricultural techniques that farm with and not against nature. Observing the devastation wrought on landscapes by traditional farming techniques, including overgrazing and annual tilled monocultures, Massy proposes alternate regenerative methods that build soil health, water retention, solar energy capture, dynamic ecosystems and social well being and cohesion. Much of this land 'repair' draws both knowledge and inspiration from indigenous land management which transformed the Australian landscape into a vast, agricultural system that supported plants, animals and humans at a continental scale.

While Massy himself acknowledges the challenge of feeding a global population now in excess of eight billion people, it would seem a useful starting point to transform agricultural practice which currently farms in spite of our landscape into something that genuinely supports it. At a lecture in Melbourne in 2017, historian Bruce Pascoe described the vast swathes of countryside utilised by indigenous people to grow grain, yam daisy and other crops,[6] and then showed photographs of freshly baked bread made from the grain collected from kangaroo grass (*Themeda triandra*), one of the few Australian plants that can be found across most of the continent.[7]

Woowookarung Park, Welcome to Country,
Uncle Bryon and Linda Zibell.
Photograph, Micky Rootes.

Walking through Woowookarung with local elders Uncle Bryon Powell and Tammy Gilson, they describe the richness of the landscape as both a spiritual and physical resource for their people; it comes as no surprise that the name Woowookarung means 'a place of plenty'.

Very large 'wilderness' repair

We would like to end with some thoughts on the 'bush', which underpins so many settlement stories. These myths continue today in countless tourism and car advertisements which depict vast wilderness and wide open spaces. These depictions work to the stereotype of a wild Australia unmodified by human activity, perpetuating a *terra nullius* or 'nobody's land' where the landscape is absent of people. Such depictions continue to shape how we view many of our iconic natural landscapes, where there is a tendency to see the landscape before us as the 'correct' state of nature; in other words, how the landscape should be without human occupation or interference. This representation drives a strong push to conserve these landscapes in accordance with this state.

Woowookarung Park, top (13 February 2013).
Photograph, Micky Rootes.
Bottom, regenerating forest (15 March 2017).
Photograph, Site Office.

Mitigate, Repair, Adapt or Evolve? Some Thoughts on Repair

47

Eugene von Guérard,
Mount William and part of the Grampians in West Victoria 1865.
Oil on cardboard, 30.3 x 40.6 cm, National Gallery of Victoria,
Melbourne, Collier Bequest, 1955 (1562-5).

Eugene von Guérard,
View from the Gaphill of the Serra Ranges.
South western portion of the Australian Grampians 1858.
Pen and ink and wash, 27.0 x 50.9 cm irreg.
(image) 33.4 x 50.9 cm (sheet),
National Gallery of Victoria, Melbourne,
Felton Bequest, 1960 (632-5).

In 2012 we began working with Parks Victoria on the planning of a long distance walk through the Grampians Gariwerd National Park, one of Victoria's most significant natural landscapes. Much time was spent understanding the 'nature' of the landscapes through which we were walking. The project coincided with two extremely helpful events. Firstly was an amazing exhibition of Eugene von Guérard's paintings and drawings at the National Gallery of Victoria,[8] which included works depicting the Grampians soon after white settlement, and secondly was the publication of

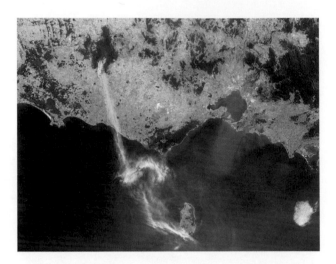

The Moderate Resolution Imaging Spectroradiometer (MODIS) on NASA's Terra satellite captured this image showing large bush fires burning in south western Victoria on 18 February 2013. Winds blew a long plume of smoke south toward the Bass Strait. About 300 firefighters using dozens of vehicles and fourteen aircraft were battling the fires, which were burning near Grampians National Park. Lightning ignited a number of fires about a week prior; two of them merged to create the large fire shown here. Authorities estimated that it had burned about 6,000 hectares (15,000 acres) by 19 February 2013. NASA image courtesy Jeff Schmaltz, LANCE MODIS Rapid Response. Caption text sourced from Adam Voiland, 18 February 2013, *Fires in South eastern Australia*, viewed 14 April 2013, https://visibleearth.nasa.gov/view.php?id=80465.

Bill Gammage's book *The Biggest Estate on Earth* in which he speculates on what von Guérard was likely seeing as he travelled through Gariwerd in 1858. Gammage suggests that the forests von Guérard sketched a century and half ago were significantly different in composition and density to the forests today, challenging the idea that the forests we now see are representative of how they always were and always should be.[9]

There has been a growing body of research dispelling the myth of the Australian wilderness as untouched by human hand and the realisation that landscapes across the continent have been shaped by sustained human intervention over many thousands of years. It is now well documented that when the white settlers first arrived in Australia, they described a landscape that appeared before them like a vast managed estate. Time and time again the words and images of the new European arrivals made

reference to a manicured, park-like landscape. It would now seem this 'place without people' has been shaped by many generations of traditional owners. The wilderness it would seem, has always been a garden. Standing on the Dunkeld golf course at dusk, it is easy to see the interaction between humans and their ecosystem, with hundreds of kangaroos happily maintaining the perfectly manicured grass.

Such a revelation is useful in understanding how we work within such beautiful landscapes, especially in light of new threats posed by climate change. During the course of the project, Gariwerd experienced a number of extreme weather events which caused considerable damage to the park, including flooding and wildfires. While many ecosystems are adapted to cope with fire, it has become clear that the extremity of such events pose a significant risk to these ecologies, and that changes in the composition and density of our forests over the last two hundred years may be a contributing factor. The 2016 bushfires in the central highlands of Tasmania exposed the vulnerability of many ecologies to the effects of climate change, with irreversible damage to a sensitive alpine ecology not evolved to deal with such intense fire. As ecologist David Bowman bluntly said of the fires, "this is what climate change looks like."[10]

It is now becoming clear that strategies for repair will be necessary across the entire country, including our most remote and precious landscapes. Such strategies now include ecological based burning regimes (or 'firestick farming') that utilise more frequent, cooler burns to stimulate ecological health and maintain a desirable composition of plants within the landscape, as well as mitigate the likelihood of more severe bushfires. Similarly, 'tenure blind' strategies allow better management of complex ecological issues that are 'blind' to the surveyors plan. These strategies challenge the primacy of freehold tenure and have more in common with the management of the pre-settlement Australian landscape by a multitude of First Nations, where the collective landscape was managed on behalf of all irrespective of geopolitical boundaries.

Techniques which have been used for many thousands of years to 'curate' the Australian landscape may once again play a vital role in caring for country and repairing our land.

Some final thoughts on repair

Repair is not someone else's problem.
Repair begins in your own backyard.
Everyone of us can initiate repair –
we can all become repairers.
Repair is needed at every scale
and in every location.
Repair operates beyond site boundaries,
geographic scales, and professional disciples.
There are opportunities for repair in every project.
Repair is both small and simple as well as large
and complex.
Just because repair is small, does not mean
it is less valuable.
Repair is often many things at once. It can take
many different forms, strategies and outcomes.
Repair can be pre-emptive by not making a mess
in the first place.
Repair favours actions over words.
Repair begins with the site and not the form.
Repair relies on collaboration rather than
competition, much like the symbiotic relationships
that underpin the diversity of our ecologies.
Repair is often messy, unclear, incomplete
and emerging.
Sometimes repair is downright ugly, challenging
our conception of what is successful.
While design is driven by aesthetics and form,
the repair of ecologies is not.
We need a more effective language to observe,
measure and quantify repair.
Without this language, the most appropriate
method of repair remains elusive.
Repair takes time. You need to develop patience
to be a repairer.
Sometimes it is difficult to see what you
are repairing.
Sometimes you feel like you don't understand
what you are repairing.
Repair is commitment.
Repair is an act of kindness.
While repair may be complicated, it does
not favour complex solutions.
The best strategies of repair may well
be the most simple.
The most radical repair strategy may well
be planting a tree.
Whether we choose to mitigate, repair, adapt
or evolve, repair will require reinserting ourselves
within our ecosystem and reigniting our
relationship with nature.
As architect Paul Shepheard so eloquently states,
"wilderness is not just something you look at; it's
something you are part of. You live inside a body
made of wilderness material." (11)

(1) City of Melbourne n.d., *Unleashing the Potential of Nature, Discussion Paper on City Ecology, Ecosystems and Biodiversity*, City of Melbourne, viewed 19 February 2018, <https://participate.melbourne.vic.gov.au/application/files/2214/2369/1370/Urban_Ecology_Discussion_Paper.pdf>.
(2) Schetzer, A 2016, 'Fighting for survival, some animals and plants are thriving in the heart of Melbourne', *The Age*, 30 April, viewed 15 February 2018, <https://www.theage.com.au/national/victoria/fighting-for-survival-some-animals-and-plants-are-thriving-in-the-heart-of-melbourne-20160428-gogzle.html>.
(3) Melbourne and Metropolitan Board of Works.
(4) "The Victorian gold rush was a period in the history of Victoria, Australia approximately between 1851 and the late 1860s." See Wikipedia n.d., *Victorian gold rush*, Wikipedia, viewed 19 February 2017, <https://en.wikipedia.org/wiki/Victorian_gold_rush>.
(5) Massy, C 2017, *Call of the Reed Warbler: A New Agriculture – a New Earth*, University of Queensland Press, St Lucia, Queensland, Australia.
(6) The 2017 Stephen Murray-Smith Memorial Lecture by Bruce Pascoe was delivered on 14 November 2017 at the State Library of Victoria, Melbourne.
(7) See Pascoe, B 2014, *Dark Emu: Black Seeds Agriculture Or Accident?*, Magabala Books, Broome, Western Australia, Australia.
(8) The exhibition *Eugene von Guérard: Nature Revealed*, curated by Ruth Pullin and Michael Varcoe-Cocks with special assistance from Humphrey Clegg, was held at the National Gallery of Victoria (NGV Australia) in Melbourne from 16 April to 7 August 2011.
(9) See Gammage, B 2012, *The Biggest Estate on Earth: How Aborigines made Australia*, Allen & Unwin, Crows Nest, NSW, Australia.
(10) Australian Politics Forum 2016, *System Collapse: Latest Stage Of AGW*, Australian Politics Forum, 30 January, viewed 19 February 2018, <http://www.ozpolitic.com/forum/YaBB.pl?action=print;num=1454149439>.
(11) Shepheard, P 1997, *The Cultivated Wilderness: Or, What Is Landscape?*, MIT Press, Cambridge, Massachusetts, USA, London, UK.

Grampians National Park, Mt Abrupt, Victoria, day after the big wet, (14 October 2014).
Photograph, David Roberts, Parks Victoria.

REPAIR AND ABORIGINAL ARCHITECTURE

PAUL MEMMOTT

The theme of the Australian pavilion at Biennale Architettura 2018 is 'repair'.

"...*Repair* will frame and reveal an architectural culture in Australia that is evolving through processes that integrate built and natural systems to effect repair of the environment, and in so doing, repair of other conditions such as social, economic and cultural ones".[1]

The potent symbolic content of the *Repair* exhibit in Venice, Italy, is a reconstruction of a temperate grassland in south-eastern Australia, with all of the Australian plants being grown in glasshouses at Sanremo, Italy, which shares a similar temperate climate, to generate this transported ecosystem. For many architectural theorists, the idea of 'repairing' the natural environment in a design project best fits the design paradigm of 'sustainability'.

The emergence of the idea of 'sustainability' in architectural design and execution has developed and gathered momentum globally throughout the late twentieth and early twenty-first centuries, accompanied by the growing concern over climate change and the gradual recognition that humankind has inadvertently catalysed the Anthropocene era! The first theoretical pillar of sustainability was environmental sustainability, which involved protecting the environment through design and selection of building materials that were biodegradable and did not lead to ecosystem over-exploitation and destruction.[2] The second theoretical pillar to emerge was economic sustainability, the third was social sustainability and the fourth and least understood pillar (and least implemented) has been cultural sustainability.[3] Environmental sustainability is clearly a central theme of the Australia's Venice Biennale Pavilion's topic of repair, especially if its meaning is more than just sustaining badly damaged ecosystems but regenerating and improving ecosystem balances.[4] But how might environmental sustainability be intertwined with cultural sustainability in good practice?

This essay explores ways by which contemporary Australian architects (including Indigenous ones) are attempting to achieve this through collaborations with Australia's First Nations peoples. I draw briefly from the actual case-study projects both submitted to and exhibited in the Australian Pavilion. This essay employs an ethnographic historical narrative technique centred on the south-east Australian grasslands to elicit a set of ecological constructs, cultural change propositions, design values and cultural principles to provide understandings of how emerging intercultural partnerships may bridge the gap between 'repairing' environments and 'maintaining' cultures, in politically and professionally sensitive contexts. It reflects a wider architectural awareness and design paradigm emerging around the globe that involves a strengthening Indigenous Architecture movement.[5] This essay draws from my forty-five years of professional life working for and being taught by Indigenous clients and directing the Aboriginal Environments Research Centre at the University of Queensland.

This essay addresses how repair might work, and *is* working in certain ways, in the contemporary field of Aboriginal Architecture in Australia. I start with the narrative that draws from the early ethnographic descriptions in South-east Australia[6] and later move to the nineteenth century contact history.[7]

On the basalt plains country

Scene: the Temperate Grasslands in what is now Victoria, South-eastern Australia, 1835.

Dooti awoke at the pre-dawn to the sound of the song-man's boomerangs clapping. She emerged from her domed *wuurn* (house) to blow the fire coals and raise flames for warmth. The winter rains had departed a month before and the bone moon was hovering low in the sky to the west with the Morning Star. There was not a breath of wind, giving perfect conditions to make the great smoke signal to invite the surrounding tribespeople to gather at *Mirraywuyay* for the annual assembly of the grassland tribespeoples. More and more boomerang percussionists joined the distant singing as the local clansmen began their ceremony for the invitation smoke. As the sun lipped above the horizon, all of the camp had to be at the side of the big swamp a kilometre away.

The local *Bunjil* (Eaglehawk) Dreaming clansmen emerged in full body paint in a single line to commence their Kangaroo fertility dance. The *Waa* (Crow) Dreaming men from the neighbouring clan stood ready with their green boughs ready to manage the fire. When the dance reached its crescendo, the senior clan Elder, *Jagajaga* took the burning firestick to the swamp edge and lit the tall fringing grass. Flames leapt high as there was much dry dead grass interspersed with green on the swamp's edges. It was the role of the *Waa* men to control the fire so that it burnt in a narrow band from north to east (clockwise) around the periphery of the 500m circular swamp. As the song men raised their pitch, the great spiral white smoke began its ascent into the still morning sky. If it remained calm, the spiral would reach the height necessary to be seen for a radius of 250 kilometres covering the territories of the seven tribes of the Plains Nation.

Later in the middle of the day, *Dooti* was on the basalt-strewn plains with her clanswomen's group, digging root foods (tubers, rhizomes, corms, bulbs). They were accompanied by some of the younger women from the neighbouring clan who were also *Bunjil*, having married in to the *Waa* clan. The women had spent most of the morning targeting *murnong* tubers (daisy roots) whose presence

across the plain was conspicuous by their bright yellow flowers. But they supplemented these with other species of orchids that had shot up after the good winter rain. Their metre-long digging sticks, water coolamon and reed baskets were placed to one side together with tied bundles of grass for thatching the domed roofs in the camp. The women were taking a break in the shade of a small patch of shrubs on the otherwise open plain, and lightly roasting a small portion of their foodstuffs for a midday snack. The gossip was about the eligibility of particular young women from other tribal groups as wives to be promised for the young boys who would undergo the 'making-men' ceremony at the forthcoming assembly. *Margurah*, a visiting senior woman was praising the virtues as well as promoting the economic preference for the daughters of the Stone-Dreaming people to the west, who controlled rituals and rights over the greenstone axe and obsidian knife quarries.

Some weeks later, when the moon had grown full:

The great assembly was now well underway. All of those invited had arrived, according to the clan messengers who had travelled with the invitation ochre and feathers a moon before. The square-up rituals had been completed to equalise emotions – resolve grievances by duel fighting and perform mourning obligations for the deceased. The *Tanderrum* ceremonies had then followed over six days to ritually smoke all of the visitors, cleansing them of any malignant spirits that may have entered upon their well-being, and then to bestow them with rights to join in the local collection of food and material resources. And then the hundreds of visitors (perhaps almost 2,000) had to be all carefully allocated to their camping places between the foothills of the woody uplands and the fast-running stream on the edge of the plain, with an allocated defecation area at the rear. They all needed access to ample firewood and freshwater, but the camping pattern was according to locational positioning and had to be preserved: each party had to be camping in the direction of their homeland. All those from one language group had to be together and broken down into clusters according to their constituent clans, which could be either *Waa* or *Bunjil* Dreaming. Public dancing corroborees had commenced in the evenings with each language group vying to be the most polished performers and at times, humorous dancers. This pattern would only be broken on the three nights of the man-making ceremony when everyone would camp around the ceremony ground in two large groups, either *Waa* or *Bunjil* group, to represent the two inter-marrying halves of the regional bloc of the plains tribespeople. These two categories of people would also be expressed during the ceremony in both sitting and dancing groups as well as styles of body paint-up and dress apparel. Husbands had to split from wives and adult children went with their father's clan. All young children were

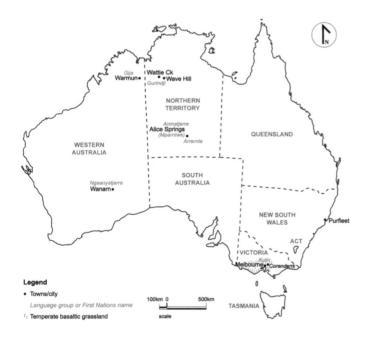

Map of Australia, places and groups mentioned in the text. Source, Paul Memmott, Aboriginal Environments Research Centre, University of Queensland.

(Overpage) John Skinner Prout, *Melbourne from Collingwood 1847*, with swamp ecology destroyed. Lithograph; 22.8 x 37.5 cm., on sheet 33.5 x 42.0 cm. Source, State Library of Victoria.

Repair and Aboriginal Architecture

December 1846 on original

separated under a chaperone, well away from the ceremony ground. These were the socio-spatial customs of the grassland peoples.

The hunting drive begins:

Jemba, the husband of *Dooti* was in charge of the right flank of the great kangaroo and emu drive which would supply the camp with fresh meat for the duration of the ceremonies. Patchwork mosaic burning had been carried out before the wet season in the drive area, and now these patches contained succulent grass shoots from the ample winter rainfall. It was these shoots that drew in the feeding kangaroos. The drive was happening on day 4, after the visitor's offerings of smoked eels and fish as well as their vegetable baskets had been enjoyed by all. The weather was favourable with a prevailing wind from the north arising in the mid-morning. The strategy was to throw an arc of

Ground. Photograph, Linda Tegg.
The beginning point of the walk (or pilgrimage way)
at Jinbarak. Gurindji elders Timmy Vincent, Kathleen
Sambo, Rosemary Johnson, Violet Wadrill, Biddy Wavehill,
Jimmy Wavehill share their stories.

people, men, women and children, across a distance of twenty or so kilometres and gradually move south over a whole day towards a V-junction between two running streams, making as much noise as possible with the aid of barking hunting dogs, and by igniting selected patches of unburnt grass to make smoky fires. As they walked, the lead beaters from the local clan would sing the songs of the ancestral beings, the two Black Snake Cousins, the Long-tail one and the Short-tail one, who created the sacred stone weir sites in these streams. According to this sacred history, the two Cousins travelled to meet up and dance together at the junction site called *Bukadi,* before travelling seaward to create the site of *Limbilimbi*, the sacred rocks off-shore that stopped the sea from advancing landwards.

This great drive would concentrate large mobs of kangaroos, flocks of emus and other animals into the stream

junction at *Bukadi* where long net traps were slung between poles and spearsmen were waiting. The right flank was led by the *Bunjil* men and the left by the *Waa* men. Once the kangaroo and emu meat was all consumed, the camp would fall back to the reed-plaited eel and fish traps set in the rock weirs left by the Snake Cousins in the Dreamtime along the two streams. This system of stone-wall traps would yield the camp's sustenance during the final days of completing the ceremonies.

There is extensive ethnographic evidence that the temperate grasslands of the plains and dry foothills were seasonally maintained by the *Kulin* Nation through the dual practices of the controlled burning of the country and tuber foraging. The annual burning just prior to the start of the wet season prepared the country for a regrowth of green shoots from the root stocks which remained unharmed below the surface. The shooting of the green grass and other herbage that occurred upon the advent of the first rains attracted herds of kangaroos from surrounding woodlands and enabled the large scale kangaroo drives to provide bulk meat for feasting. But the burning also prevented the growth of newly shooted shrubs, preventing scrublands or woodlands from spreading into the plains, and thus provided a technique of maintaining a stable equilibrium of the plant communities in the plains habitat. The second practice was the foraging for tubers and other edible plants, a task carried out by groups of women who divided themselves according to their principal totemic divisions (Crow and Eagle-hawk). In particular the *murnong* (*Microseris lanceolata*), later to be called the 'daisy root' by the colonists and new settlers due to its yellow-petalled flower, was a favourite target. *Murnong* plants were easily located by the flowers, and the women used sharpened sticks to dig some 15 centimetres to detect, follow down, expose and withdraw the tubers. This was in effect a form of patchwork hand ploughing that loosened the soil in which more *murnong* could grow from the flower seeds during the following season, and which gradually increased the distribution and yield of the tubers throughout the plain. The environmental impact of these practices over millenia was unnoticeable to the Eurocentric eyes of the new settlers who presumed they were in a wilderness rather than a carefully maintained and manicured landscape.[8]

Aboriginal land management occurred in every region of Australia involving in each case, a particular array of different practices. These usually included fire management,[9] fish (and sometimes eel) farming,[10] the protection of sacred sites identified as the reproductive habitats of individual species, rituals for these species, and beliefs of maintaining the collective balance of all species, both plants and animals.[11] In return, the sustainable use of plant and animal products provided food, shelter and artefacts for human and cultural sustainability. The human shaping of the entire continental landscape was perpetuated through recurring practices over millennia.

The implementation of land management practices was preceded by the gradual territorialisation of the continent's regions over fifty or more millennia. Groups became established in specific territories and constructed environmentally-based identities, languages, totemic affiliations and kinship structures. The identity of these groups became expressed in the socio-spatial behaviours at larger scale camps and social settings,(12) as demonstrated at the *Mirraywuyay* gathering of the grass-plains peoples. It was also expressed through groups' ceremonial expressions in maintaining and celebrating the sacred sites in their respective countries which collectively provided the basis for a sense of having a 'cultural landscape' together with the ecological relationships that evolved in the cohabitation in the environment.

Certain Aboriginal socio-spatial behaviours have been retained, albeit adapted, and in some cases simplified by many Aboriginal groups across Australia. Types of Aboriginal spatial behaviours have thus been understood and incorporated into designs by *Repair* architects including avoidance behaviours between particular kin (mother-in-law and son-in-law avoidance, gender-separated group activity spaces) as at the Walumba Elders Centre in the Warmun community on Turkey Creek (remote north of Western Australia), designed by iredale pedersen hook, and further described in the Projects section of this catalogue/book.

How does this historical understanding relate to the exhibition? The educational symbolism of Aboriginal Architecture is readily analysable into three identity concepts originally formulated by Keeffe.(13) The first identity concept is that of making reference to classical associations from the pre-colonial era. In the submissions for *Repair* exhibition, an important example is the representation of the seasonal calendar in the landscape design and educational messaging at the Ngarara Place of the Ngarara Willim Centre (included in this catalogue/book) designed by Greenaway Architects in the city campus of RMIT University (Royal Melbourne Institute of Technology) which links together the climatic, floral and faunal changes of environmental transformation that were so acutely monitored by the traditional peoples of the *Kulin* Nation in their hunting-gathering-fishing lifestyles. This knowledge is further embedded in other projects (for example, Perth Stadium Park by Hassell) which not only select food-bearing plants as landscaping, but also purposefully choose plants whose fruitings will attract particular animals and birds, reactivating the chain of connection in the seasonal cycle. Traditional Aboriginal socio-religious lifeways fitted into this seasonal calendar as exemplified by the assembly at *Mirraywuyay*. I shall discuss the other two identity concepts defined by Keeffe(14) in due course.

Tangentyere Design & University of Newcastle, Essential Infrastructures, Anthelk-Ewlpawe Town Camp, Alice Springs (Mparntwe), Northern Territory. Anthelk-Ewlpawe (literally means 'flood debris'), is on Charles Creek and is a lineal decentralised settlement situated beside a normally dry riverbed, interspersed with rocky outcrops, and containing the travel routes of at least three Dreamings, the most commonly known being the Dingo (Artnwere) on the south side. The Central Arrernte people have an intense cultural landscape in Alice Springs (Brooks 1991). This project is as much about repairing the infrastructure and well-being inequities between the Town Camp people and the more affluent townspeople. Tangentyere Design is an architectural practice established and directed by Tangentyere Council to respond to the needs of some nineteen Town Camps.
Photograph, Chris Tucker.

ARM Architecture, Barak Building, Melbourne. The apartment building
with the staring face of the Elder, William Barak from the 1800s,
gazes down Melbourne's central axial Swanston Street to
the Shrine of Remembrance (2.8 kilometres away).
Photograph, Peter Bennetts.

Colonial impacts

The narrative returns. The year is 1881 and the scene
is a rural roadway leading into Melbourne:

Dooti is now a very old woman, but still strong and animated,
riding on the tray of a horse-drawn wagon with some
younger Aboriginal women and children, and led by their
men-folk who are walking in front. She is 'calling the country';
calling out the *Kulin* Nation's names of each hill, creek,
and waterhole that they pass as they travel, occasionally
weeping, singing to the country, then reminiscing about her
experiences and memories in each place during her younger
years when people were under the old Law, and before the
great disease-time which came with the white men and killed
4/5 of their plains-people.
    Dooti is talking to her grandchildren and her great grand-
daughter *Bulthuku* (also called Jane), in particular, lamenting
the loss of the food resource places and the destruction
of sacred sites. She is encouraging *Bulthuku,* but with a
chastising tone as if she will not take notice, to remember
that her cultural identity is based on the Dreaming in their
country. The wagon enters and moves through the growing
suburbs of Melbourne with sprawling estates and industrial
coal and steam-powered factories. The travelling group who
are all extended family, lament on the impact and loss of the
cultural landscape....*Dooti* is calling the names of sacred sites
and of her ancestors whose spirits she believes are still at
those sites; all being subsumed by the fast-expanding
urban development.

Once the steam engine-driven industrial era reached
Australia in the late 1800s, the colonial conversion of the
continent for economic purposes irreversibly damaged
the ecology and habitats, either by urban expansion,
pastoralism, mining, farming, logging, over-fishing, draining
and damming waterways, and feral animal and plant
introductions, all bringing the onset of the Anthropocene
in the Southern Hemisphere. The differential spread of the
frontier over 180 years had variable impacts in different
ecological systems.

The party of *Dooti* and her relatives is travelling
in protest, along the 65 kilometre journey south from their
Aboriginal farm station of Coranderrk to Melbourne.
    They intend to petition the Colonial Parliament against
the actions of the Aborigines Protection Board which has
been trying to sell their Coranderrk farm station, and which
through imposed management conditions has undermined
the initiatives of the *Kulin* plainspeople to be economically
self-sufficient. This is despite their earlier successes at self-
governance, farming, house-building and commercial hop-
processing, from when they voluntarily took up residence
there in the 1860s with the help of Protector Thomas and
Missionary John Green, after a time of starvation and land
loss. Worse still, the Board wants to force tribespeople
who have some white (Anglo-Celtic) blood to leave their
old people at Coranderrk and live in cities and work for
white people, and assimilate. The group of protesters is
led by the last strong clan spokesmen who are grounded
in the old Law, the *Ngurangaeta* leaders, William Barak of

the *Woiwurrung* and Thomas Banfield of the *Taungurung*. *Dooti* is from the older generation again and a reference point of wisdom for the whole protest group. This is the tenth protest march which the group have made to the government in Melbourne since 1863, when they had delivered gifts to be sent for Queen Victoria and Prince Albert in return for their granted land rights. Unfortunately the Queen did not hear. *Bulthuku* (Jane) was left angered and bitter.

In Aboriginal belief, the first travellers across the Australian continent were the ancestral heroes of the Dreamtime who created numerous sites as they travelled in which they deposited their sacred energies, perpetually left behind. In classical Aboriginal societies (before the colonial invasion), these creative acts were re-enacted and celebrated in ceremonies, as in the case of the Black Snake Cousins who travelled through the grassland country creating the weirs. Today the popular term 'Song-lines' is often used to describe these lines of travel and the creation sites at which songs, sacred histories and ceremonies and sometimes sacred objects were left behind. However, travel routes of cultural significance to Aboriginal people have also been generated during the colonial era, as was the case with the protest marches from Coranderrk to Melbourne. Another protest example is embedded in the *Repair* exhibit 'Wave Hill Walk-off Pavilions' by the Bower Studio, University of Melbourne – also this work is further discussed in this catalogue/book.

These pavilions were designed to commemorate and provide a modern pilgrimage route for retracing the steps of the *Gurindji* people along their Wave Hill cattle station 'walk-off' route that followed their strike in 1966 over decades of impoverished working conditions for stockmen and domestics under the control of the British Lord Vestey's pastoral empire. In the same way that the introduced pastoral stock destroyed the ecology of the Victorian grasslands, the imposition of the cattle industry in the Northern Territory severely damaged the *Gurindji* country, including its sacred sites and biodiversity as well as the intertwined land management practices. The broader vision of the 'walk-off' was to 'repair' the country and has involved ceremonial revitalisation and more recently Aboriginal ranger programs. The three architectural/educational installations along the route mark the 50th anniversary of this historical event which eventually catalysed the return of lands and/or rights in land to Aboriginal peoples across Australia in a cascading succession of political processes including land rights legislations, Native Title legislation and other federally-funded land purchase options. These lineal travel routes in the Australian landscapes or urbanscapes thus generate significant cultural properties for place design initiatives in collaboration with Indigenous Traditional Owners.

This introduces the second and third categories of identity concepts in Aboriginal Architectural semantics or meaning (as inspired originally by Keefe;[15] the second is architectural expression by design reference to significant contact history[16] experiences as a way of embedding and expressing important identity elements. The Wattie Creek installations thus make reference to the iron humpies (self-built shelters) of pastoral camps, a symbol of sedentarised colonial lifestyle for many Aboriginal people.

The third category of semantic reference is that of resistance or oppositional statements, and the Wattie Creek project again qualifies here as celebrating the *Gurindji* peoples' pastoral strike and 'walk-off' and their long wait for land rights. A comparable symbolism in a modern architectural project that draws on semantic inferences from the Coranderrk protests is described below.

Understanding environmental change

There was a tendency in both colonial and post-colonial thought and writing to create and perpetuate a dichotomy between the city and the bush, the settled cities and farms of the east-coast versus the interior and northern wildernesses. However, the artificial colonial landscape versus the natural wild landscape myth has been gradually deconstructed in the late twentieth century with improved ethnographic models and understandings of ancient Aboriginal land management practices, as well as ecological understandings of how European land practices brought irreversible damage.[17]

A different way of thinking then, is that all ecosystems both in urban, rural and remote areas have been undergoing successive transformations over centuries and millennia as a result of human interventions, starting with Aboriginal pre-colonial era, then followed in the colonial era by impacts such as pastoral grazing, farming, timber-getting, land clearing, feral plant and animal introduction, soil erosion, atmospheric pollution culminating in the emerging Anthropocene with the likelihood of severe climate change. The proposition of restoring a landscape to some pristine imaginary model of an earlier non-human ecosystem becomes questionable if not impossible to model let alone achieve. What sense can we make then from the exhibition theme of *Repair*? The Biennale theme has been framed as a provocation to interrogate in what way to repair – accepting we can't go backwards. Is there something that we can call 'partial repair' around which one can identify some sound ecological planning principles that mitigate against loss of species and support a healthy reproductive ecosystem? The exhibition asks for ongoing interrogation around these questions.

Situating projects within Aboriginal Cultural Landscapes

A challenge then for contemporary architects is how to relate a project with some moral integrity, to a changed cultural landscape, often an irreversibly changed landscape.

The UNESCO definition of a cultural landscape derived from a context of landscape conservation values is as follows:

"Cultural landscapes are those where human interaction with natural systems has, over a long time, formed a distinctive landscape. These interactions arise from, and cause, cultural values to develop. Managing these values, with their material, physical evidence and nonmaterial associations, so that they remain of outstanding universal value, is the particular challenge for World Heritage cultural landscape managers."[18]

Awareness of the many salient constituent places in an Aboriginal cultural landscape, both from the pre-colonial and post-colonial eras, leads to the challenge of how to position a building or development in such a landscape. One exemplar in the *Repair* submissions is the Charles Creek Town Camp development by Tangentyere Design in Alice Springs which is occupied by a mixture of *Arrernte* and *Anmatjerre* speaking peoples within the intense mythological landscape of *Mparntwe*, in proximity to sacred Dingo sites. Daily cultural practices are embedded within proximity to the sacred sites, as a type of cultural sustainability. Another exemplar is the case of the post-flood design of the Walumba Elders Centre; here the *Gija* people expressed the sense of the catastrophic flooding of their community in terms of a dance ceremony (*Girrirr Girrirr*) involving a travelling Cyclone Dreaming from the northern saltwater people. Ongoing practice of ceremony was an essential component of this design brief.

But this sense of connection to the surrounding landscape, whether it be a bush or urban setting, relates also to the principle of external orientation. A recurring design principle in architectural briefs over many decades has been a preference by Aboriginal clients to be visually connected to the exterior in many settings.[19] In fact this spatial principle dominates over any request for symbolism in projects. External orientation is also a stated design principle in a number of the *Repair* projects: for example at Wanarn Clinic for the *Ngaanyatjarra* of the Western Desert, as well as at Biripi Health Clinic at the former Purfleet Mission on the East Coast, both by the Kaunitz Yeung Architecture firm.

Further on contemporary architectural approaches

But the narrative is not yet complete.
We must turn towards the present and consider the future. The year is 2018.

A young fair Aboriginal woman in a Melbourne classroom is telling the teacher and her class about her identity, stating that she is *Namba*, the great-grand-daughter of *Jemba* and *Dooti*, and a Traditional Owner of Melbourne by her bloodline. The class consists of Aboriginal-identifying young adults engaged in a land management course. They are to be rangers in a new National Park/Conservation area on the basalt grasslands to the north. They are being addressed by an Aboriginal architect named Jandamarra Fitzroy who discusses principles of ecological planning and the need to think about cultural landscapes in urban design in conjunction with environmental sustainability, and why Koories (southern Aboriginal people) need to be global leaders in carrying out local initiatives to care for country and so reverse development impacts, as well as redress lingering post-colonial attitudes.

He challenges the group by projecting an image of the controversial building with a face sculpted on its facade recently constructed in Melbourne; then asks some questions:

Does this building rejuvenate a spiritual meaning into the urban landscape of Melbourne? Does it invoke a memory of the old feeling of country, a place of natural and spiritual livelihood? He asks the class: Does the gaze of William Barak down the axis of Melbourne's CBD invoke the past values of the cultural landscapes of the Kulin Nation?

Namba replies that seeing Grandfather Barak's face always gives her a good spiritual feeling of his presence and reminds her of the old tribal ways. She says 'If somebody doesn't know what it means, it will make them ask, and they might learn something about *Kulin* culture and the theft of our land! We still feel him with us.'[20]

The posing of such questions forces us to consider whether an intertwining of both environmental and cultural approaches to sustainable design involves a respect and consideration for spiritual presences which are believed by different Indigenous peoples to continue to exist in an environment, irrespective of it being a remote, rural or urban setting. In short, according to belief, Aboriginal cultural landscapes contain a range of spiritual presences which animate them for those who appreciate and believe in them, as well as which have protective agency when people damage the environment in particular ways. Acknowledging the spiritual power of place has been a challenge for architects throughout the ages whether it be within the Greek, the Gothic, the Zen, the Inca or other traditions.

Spiritual presences are also incorporated into the *Repair* display reflecting this value of respect for cultural belief. The Aboriginal custom of smoking both people and environments (as was portrayed at the *Mirraywuyay* Camp) was aimed at cleansing away malignant spirits that could affect the well-being of a group's living spaces and its occupants. In several contemporary *Repair* projects, the architects have recognised and designed facilities for ritual smoking (despite onerous fire safety regulations), viz the Walumba Elders Centre at the remote Warmun community, and Ngarara Place in metropolitan Melbourne.

Environmental change and cultural change intertwined

There is thus an argument about Aboriginal cultural change that needs to be expressed. Just as the ecology has been gradually transforming as a result of successive human economic, territorial and religious activities, so has Aboriginal culture been transforming due first to its own internal innovations and diffusions over millennia, but second, due to the impacts of the colonial and post-colonial cultures of the new settlers and their descendants. So much so that in the Land Claim (and Native Title) courts, lawyers and anthropologists argue as to whether a particular group claiming Indigenous title over an area has retained its traditional system of laws and customs through a gradual transformation and adaptation of the old classical system despite the destructive impact of the foreign intruding cultural system...or alternatively, whether the old system is so adversely impacted by the new, that it no longer exists as a coherent system; that is, too many vital elements and binding forces have been lost or removed and it can no longer reproduce itself in a systemic way. This is the grim politics of the Native Title court.

We can draw the parallel here with an ecosystem that loses so many constituent fauna and flora species and micro-organisms together with the introduction of new competitive and destructive species (for example, rabbits, foxes, cane toads), that the integrity of the old system is no longer recognisable in any meaningful way. This leads us to link environmental sustainability with cultural

sustainability introducing a more profound way to think about what repair can mean in an architectural or urban design project, and especially in an Indigenous collaborative project. For a cultural system that emphasises relational self-identity (or personhood), this implies that humans define themselves in relation to environments and conversely that environments contain something of the nature of humans (forms of totemism).(21) To sustain one without the other becomes counter-productive to the well-being of both. Thus, maintaining the sustenance of healthy environments and healthy humans becomes an intertwined endeavour. This is why so many contemporary Aboriginal ideologies and practices of healing, emphasise being on country, understanding identity in relation to country, and knowing about being placed or grounded or rooted in country.(22) This in turn opens up an ongoing avenue of exploration in the examination of good-practice project exemplars. What projects can be identified that combine the management and repair of the environment with the management and repair of cultural well-being in an holistic approach?

What are the current cutting-edge best practices in Australian sustainable architecture that combine both environmental and cultural sustainabilities? This is examined further from the case studies being profiled in the exhibition, and elsewhere in the catalogue within the following piece by Dyirbal researcher Carroll Go-Sam. These projects cover a range of examples and principles but link in some way to both repair of landscape and repair of culture, and their intertwining.

iredale pedersen hook, Walumba Elders Centre, Warmun, Western Australia.
The central space in the Walumba Elders Centre with circular pit used for smoking ceremonies designed to spiritually cleanse visitors and guests by being immersed in smoke that repels malignant entities, being enjoyed here by local children. The Centre is raised in response to river flash flooding which occurs periodically but at a time scale of centuries (notwithstanding possible climate change).
Photograph, Peter Bennetts.

(1) See Australian Institute of Architects 2017, *The Australian Pavilion Biennale Architettura 2018: News: Sowing Seeds for 2018 Venice Architecture Biennale – Creative Team Announced*, Australian Institute of Architects, 23 August, viewed 22 February 2018, <http://wp.architecture.com.au/venicebiennale/sowing-seeds-for-2018-venice-architecture-biennale-creative-team-announced/>.

(2) See OECD (Organisation for Economic Co-operation and Development) 2001, *Sustainable Development: Critical Issues*, OECD, Paris, France; U.N. General Assembly 2002, *Report of the World Summit on Sustainable Development Johannesburg*, South Africa, 26 August – 4 September, United Nations, New York, USA.

(3) See Memmott, P & Keys, C 2015, 'Redefining architecture to accommodate cultural difference: designing for cultural sustainability', *Architectural Science Review*, vol. 58, no. 4, pp. 278-289.

(4) Girardet, H 2013, 'Sustainability is unhelpful: we need to think about regeneration', *The Guardian*, 10 June, viewed 4 January 2018, <https://www.theguardian.com/sustainable-business/blog/sustainability-unhelpful-think-regeneration>.

(5) See Memmott, P and Go-Sam, C 2003, 'Synthesizing Indigenous Housing Paradigms: An Introduction to TAKE 2', in P Memmott & C Chambers (eds), *TAKE 2: Housing Design in Indigenous Australia*, Royal Australian Institute of Architects, Canberra, ACT, Australia, pp. 12-17; Mainar, JM & Vodvarka, F 2013, *New Architecture Indigenous Lands*, University of Minneapolis Press, Minneapolis, USA; McGaw, J & Pieris, A 2015 *Assembling the Centre: Architecture for Indigenous Cultures – Australia and Beyond*, Routledge, London, UK and New York, USA; Grant, E, Greenop, K, Refiti, A & Glenn, D (eds) 2018, *The Handbook of Contemporary Indigenous Architecture*, Springer Nature, Singapore.

(6) See Dawson, J 1881, *Australian Aborigines: the languages and customs of several tribes of Aborigines in the western district of Victoria*, George Robertson, Melbourne, Victoria, Australia; Smyth, RB 1878, *The aborigines of Victoria: with notes relating to the habits of the natives of other parts of Australia and Tasmania*, J. Ferres, Government Printer, Melbourne, Victoria, Australia; Howitt, AW 1904, *The Native Tribes of South-east Australia*, Macmillan and Co., London, UK.

(7) See Barwick, DE 1984, 'Mapping the past: An atlas of Victorian clans 1835-1904' in *Aboriginal History - Part 1*, vol. 8, pp. 100-131; Barwick, DE 1998, 'Rebellion at Coranderrk' in LE Barwick & RE Barwick(eds), *Aboriginal History Monograph 5*, Australian National University, Canberra, ACT, Australia. The names of people and places to follow in this essay have been partly fictionalised to preserve anonymity and confidentiality but the ethnographic model of events aims to reflect a sensitive appreciation of what life was like in this context.

(8) Gott, B 1999, 'Koorie use and management of the Plains' in *The Great Plains Crash. Proceedings of a conference on the grasslands and grassy woodlands of Victoria*, Indigenous Flora and Fauna Association, Melbourne, Australia, pp. 41-45; Gott, B, Williams, N & Antos, M 2015, 'Humans and grasslands – a social history' in N Williams, A Marshall & JW Morgan (eds), *Land of sweeping plains: managing and restoring the native grasslands of south-eastern Australia*, CSIRO Publishing, Clayton South, Victoria, Australia, pp. 6-26; Presland, G 2008, *The Place for a Village: how nature has shaped the city of Melbourne*, Museum Victoria Publishing, Melbourne, Victoria, Australia, pp. 118-120.

(9) See Lourandos, H 1997, *Continent of Hunter Gatherers: New Perspectives in Australian Prehistory*, Cambridge University Press, Cambridge, UK; Latz, PK 2007, *The Flaming Desert*, IAD Press, Alice Springs, Northern Territory, Australia.

(10) Rowland, MJ & Ulm, S 2011, 'Indigenous Fish Traps and Weirs of Queensland', *Queensland Archaeological Review*, vol. 14, pp. 1-58; Builth, H 2014, *Ancient Aboriginal Aquaculture Rediscovered - The Archaeology of an Australian Cultural Landscape*, LAP Lambert Academic Publishing, Saarbrucken, Germany.

(11) Strehlow, T 1970, 'Geography and Totemic Landscape in Central Australia: A Functional Study' in RM Berndt (ed.), *Australian Aboriginal Anthropology*, AIAS, Canberra, ACT, Australia, pp. 92-140.

(12) Memmott, P 2007, *Gunyah, Goondie and Wurley: The Aboriginal Architecture of Australia*, University of Queensland Press, St Lucia, Queensland, Australia, chapter 5.

(13) Keeffe, K 1988, 'Aboriginality: Resistance and Persistence', *Australian Aboriginal Studies*, no.1, pp. 67-81.

(14) Ibid.

(15) Ibid.

(16) Implying culture contact between the Indigenous peoples and the British colonisers.

(17) See Gammage, B 2011, *The Biggest Estate on Earth: How Aborigines made Australia*, Allen & Unwin, Crows Nest, NSW, Australia; See Pascoe, B 2014, *Dark Emu: Black Seeds Agriculture Or Accident?*, Magabala Books, Broome, Western Australia, Australia.

(18) Mitchell, N, Rossler, M & Tricaud, P 2009, *World Heritage Cultural Landscapes. A Handbook for Conservation and Management. World Heritage paper No 26*, UNESCO World Heritage Centre, Paris, France, p. 5.

(19) Memmott, P & Chambers, C 2003, op. cit., pp. 33-34.

(20) Please note the names are fictional in this piece except for that of the ancestor William Barak.

(21) Myers, F 1989, 'Burning the Truck and Holding the Country: Pintupi Forms of Property and Identity', in EN Wilsen (ed), *We Are Here. Politics of Aboriginal Land Tenure*, University of California Press, Berkeley, USA, pp. 15-42.

(22) Burgess, CP, Johnston, FH, Bowman, DMJS & Whitehead, PJ 2005, 'Healthy Country: Healthy People? Exploring the health benefits for Indigenous natural resource management', *Australian and New Zealand Journal of Public Health*, vol. 29, no. 2, pp. 117-122; Burgess, CP, Johnston, FH, Berry, HL, McDonnell, J, Yibarbuk, D, Gunabarra, C, Mileran, A & Bailie, RS 2009, ' Healthy country, healthy people: the relationship between Indigenous health status and 'caring for country'', *The Medical Journal of Australia*, vol. 190, no. 10, pp. 567-572; Schultz, R & Cairney, S 2017, 'Caring for country and the health of Aboriginal and Torres Strait Islander Australians',*The Medical Journal of Australia*, vol. 207, no. 1, pp. 8-10.

GAPS IN
INDIGENOUS REPAIR

CARROLL GO-SAM

The *Repair* Exhibition for the Biennale Architettura 2018 explores uniquely Australian approaches to architecture that primarily catalyse ecological repair, within and around other related social and cultural systems. It presents an opportunity to ask whether considered attention has been given to the convergence of Indigeneity, ecology and architecture? The short answer being, that to date it hasn't. From environmentalism, conservation and sustainability we learn of potential benefits from Indigenous engagement to create meaningful outcomes. Complementary understandings of the potential between biodiversity conservation, land management and resource usage are found in Indigenous ecological knowledge (IEK). IEK has its roots in anthropology and ecological science, an approach that captures synergies between Indigenous ecological and social interactions.[1] It can inform and provide substance to emerging directions in repair architecture and Indigeneity. Its value is in understanding land stewardship as one component of complex ecological and social systems. A distinctly narrow lens is centred on three remote projects submitted: Wave Hill Walk-off Pavilions, Walumba Aboriginal Centre and Jabiru Rejuvenate. Each has varying degrees of ecological repair that intersect in different ways with architecture, yet all emerge from social contexts shaped by tainted historical legacies, intergenerational change and shifting government policies. The projects selected for discussion here explore more than land stewardship, they also illustrate different and complex challenges faced in remote Indigenous Australia by architects and Indigenous stakeholders from unexpected events.

The title above implies evident gaps in approaches to architectural repair and Indigeneity in Australian architecture, this is due in part to its immaturity. Repair also faces stiff competition from agendas loaded down by structural inequalities and the contingencies of separation from major markets in tourism, mining and pastoralism. Remote Indigenous economies are dominated by dependencies on government funded services, agencies and programs delivered to settlement residents and less characterised by small Indigenous micro-economies in tourism, arts and other enterprises. This review acknowledges that repair is an emerging pursuit in Indigenous architecture, beset by other pressing social, economic and cultural priorities. Yet, although stark realities of under development and poor development impact in different sectors of Indigenous Australia, repair rallies architectural stewardship of land. This is a position that could align with Indigenous stewardship of country (or traditional lands) while recognising that customary environmentalism has undergone significant transformation by modernity.[2]

Australia is an arid and semi-arid continent with 70% of its land mass receiving less than 250 millimetres of rain. Conversely, nearly 25% of Australia, largely its northern region, is defined as monsoonal. Both contribute to relatively intact rich biodiverse regions that bolster national wealth.[3] In Australia the population majority reside in cities and urban centres in southern states. Almost 4/5 of Indigenous Australians live in urban areas and 1/5 live in remote areas. This statistic however deceptively fails to explain the significance of finer grained geographic dissimilarities of wealth distribution that too easily mask lower levels of development, services and outcomes.[4] Not all socio-economic circumstances are equal within urban centres and even greater challenges exist in remote areas. Other broader social, economic and environmental vulnerabilities faced by Indigenous Australians in comparison to the general population are further heightened in rural and remote Australian settings. While *Repair* explores growing interests in how healing relationships between ecosystems and architecture might interact, the emphasis of Australian government programs and in turn social architecture are caught up in alleviating, intervening and closing gaps in inequalities.

Supplanting sustainable architecture

Architecture is deeply intertwined with aspirations for economic growth and maintaining the status quo of consumptive growth[5] without monitoring the cost or actioning regeneration. Damaged ecosystems upon which human communities rely are in resource deficit, giving rise to concerted efforts in previous decades to reverse the state of play through sustainability measures. Sustainability principles sought to constrain economic prosperity while straddling tangible and intangible concepts of ecological integrity, human rights along with symbolic and iterative change. (6) According to Girardet, the sustainability solution became the problem due to its ineffectiveness to garner change and diffuse application. Triple bottom line accountability disintegrated into a code for unregulated growth. (7) Washington however, questions the wholesale abandonment of sustainability, just because the term has become vexed, arguing that other issues are equally "contestable, such as democracy, justice or freedom", yet these have not been discarded. (8) Girardet advocates regeneration which is synonymous with the notion of repair. Repair/regeneration is thought to evoke needed change by dispensing with the global orthodoxy of sustainable development. In Australia self-conscious application of sustainability agendas in architecture followed international shifts in the 1980s. (9) Sustainable architecture first appeared in remote Indigenous settlements under community planning, bioregional development, infrastructure and livelihoods in late 1990s and beyond. (10) According to Indigenous ecological ethnographer, Douglas serious attention to Indigenous ecological knowledge only emerged in the 1980s due to perceived linkages with sustainable development and environmental conservation. (11)

Emphasis on sustainable Indigenous communities in remote locations, have remained preoccupied with reducing severe disparities and increasing access to fundamental resources. Indigenous settlements in arid zone regions are frequently characterised by economies and services they lack. In comparison to urban counterparts there is a predominance of "sub-standard infrastructure," "poorly designed housing, inappropriate household technologies and unnecessarily high demand for utilities". (12) In the mid-2000s radical policy shifts of Australian governments towards servicing of discrete remote settlements sought to close communities. Many settlements where Indigenous people reside and are the majority were considered economically unsustainable due to high costs of servicing small populations. Then later, these settlements were recast as culturally unsustainable due to rising reports of social disintegration and interpersonal violence. Paradoxically, Federal and State governments increasingly justified remote community closures and withdrawal of services, on the basis that small scale settlements with 200 or less residents were unsustainable, forcing residents to relocate to larger towns where pooled resources and rising costs were presumably better managed. (13) Indigenous Australians have continued to contend with policy impacts of remote service delivery withdrawal, while sustainability had become a loaded term.

Altered climates, the repair heuristic and Indigenous ecological knowledge

Adding to socio-economic challenges faced in remote Australia are environmental and ecological changes due to altered climates and extreme weather events. In coming decades remote Indigenous Australia, will bear a disproportionate burden of the impact of climatic change (cyclones, storms, floods, sea surges, heatwaves, droughts and bushfires) (14) while being the least beneficiaries of financial benefits derived from national wealth. (15) The regenerative concept of repair targets the macro scale of urban development of cities where the majority of human populations reside, but also encounter the effects of problems due to density. The repair heuristic primarily seeks to implement restorative relationships, between cities and natural systems that humans are dependent upon. It advanced initiatives such as greening urban environments and halting urban growth, but does not want to be confined to these strategies. In essence repair advocates the orthodoxy of regenerative systems. Its apparent weakness is that it lacks strategies for issues at extreme ends of the scale. Hyper-scaled global problems require global cooperation in a climate of national self-interest. Issues impacting on dispersed, small scaled settlements with comparatively intact ecological environments separated from large economies, appear irreconcilable with centres of economic power and social interaction. (16)

Disciplinary shifts in western anthropology and biological science increased attentiveness to Indigenous ecological knowledge by shifting focus from purely quantifiable scientific data to include social aspects of ecology. Indigenous ecological knowledge systems are thought to hold the key to Indigenous resilience and cultural maintenance. Albeit in contexts of transformative change. Indigenous ethnographer, Josie Douglas describes, Indigenous ecological knowledge in Central Australia as more than "environmental programs, developmental theories or the nexus between Indigenous and Western or scientific knowledge". (17) Indigenous ecology is akin to "knowledge-practice-belief ecology". (18) Simply stated, it is a proposition where human agents are not excluded from ecology. (19) Hence, ecology is dependent on human agents and both are affected by associated beliefs, accounts and behaviours. Interactions between everyday lived experiences and ecology are used to explain environmental and ecological phenomena. To some Indigenous people these practices and beliefs perpetuate the "sentience of country". (20) However, the danger is that Indigenous ecological knowledge can be confined to caretaker roles of the environment that exclude other important socio-cultural and economic contexts. For example, many of the drivers of ecological activities, programs and research action involving Indigenous people, such as Caring for Country and Indigenous Ranger Programs, are workforce employment programs. The inseparable relationship between the social and ecological, needs to reflect how Indigenous lifeways are punctuated by the complexities of modern life demands in the context of transformations.(21)

Existing gaps and translating repair

The review team consisting of Paul Memmott, Reuben Berg and myself evaluated twenty-one submissions that explored Indigeneity and degrees of the central theme of environmental repair. A slim majority of submissions had their origins in metropolitan cities, but a significant number were located in non-urban centres, where vastly different challenges prevail for Indigenous Australians. The review was moderated by *Repair* creative directors, Baracco+Wright Architects whose stated core objectives emphasised the intersection of architecture and restorative ecological repair, hence their selections differ, with overlaps with the projects selected by the author. Repaired ecological environments were confined to living biotic and abiotic environments as a core pursuit, where architecture catalysed or actively sought out to repair the place it is situated in. It was indeed challenging to single out projects that represented strong examples of cutting-edge dialogue between architecture, ecology and Indigeneity that simultaneously effected repair by positively reshaping and relieving duress on environments.

In general, within Indigenous architecture there exists capacity to reproduce or acknowledge Indigenous ways of knowing, but sometimes Indigeneity is constructed as a shallow enterprise. This occurs due to a failure to pursue collaborations with Indigenous clients/stakeholders resulting in schemes lacking depth. The emerging pursuit of ecological repair in architecture likewise risks being fixed as marginal to the architectural object. Many project submissions were overly attentive to other concerns, bypassing the sought interdependence with ecological repair, instead emphasising civic, historical, social, economic and cultural constructs as repair. The lack of considered attention to the core theme of repair in Indigenous architecture with neither an ecological emphasis nor penetrating understanding of Indigenous culture caused a brief reflection and hiatus within the evaluation team. Could reframing Indigenous architectural repair include civic, cultural, economic and social themes as repair? And could broadening repair withstand sustained scrutiny? This expansion became fraught due to a number of limitations. Architecture has too often been reified as a catalyst for change or social repair, just by its themed Indigenous content, when at best such architecture enables pre-existing social or civic environments. Ideological framing of Indigenous themes and acknowledgements of traditional owner groups in architecture, often mistakenly equate recognition of social identities, as repair. How can architectural propositions differ in novel ways from ongoing acts of recognition and reconciliation to achieve repair? This intention needs to be made explicit or there are perils in miscategorising, marginalising and trivialising Indigenous social and civic architecture as repair.

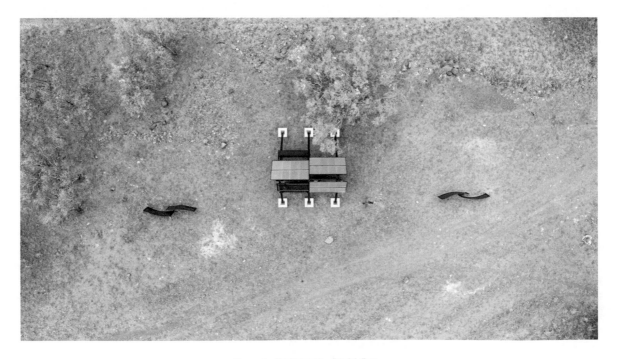

Ground. Photograph, David Fox.
Bower Studio, University of Melbourne,
Wave Hill Walk-off Pavilions,
Junani, Northern Territory.

As an Indigenous person, I was particularly attentive to projects with a visible level of Indigenous agency, not only because they conveyed Indigenous stakeholder engagement and collaborations, but they also demonstrated greater capacity to reflect meaningful responses to Indigenous and other shared realities. A key concern was how did these projects not only respond to the architectural brief, but how did intercultural interactions influence the architectural outcome. The projects chosen show an integration of built and natural ecological systems reflective of Indigenous influence, concerns and worldviews. The selected projects represent economic activities (pastoralism and mining) or climatic events (flooding) that all had social and ecological impact. All three sites have tainted histories, yet each have value as outcomes of ongoing Indigenous resilience. Summarily, the chosen projects involved a combination of discernible levels of Indigenous agency and are unequivocally powerful narratives about historical and contemporary Indigenous Australia.

Three projects – Wave Hill Walk-off Pavilions, Walumba Elders Centre and Jabiru Rejuvenate – have been selected for discussion because they present distinct examples of relationships between indigeneity and repair. In this mix there are two built and one unbuilt project, each juggle priorities about place, economy, culture and remoteness. Two projects are located in the Northern Territory. Wave Hill is a former pastoral holding and Jabiru will soon be a former mining town. Walumba Elders Centre project at Warmun (Turkey Creek) in Western Australia arose

out of a major flooding event in 2011. All three sites are classified as very remote Indigenous settlements based on distance from major town centres or regional cities. Acknowledging there are different ways of seeing and doing repair between Indigenous and other Australians, this review aims to focus on collaborative architectural projects with ecological aspirations and outcomes. Each project illustrates the elusive nature of repair in remote Indigenous contexts by not adhering to strict definitions in the brief of repairing ecologies. They typify shifting relationships between Indigenous traditional owners lifeworlds, settler environments and changing ecological conditions.

WAVE HILL WALK-OFF PAVILIONS, BOWER STUDIO, UNIVERSITY OF MELBOURNE [22]

This project is located on Gurindji country in the Northern Territory and consists of three pavilions at Jinbarak (Pavilion 1), Junani (Pavilion 2) and Kalkarindji (Pavilion 3).

Project background

The Gurindji people – Northern Territory occupy a significant place in the formation of the Aboriginal Land Rights and self-determination political movements in Australia. Their prolonged nine-year battle advocated for equal wage payments in the pastoral industry, and evolved into advancing land rights. [23] The Wave Hill 'walk-off' or strike

Ground. Photograph, Linda Tegg.
Gurindji elders Timmy Vincent, Kathleen Sambo,
Rosemary Johnson, Violet Wadrill, Biddy Wavehill,
Jimmy Wavehill share their stories.

was equally about human rights violations and indentured labour conditions arising out of a legacy of historical violence and oppression dating back to settler incursions in 1855. Massacres, sanctioned violence and indiscriminate killing of Gurindji, Malngin, Bilinarra and Mudburra men, women and children continued as late as the 1940s. The Wave Hill pastoral holding commenced operations in 1882 by Nat Buchanan. At the time of the Wave Hill walk-off British-based Vesteys, an international meat company, owned and retained ownership until the 1990s.(24) The station ran 40,000 cattle and employed Aboriginals from the surrounding region – Gurindji, Mudburra and Warlpiri. Wave Hill had the largest number of Aboriginal stockmen and house servants of any pastoral station in the Northern Territory.(25) The Aboriginal workers were in servitude under the prevailing national system of subsistence rations (dry bread and salted beef, tea, flour and sugar).(26) The policy of no wage or low wage prevailed in Australia and remained in some States up until the late 1960s and in other States the 1980s.

In August, 1966 Aboriginal traditional owners withdrew their labour from Vestey's with the support of a large collective that included the Northern Territory Council for Aboriginal Rights, Federal Council for the Advancement of Aborigines and Torres Strait Islanders, the Communist Party of Australia, North Australia Workers Union, Commonwealth parliamentarians and prominent Australian writer, Frank Hardy. Vincent Lingiari and Pincher Nyurrmiyari and other Aboriginal leaders staged the longest workers strike in Australian history. What initially began as negotiations for equal pay transformed into exposing human rights violations, later catalysing into a Land Rights campaign. Grievances expressed by Gurindji extended far beyond oppressive servitude, chronicling abuses of sexual exploitation of Aboriginal women, racism and poor living conditions. Other demands for the return of their traditional lands surfaced later as Gurindji were emboldened by external support and increasing national attention. The writer Frank Hardy chronicled the event in the book, *The Unlucky Australians*.(27) Hardy described what he witnessed in the pastoral industry as an apartheid system operating in Australia. Although, Hardy downplayed his role in the eventual successful outcome of the political actions, he is viewed as a pivotal player amongst many. These included Aboriginal activists, Union officials and others who were able to articulate and strategically manoeuvre the assertion of Gurindji rights through Commonwealth government structures and national media.(28)

The change to the Whitlam Labor government in 1972,(29) later resulted in one of Whitlam's defining moments as a visionary political leader who initiated the slow beginnings of restitution to Aboriginal traditional owners. After travelling to Dagaragu (formerly Wattie Creek) on 16 August, 1975, Whitlam's symbolic gesture of pouring soil into the hand of Vincent Lingiari, became a national moment. Whitlam however, was unable to ensure the realisation of promised land restitution and it would be another eleven years before the Gurindji ownership was recognised under Commonwealth NT Land Right Act (1976).(30) In plotting their path to self-determination the Gurindji planned to variously operate their own pastoral station and mining lease, realising their future was uncertain without financial income.(31) The Wave Hill Walk-off Pavilions commemorate the 50th Anniversary of Whitlam's handing over of Northern Territory's pastoral lease title deeds. The gesture effectively granted equal access to lease land, one that had previously privileged non-Aboriginal Australians.(32) However, to many Gurindji, obtaining land rights in 1986 was a more significant achievement.

Project description

Gurindji is located on the edge of monsoonal savannah and desert climatic zones with seasons ranging from very hot to dry, to periods of high rainfall leading to flooding. The site of the commemorative pavilions is located in the vicinity of Kalkarindji, (population: 334, Australian Bureau of Statistics 2016) 460 kilometres south-west of Katherine in the Northern Territory. The nationally listed heritage trail is on Gurindji traditional lands totalling 3,250 square kilometres. Bower Studio was invited by Gurindji to design and construct three commemorative pavilions situated along a 22 kilometre listed heritage trail, commencing at Jinbarak, then onto Junani and ending at Kalkarindji. The trail follows former pastoral boundary fence lines and crosses the Buntine Highway, a partly sealed narrow road that links to the town of Katherine. Bower Studio is a consult/design/build Masters of Architecture Studio at Melbourne University operating at numerous national and international sites. The pavilions are A-framed prefabricated steel ribs on raised concrete pad footings, clad with perforated and laser cut metal sheeting. Curved sheets of corten steel and corrugated iron mark and memorialise the pathway taken by the strikers from Wave Hill to Daguragu. The panels were transported and assembled at the three sites along the trail. The design includes interpretative sign panels, seating and landscape elements conveying Gurindji stories and outlining their attachments to land.

The Pavilions operate as informal classrooms shared with younger Gurindji generations and visitors. Both elders and Murnkurrumurnkurru (waterhole near Kalkarindji) – the name given to a group of six Gurindji rangers – carry out reconstituted traditional and transformed ecological practices that include fire management, cultural site and biodiversity work, weed and feral animal management and work on Judbarra (Southern Gregory) National Park.(33) The Pavilions symbolise and memorialise Gurindji self-determination marking the failings and celebrations of nationhood. At the micro-level Gurindji continuity and revival of ecological practices have been transformed to work on country programs that include environmental management funded by the Commonwealth government.

The architecture has not facilitated this transformation because the practice was in place prior to the pavilions construction. Rather, the Pavilions enable and centre aspects of the caring for country program and its overlay with memorialisation in the vast interstitial arid-tropical zone of Gurindji country.

WALUMBA ELDERS CENTRE – AGED CARE FACILITY, IREDALE PEDERSEN HOOK(34)

This project is located in Warmun, on Gija country, in the East Kimberley area in Western Australia.

Project background

On 13 March 2011 wet season rains overflowed the banks of Turkey Creek creating flash flooding inundating the adjacent river valley settlement of Warmun/Warrmarn (population: 366, Australian Bureau of Statistics 2016), East Kimberley. Jadagen refers to the time of the big rains and it is one of five seasons that Gija equate with the wet season. For Gija people flooding events are not natural disasters, but are spiritually interpreted as ancestral warnings or reminders to the living to keep their cultural practices strong (dances, rituals, song cycles).(35) Due to a monsoonal trough and slow moving tropical low, four times the average rainfall poured a total of 500 millimetres, causing Turkey Creek to

iredale pedersen hook, Walumba Elders Centre, Warmun, Western Australia. Photograph, Peter Bennetts.

iredale pedersen hook, Walumba Elders Centre, Warmun, Western Australia. Photograph, Peter Bennetts.

rise nine metres in four hours. The flood torrent first moved towards low-lying houses and then onto the Walumba Aged Care Facility. Next was the Warmun Art Centre and the school. By nightfall most residents had been evacuated to higher ground at the Warmun Roadhouse and the adjacent Mirrilingki Catholic Centre, but some residents were still isolated and surrounded by rising waters on the opposing side. Two days were spent air lifting 275 residents to Kununarra, country of the Mirriwoong people who generously hosted the evacuees.

After assessing the damage by the Warmun Re-establishment Taskforce, it was concluded that 80% of the buildings in Warmun were either destroyed or significantly damaged. Detailed hydrological modelling was followed by new town planning recommendations that required future developments to have minimum floor levels 200 millimetres above the 2011 flood, approximately 3 metres above ground level. This required the relocation of Warmun and abandonment of the much of the original town site. Although some core services remained in the flood zone they had to conform to the new minimum floor level requirement. The new town layout was designed in partnership with the Warmun community. After fifteen months, the town had twenty-four essential facilities rebuilt, fifty-six new houses and twenty houses refurbished and restored.(36)

However, major flooding events are not the only dangers Warmun community had to contend with. In the aftermath of the flood rebuilding an unscrupulous opportunist and conman, Craig Dale approached Warmun community with a new proposal to construct additional staff housing, not included in the original rebuild plans coordinated by the Western Australian (WA) Housing Authority. At this moment of great vulnerability, Dale convinced the community board that WA Government would pay for the costs of the additional housing. Dale was then an approved construction contractor working on the Warmun reconstruction under a government approved service provider. Stipulating that Warmun had to pay his company, Five Day Holdings P/L in advance of doing the work, Dale eventually secured $3 million in multiple payments from Warmun, without intending to fulfil the contract. The funding shortfall resulted in Walumba Aged Care Centre unable to secure funds to operate as registered aged care facility. Consequently, the building was never occupied and remained empty for several years up until late 2017.(37)

Project description

The new Walumba Aged Care Centre site was selected by community elders to be adjacent to the school and close to the community centre within the 2011 flood zone. The building floor level was set at 2.4 metres above the natural ground to avoid future flooding. Responding to the pragmatic requirements of the new town plan, the architects elevated the building form and circulation spaces, creating exterior spaces for communal gathering. The building's staggered mass allows future flood waters to flow between and below the new Centre. Its preferred location and proximity to the school was seen as providing a centred place within Warmun, marking elders' return to country at the centre of community activity. Additionally, it created opportunity for transmission of Gija

knowledge between generations, a landscaped gathering space at the ground level, further symbolising the reconstruction of Warmun both physically and spiritually.

The ongoing stalled operation of the respite centre and non-occupation of the building by elders did not prevent day to day micro needs of elders being cared for by Home and Community Care (HACC) and Aged Care staff in shared accommodation or with their families. Planting of Snappy Gum trees used in smoking ceremonies, along with bush medicine and bush tucker plants in the landscaping brought these resources closer to the built and cultural environments. At the macro scale building sight lines overlook key creation dreaming sites around the river valley and a ceremonial tree where a lodged fridge remains five metres above the ground memorialising the flood. The building was recognised under several national and international architectural awards programs for its ecological, social and sustainability innovation.(38) The realpolitik of securing funding and managing related services in remote Australia overshadows the buildings architectural rhetoric as a facilitator of repair. An outcome not achievable if the building lay vacant for several years with elders located elsewhere in the community. Architectural hubris was equally shaken as was the strained resilience of the Warmun community.

dB(A) Decibel Architecture, Jabiru Rejuvenate, masterplan, 2028, Northern Territory.
Image, dB(A) Decibel Architecture.

JABIRU REJUVENATE,
DB(A) DECIBEL ARCHITECTURE

This project is located in Jabiru, in the Kakadu National Park, on Mirarr – Bininj/Mungguy country, in the Northern Territory.

Project background

Jabiru is situated within the heritage listed Kakadu National Park, Northern Territory. Kakadu is approximately 20,000 square kilometres of natural biodiversity, various landforms, habitats and wildlife.(39) In the late 1970s Mirarr people opposed the establishment of Uranium mining lease at Ranger (1976) and later at Jabiluka (1982) and Koongara (2010) in and near Kakadu. The impending expiration of the Ranger mining lease in 2021, held by Energy Resources Australia (ERA), had created an uncertain future for Jabiru town (population: 1,081, Australian Bureau of Statistics 2016) which was built in 1982 as service hub for mine workers, business operators, visitors to Kakadu National Park and traditional owners. In 2016, it had a population of 1,100 people (rounded up), with almost 1/4 (24%) being Indigenous. Many of the towns' health and education services and infrastructure were predicted to be severely affected when the majority non-Indigenous population dramatically decreases after the mine closure. The Jabiru Steering Committee comprised of traditional owner representatives, the mining company ERA and Commonwealth, Northern Territory and West Arnhem Regional Council are working to progress a viable future for Jabiru post-mining. Kakadu has a vibrant tourism industry which Mirrar propose is the future foundation for economic development.(40)

Aboriginal environmentalism had formed alliances with different green groups over gold and uranium mining operations in Kakadu. Aboriginal ecological knowledge strives for customary traditional maintenance of the cosmological status quo between plants, animals and ceremonial life. This belief has underlined opposition to mining activities and its disturbance of the ground. Aboriginal concerns were initially a secondary priority to western conservation ecological and mining objectives. However, when another mining operation was halted by the Hawke Labor government(41) in 1991 on the basis of responding to traditional owner's concerns about sites, sacred sites had achieved centre stage. The currency of sacredness was quickly co-opted by conservation groups and applied in oppositional tactics. However, in later years tensions arose between Mirrar traditional owners and anti-nuclear protesters about protest methods. The Mirrar not supportive of confrontational road blockades, clashed with green activists who were unconcerned with Aboriginal directed control of campaigns on the country. Instead activists prioritised environmentalism leading to a dissolution of alliances.(42) The present day Mirrar concerns about Jabiru and Kakadu are anxious about how traditional owners can forge an economically secure future through expanding access to biodiverse and cultural assets of Kakadu by revitalising the township as a tourist destination.

Project description

Since 2001 traditional owners have attempted to develop a grand vision to reimagine Jabiru as eco-tourism hub. This ambitious unbuilt architectural vision is based on optimistic assumptions of accelerated population growth (3,000 residents), diverting tourism traffic, and capturing other visitors seeking to experience ecological and cultural tourism. Jabiru Rejuvenate includes a Kakadu arrival hub with a visitor facility and bus terminal for tour services linking them to the vast Kakadu Park region. The project seeks to respond to traditional owner concerns about drive-in, drive-out tourism that fragments access. Jabiru Rejuvenate proposes to salvage existing infrastructure creating a revitalised place for cultural exchange, mutual respect and learning exchanges with visitors. The Jabiru Masterplan 2028 envisions visitor accommodation, new cultural centre, Lakeside precinct with wetlands walk and expanded residential clusters. The revised town plan is focused on linking tourist facilities to new wildlife trails alongside housing subdivisions. New residential layouts reflect Aboriginal family kinship groups in corresponding housing clusters. A new path will be created connecting Jabiru to Bowali Centre designed by Glenn Murcutt and Troppo.

As a consequence of deep mining operations several mining pits exist onsite, for example Pit 1 is 170 metres deep measuring 39.3 hectares.(43) The design seeks an alternate plan to standard back filling the pit and revegetation. Instead proposing to replace reliance on diesel power generation with renewable geothermal and solar energy. Using principles of sustainability, the objective aims to rehabilitate, rejuvenate and repurpose existing buildings and infrastructure where possible. Some of the ambitions of the scheme attempt to thwart the proposed ERA draining of the artificial recreational lake by reshaping it to create an active edge and wetlands. It remains to be seen whether this bold vision can turn the tide of standard approaches to land reparations. It requires the support of risk adverse governments, however its aspirations for repair reflect intercultural solutions more aligned with Mirrar ecologies.

Emerging repair

Repair seeks to tackle the realities of big issues facing our cities, but it is evident that issues of climate change in the anthropocene are felt everywhere. Outside city domains in vast, remote and relatively biologically intact landscapes, Indigenous people face other threats in addition to climate change. This means that challenges to achieve recognition, governance, and self-determination exist as realworld hurdles to livelihoods and well-being. These projects signal how Indigeneity, ecology and emerging architectural repair have been conceptualised, theorised, represented and practised. The solutions respond to remote circumstances, across built and unbuilt projects, ranging from small to larger propositions. But, gaps in achieving the objectives of repair remain. The Wave Hill Walk-off Pavilions illustrated how small acts of repair initiated in land care projects prior to the architecture count, albeit in limited ways to the livelihoods of Gurindji rangers. They highlight fragile futures for Gurindji people on country. Repair here is tied to their dependence on external funds. The Walumba Elders Centre provides an example of Indigenous ecological knowledge and different ways of seeing and memorialising flooding events. After Warmun's rebuilding, Gija resilience and trust was tested. Sometimes well considered architectural solutions attentive to repair are halted by events external to the project. The unused building creates ongoing ambiguity about the Elders Centre, its achievements and future use, leaving a gap in repair. This has led to unresolved frustration for Gija, which governance support could remedy. And finally, the visions grand of Jabiru Rejuvenate reimagined as an Indigenous eco-tourism hub shares the optimism of repair. The scars and gouges of mining are being repaired, but more than environmental repair alone is needed. Vast resources devoted to environmental repair after mining need to consider contributions to building a future, under Mirrar control connecting tourism to country. Emerging architecture of repair could pursue novel ways that consider both the ecological with the social, working effectively with Indigenous stakeholders devising solutions that enhance livelihoods in challenging settings.

(1) Douglas, J 2015, 'Kin and knowledge: The meaning and acquisition of Indigenous ecological knowledge in the lives of young people in Central Australia', PhD thesis, Charles Darwin University, Northern Territory, Australia, pp. 31-33.

(2) Smallacombe, S, Davis, M, Quiggin R et al. 2007, *Scoping project on Aboriginal Traditional Knowledge*, Report 22, Desert Knowledge CRC, Alice Springs, Northern Territory, Australia, p. 7.

(3) See Australian Government, Department of Environment and Energy n.d., *Outback Australia - the rangelands*, viewed 20 February 2018, <http://www.environment.gov.au/rangelands>.

(4) Australian Government, Australian Institute of Health and Welfare 2015, *The health and welfare of Australia's Aboriginal and Torres Strait Islander peoples: 2015*, p. 9, viewed 18 February 2018, <https://www.aihw.gov.au/reports/indigenous-health-welfare/indigenous-health-welfare-2015/contents/table-of-contents>.

(5) Washington, H 2015, *Demystifying Sustainability: Towards Real Solutions*, Routledge, London, UK and New York, USA, p. 114.

(6) Newman, P 2006, 'Sustainable Indigenous Communities: Applying the Eleven Sustainability Principles', in G Ho, K Mathew & M Anda (eds) 2009, *Sustainability of indigenous communities in Australia: Selected papers from the National Conference (12-14 July 2006)*, Murdoch University, Perth, Western Australia, Australia, pp. 5-15.

(7) Girardet, H 2015, *Creating Regenerative Cities*, Routledge, Abingdon, Oxon, UK, and New York, USA, p. 2.

(8) Washington, H 2015, op. cit., p. 29.

(9) Go-Sam, C. and Keys, C. 2018, 'Mobilising cultural sustainability in architecture: Are we there yet?', in E Grant, K Greenop, A Refiti & D Glenn (eds), *The Handbook of Contemporary Indigenous Architecture*, Springer Nature, Singapore.

(10) Beale, T 2006, 'Energy Service Levels for Remote Indigenous Communities', in G Ho, K Mathew & M Anda (eds) 2009, *Sustainability of indigenous communities in Australia: Selected papers from the National Conference (12-14 July 2006)*, op. cit., p. 74; Fisher, S 2006, 'A Light that Never Goes Out: Livelihoods and Reality on the Margins', in G Ho, K Mathew & M Anda (eds) 2009, op. cit., p. 22.

(11) Douglas, J 2015, op. cit., p. 30.

(12) Memmott, P et al. 2013, *Aboriginal responses to climate change in arid zone Australia: regional understandings and capacity building for adaptation: Final Report*, National Climate Change Adaptation Research Facility, Gold Coast, Queensland, Australia, p. 12.

(13) Go-Sam, C & Memmott, P 2016, 'Dossier: Remote Indigenous Settlements - more than tiny dots on a map', *Architecture Australia*, vol. 105, no. 5, September/October, pp. 53-54.

(14) Memmott, P et al. 2013, op. cit., p. 11, 25; Rigby, M 2018, 'Yam Island homes destroyed as king tide raises calls for better flood protection', *ABC News*, 6 February, viewed 15 February 2018, <http://www.abc.net.au/news/2018-02-06/yam-island-locals-lose-everything-as-king-tide-causes-floods/9397794>.

(15) Vincent, E & Neale, T 2017, 'Unstable relations: a critical appraisal of indigeneity and environmentalism in contemporary Australia', *Australian Journal of Anthropology*, vol. 28, p. 304.

(16) Girardet, H 2015, op. cit., pp. 2-4; Washington, H 2015, op. cit., pp. 100-101.

(17) Douglas, J 2015, op. cit., p. 30.

(18) Ibid.

(19) Ibid.

(20) Ibid., p. 22.

(21) de Rijke, K, Martin, R & Trigger, D 2016, 'Cultural domains and the theory of customary environmentalism in Indigenous Australia', in W Sanders (ed.), *Engaging Indigenous Economies: Debating Diverse Approaches*, Research Monograph, no. 35, ANU Press, Acton, ACT, Australia, pp. 43-53.

(22) A description and images of this project are included in this catalogue/book.

(23) Hollier, N 2006, 'The Unlucky Australians. When Frank Hardy went bush he made some alarming discoveries', *The Age Book Reviews*, 8 September, viewed 15 February 2018, <https://www.theage.com.au/news/book-reviews/the-unlucky-australians/2006/09/08/1157222319244.html>.

(24) Meakins, F 2016, 'Friday essay: the untold story behind the 1966 Wave Hill Walk-Off', *The Conversation*, 19 August, viewed 28 January 2018, <https://theconversation.com/friday-essay-the-untold-story-behind-the-1966-wave-hill-walk-off-62890>.

(25) Ward, C 2016, 'An historic handful of dirt: Whitlam and the legacy of the Wave Hill Walk-Off, *The Conversation*, 21 August, viewed 28 January 2018, <https://theconversation.com/an-historic-handful-of-dirt-whitlam-and-the-legacy-of-the-wave-hill-walk-off-63700>.

(26) Zillman, S & and O'Brien, K 2016, 'Wave Hill 50th anniversary: Stockmen who walked off station pause to remember', *ABC News*, 19 August, viewed 28 January 2018, <http://www.abc.net.au/news/2016-08-18/wave-hill-stockman-remember-50th-anniversary/7760708>.

(27) Hardy, F 1968, *The Unlucky Australians*, Nelson, Melbourne, Victoria, Australia.

(28) Attwood, B 2000, 'The Articulation of "Land Rights" in Australia: The Case of Wave Hill', *Social Analysis: The International Journal of Social and Cultural Practice*, vol. 44, no. 1, April, pp. 3-39.

(29) "Edward Gough Whitlam AC QC…(11 July 1916 - 21 October 2014) was the 21st Prime Minister of Australia, serving from 1972 to 1975. The Leader of the Labor Party from 1967 to 1977, Whitlam led his party to power for the first time in 23 years at the 1972 election. He won the 1974 election before being controversially dismissed by the Governor-General of Australia, Sir John Kerr, at the climax of the 1975 Australian constitutional crisis. Whitlam remains the only Australian prime minister to have his commission terminated in that manner…The Whitlam Government implemented a large number of new programs and policy changes, including the termination of military conscription, institution of universal health care and free university education, and the implementation of legal aid programs". See Wikipedia n.d., *Gough Whitlam*, Wikipedia, viewed 21 February 2018, <https://en.wikipedia.org/wiki/Gough_Whitlam>.

(30) Ward, C 2016, 'op. cit.

(31) Attwood, B 2000, op. cit., p. 26.

(32) Ward, C 2016, op. cit.

(33) See Central Land Council n.d., *Building the Bush: CLC Rangers, Central Land Council*, viewed 2 February 2018, <https://www.clc.org.au/index.php?/articles/info/clc-rangers1/#Munguru%20Munguru>.

(34) A description and images of this project are included in this catalogue/book.

(35) See The Cross Art Projects 2013, *Jadagen Warnkan Barnden: Changing Climate in Gija Country - 31 August to 21 September 2013*, art exhibition review, The Cross Art Projects, viewed 21 February 2018, <http://crossart.com.au/98-2013-exhibitions-projects/197-jadagen-warnkan-barnden-changing-climate-in-gija-country>.

(36) Government of Western Australia, Department of Housing and Warmun Taskforce 2013, *Warrambany of Warrmarn: the flood of Warmun, 13 March 2011*, viewed 21 February 2018, <http://www.housing.wa.gov.au/HousingDocuments/Warrambany_of_Warrmarn_The_Flood_Of_Warmun.pdf>.

(37) McDonald, A, Besser, L & Russell, A n.d., 'Warmun: A tale of two disasters: a Four Corners investigation', *ABC News*, viewed 18 January 2018, <http://www.abc.net.au/news/2016-06-06/warmun-a-tale-of-two-disasters/7462544>.

(38) Wright, L 2016, 'Iredale Pedersen Hook wins international prize', *ArchitectureAU*, 20 June, viewed 18 February 2018, <https://architectureau.com/articles/iredale-pedersen-hook-wins-international-prize/>.

(39) See Parks Australia 2015, *Kakadu National Park*, visitor guide, Parks Australia, viewed 18 January 2018, <https://parksaustralia.gov.au/kakadu/pub/visitor-guide.pdf>.

(40) Northern Territory Government, Department of the Chief Minister 2018, *Information update 2 - A strong future for Jabiru*, 6 February, viewed 2 February 2018, <https://dcm.nt.gov.au/news/2018/february-2018/a-strong-future-for-jabiru-information-update-2>; Gundjeihmi Aboriginal Corporation n.d., *Uranium Mining*, Gundjeihmi Aboriginal Corporation, viewed 2 February 2018, <http://www.mirarr.net/uranium-mining>; Everingham, S 2017, 'Kakadu National Park: Jabiru residents in limbo as governments, mining company contemplate town's future', *ABC News*, 20 July, viewed 2 February 2018, <http://www.abc.net.au/news/2017-07-18/jabiru-residents-in-limbo-as-uranium-mining-draws-to-a-close/8718432>.

(41) "Robert James Lee Hawke AC, GCL (born 9 December 1929) is a former Australian politician who was the 23rd Prime Minister of Australia, serving from 1983 to 1991. He held office as the leader of the Labor Party". See Wikipedia n.d, *Bob Hawke*, Wikipedia, viewed 21 February 2018, <https://en.wikipedia.org/wiki/Bob_Hawke>.

(42) Vincent, E & Neale, T 2017, op. cit., pp. 307-310.

(43) ERA-Energy Resources of Australia Ltd. n.d., *Sustainability: Ranger Mine Site*, ERA-Energy Resources of Australia Ltd., viewed 3 February 2018, <http://www.energyres.com.au/sustainability/progressive-rehabilitation/ranger/>.

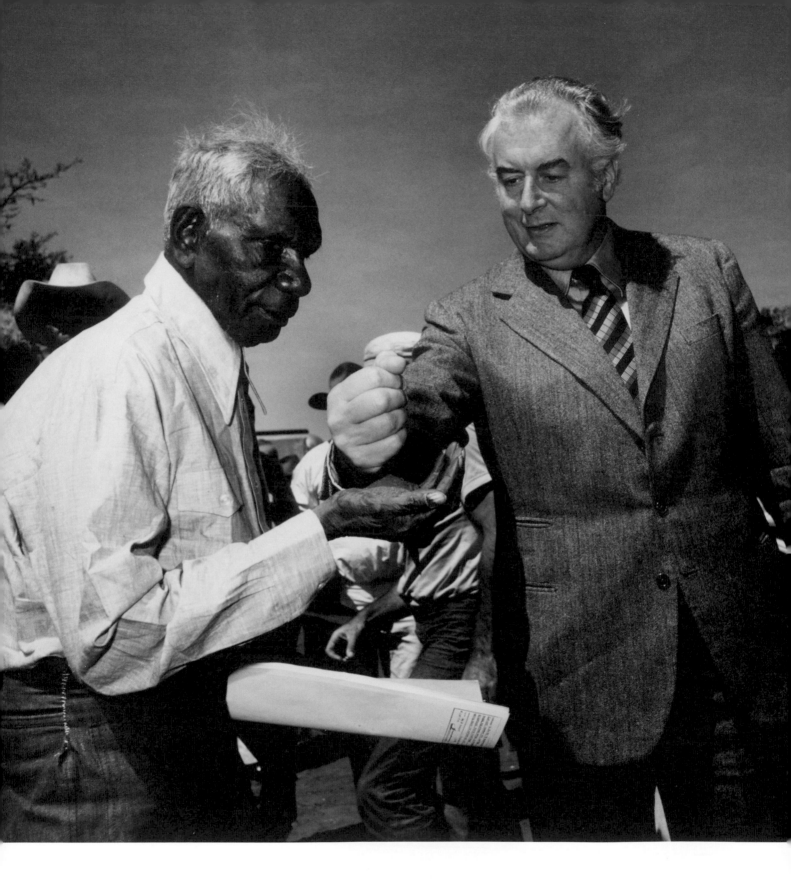

Prime Minister Gough Whitlam pours Daguragu soil
into the hands of traditional land owner
Vincent Lingiari (Gurindji elder), Daguragu
(Wattie Creek), Northern Territory, 1975.
Photograph, Mervyn Bishop, © Commonwealth.

WIDENING OUR GAZE   TIM O'LOAN

Only when you recognise the enduring value of something would you consider repairing it. When considering the act of 'repairing' in the urban context, it is easy to grasp for similes and analogies, such as the tailor repairing a jacket, the sub-editor repairing a sentence, or the surgeon repairing the tissues of the body. Repair also moves beyond the physical; we can repair relationships, cultural systems and organisations. The term is also strongly allied to the acts of restoration and reformation. However repair is distinctive in that it does not seek to simply return the subject back to a former version of itself, it seeks to promote an adaption to an evolved condition. Repair often concerns itself with the use of materials or means at hand, in the case of design these are often the contemporary technologies and prevailing design ethics of the day.

The more pragmatic and urban minded observer may move immediately towards a literal interpretation: patching bitumen; renewing streetscape planting; building new rail lines; or restoring historically significant buildings and districts. Simplistically these all appear to require a pre-existing state to be returned to; a master plan. However more often than not there are modifications made, small developments in how that particular 'piece of city' is repaired; improvised improvements on the pre-existing condition. Repair is not interested in the creation of a completely new system, fabric, field or object per se, it concerns itself with the development of an existing one. Repair is an act of nurturing and cultivating what is recognised as being of importance, something that continues to be necessary. Yet it is able to be improved in an iterative process based on cycles of observation and action, more similar perhaps to the scientific and medical methods than that of our contemporary approach to property and infrastructural development.

Therefore and most critically the act of reparation is one that is carried out in concert with its context. The repairer must understand the language, territory and culture in which they operate and be capable of acting within it. When considering the tension in design practice between the 'field' and 'object', the clear answer is, understand and act with and within both. Architecture acting through the creation of objects alone cannot hope to genuinely repair an ecosystem, a culture or a city; no more than a landscape architect acting solely through infrastructure, the public realm or ecological systems can hope to achieve the same. I have taken the position in this essay, perhaps naively, that repair is too big and important a task to be led by a single profession. It is not the sole role of an architect, landscape architect, ecologist, planner or engineer. All must be understood as 'designers' of our urban environments and held to account equally. As in medicine there is a 'division of labour', with condescension between specialisations, however without the full breadth of combined knowledge the practice of modern medicine would not be as effective as it is today. If I may indulge myself even further I might add that the humble 'general practitioner' in medicine provides a good comparison to the role of the urban designer in the creation of our cities.

The assemblage of evidence from a range of design professions that makes up the Australian Pavilion's exposition *Repair* at the Biennale Architettura 2018 shows that we do not yet have a definitive set of projects that successfully demonstrate repair across all scales and systems. We do however offer this collection as a series of moments that point towards an Australian approach to urban design that genuinely seeks to achieve our own version of repair.

A repaired item is something that has enduring value, which may have been forgotten at some stage, but which is once again deemed essential, albeit with a few modifications.

Instead of taking the view that we re-examine a global architectural tradition and attempt to find Australia's place within it, I intend to start not by looking at architecture at all. Taking the view of the 'urban designer/GP' I will start with the whole body, corpus omnium.

Recognising our 'pre-existing' condition

When a society seeks to repair its cities, it has reached a point of maturity where it is able to collectively recognise what is most fundamental to it. For Australian urban design to genuinely seek to repair significant aspects of its physical and cultural environment signals an important stage in the development of this nation.

In his book *The Australian Ugliness*, published in 1960,(1) Robin Boyd runs an unrelenting and well-argued critique of the Australian city as being devoid of a deep consideration of cultural basis and geographic influence. To pose the question of 'repair' in Boyd's time would have been met with blank looks...repair what?

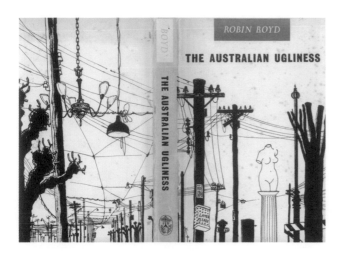

The Australian Ugliness, cover, by Robin Boyd, 1960.

Although to be fair, at the time of publication the West, including Australia, had just defeated global fascism using extreme force and was in the thrall of an ideological battle against Communism. There was an atmosphere of triumphalism and unquestionable resolve in the system of capitalistic democracy. Boyd's deliberate use of the word 'ugly' describes not just the physical condition of the Australian urban environment, but also the ideologies that drove its development. Ugly, then, is a condition to be repaired; beauty is the condition to be restored. But who's idea of beauty? Particularly during this so-called American Era, the idea of 'freedom' has been hoisted up as ideologically beautiful and even by some as the 'original and natural condition of humankind'.

Freedom was the catch cry and the West's 'enlightened' democratic system, driven by a capitalist ethos that worshiped exponential rates of economic growth, was its method. This pervasive mood is eerily similar to Australia's colonial 'squattocratic' land grab of the early nineteenth century where thousands of 'free' Anglo-European settlers fanned out from Sydney and other port towns inland to 'claim' land from the existing custodians – and all with the blessing of the colonial government. As such, this liberal free-for-all sat comfortably with the very foundations of early Australian society immediately post the European invasion. To settle more land and produce more 'city' was proof that 'western civilisation' through un-checked consumerism was winning against its ideological rival, Communism.

Terra nullius – an archaic legal term meaning "nobody's land" – was alive and strong in our cities in the mid-twentieth century, although this time it was a case of claimed intellectual and cultural absence, rather than the absence of current inhabitants and custodians. Urban design and architecture were one of the primary tools in establishing and confirming this ideological, physical and spiritual dominance.

Terra nullius infers that a particular part of the earth has no current 'owner' and is therefore free to be claimed. In declaring this, the current relationship between original inhabitants and their land is rendered void. In very simple terms, if the Aboriginal nations' habitation and stewardship of Australia was the 'pre-existing condition' that *terra nullius* sought to dissolve, then the largest and most profound type of repair we can pursue would be correcting this historic injustice. A profound cultural and ideological repair is a significant task for anyone. As urban design was part of the establishment – a tool used in defining the power to 'freely' dominate – it must now be employed to help repair the physical and cultural conditions it sought to replace. Together with the allied design disciplines of landscape architecture and architecture, the profession should be at the forefront of repairing Australia, culturally and physically.

As a side note, two years after *The Australian Ugliness* was first published the Australian government finally allowed Australia's Aboriginal people to vote. Repair in Boyd's time was a very different question in a very different Australia that we see today. Clearly both the Aboriginal and European cultures pre-settlement can never return to their pre-existing condition, we are forever entwined. Repair in our time is to work through what is useful and build upon it, identify what is not useful and purge it, a type of cultural ecology. So considering this, how can urban design act? Boyd understood the cultural crisis and was on a pathway, albeit unfinished, to repair aspects of our environment and culture through the creation of responsive built form sensitive to their environment and beginning to define a unique Australian position on our cities. He knew that 'other' systems, such as the study of biology and the environment could be used to more accurately affect a greater repair to the way in which we occupy this land.(2)

Scaling-up our moments of repair

There are moments in our practice of architecture, landscape architecture and urban design that point to how this repair is starting to take root. As small as they are these are the moments to be indentified and built upon. Examples such as iredale pederson hook architects' Walumba Elders Centre in Gija Country in the East Kimberly show how a micro intervention in a vast landscape can at the very least sustain the relationship the Gija people have with their land. Most Australians would love to believe that interventions such as these repair the relationship between Aboriginal culture, European settled society and the land.

iredale pedersen hook, Walumba Elders Centre, Warmun, Western Australia.
Photograph, Peter Bennetts.

In reality this is a small, but intelligent, gesture. A large part of this intellect is demonstrated through the interplay between the landscape and architecture, both informing each other.

This is a rarely seen relationship in our more urban areas, where the imperative for architecture to respond to – and be shaped by – the physical process of the greater urban and ecological context are not so great. The project serves both the pragmatic needs of the elders and their wider community. Its true value lies in the designers' ability to observe and then provide a series of internal and external spaces that support the connections of family and culture. A large part of this is the connection to the land, and specifically the ecology, hydrology and geomorphology. Repair is enacted through the reparation of these systems, growing back the fragile flora and fauna communities and establishing the soil structures that had successfully evolved alongside the people in this landscape over centuries.

Nonetheless, this is but an intervention in a vast cultural and physical landscape that has been greatly damaged. The real repair would commence if such an approach could be 'scaled up' and used to support and sustain much larger rural and urban communities. Culture and connection to land are one and the same; however, the process of observing and the responding to intricate and not immediately obvious cultural connections is an approach that the Australian urban designer needs to pay far more attention to if we are to repair this cultural rift. Such a project demonstrates that repair is more than

the literal return to a previous condition and allows an exploration of social, spiritual and cultural reparation.

Boyd's 'featurism'(3) and all of the ills that he associates with it is born from a lazy intellectual approach to the creation of our built environment; it is the creation of 'new things' just for the sake of it; it is not investing time in working with the prevailing cultural and physical systems. Occasionally, we need to literally create a 'new thing' such as the Walumba Elders Centre to repair previous damage; however, even this project draws heavily from the most important aspects of the 'pre-existing condition' to create a thing that provides an evolved version of what was before it.

Landscape architecture, at its best, is continually drawing from an interpretation of the land and context in this way. Where it does not, it becomes an obvious flaw; it becomes horizontal featurism, and it is open to criticism that it is merely serving to fill in the space between the buildings rather than reflect an evolved version of the 'pre-existing' condition. Architecture, it must be pointed out, seems to have a choice and far too often chooses the 'new' or self-referential. When architects work closely with landscape architects they do not necessarily 'keep each other honest' and avoid this featurism; however, what the Walumba Elders Centre and many other similar projects do demonstrate is an ability for the 'pre-existing conditions' to be more richly interpreted. Only when we see this becoming a more ordinary and expected way of working will we be able to 'scale-up' this approach to our cities.

The oldest continent with the shortest memory

The current evidence does not provide an overwhelming body of Australian work to prove that we have started to repair our connection to the land and our communities, old and new, at a great scale. There are certainly many bright lights showing that redemption is something that we are capable of; however, the pace at which our 'new world' nation continues to build over the older systems is outstripping the conscious acts of repair. In moving towards a more self-aware attempt at reconciling our urban necessities with the land, we begin to question what a returned or repaired condition needed to be. In short, we are still searching, as this exhibition demonstrates.

We can, however, start with a few basic self-evident facts of our 'condition'. Australia is the oldest continent with the thinnest average topsoil and the greatest disproportion of coastal and interior distribution of population compared with all other continents. These facts provide clues as to why the interior of our country cannot be easily compared to any other. They also point towards the importance of working effectively with both fresh water and marine environments and the ecologies and cultural systems that they support.

As Australians, socially and culturally, we have in past patted ourselves on the back for being 'multicultural'. It is true that in our major cities, particularly those along our eastern and southern coastlines, we host some of the most 'international' communities in the world, with 24% (Melbourne) and 26% (Sydney) of residents having been born outside of Australia. The similarities with Vancouver must also be noted. This city hosts more residents who were born overseas than any other. However Australia, like Canada has a difficult post-colonial past with exceptional challenges in reconciling the rifts between the original people of the lands and the new settlers. As the 2016 Venice Biennale Canadian Pavilion exhibition *Extraction* by Pierre Bélanger[4] powerfully demonstrates we are still both a long way from achieving a cultural repair in this respect.

Ironically, despite Australia's international connectedness and apparent acceptance of other cultures we are one of the least connected countries to the older knowledge and customs of the local 'indigenous' communities and by extension of our shared land. We seem to trade our access to other cultures for a loss of our local knowledge. What we are becoming more and more aware of, however, is that divisions and overt acts of disrespect amongst the various multicultural 'peoples of Australia' are causing repugnant rifts through our society. The majority of these rifts are formed and displayed in our largest cities.

Measuring rather than feeling our land

One of the major emergent social and political forces on the twentieth century has been the increasing urgency to reconcile humankind's relationship with the planet that sustains us. From Virgil to the Transcendentalists, variations on this theme have existed for millennia. However, in keeping with our western post-enlightenment thirst for pragmatic and evidence-based confirmation the spiritual or philosophical imperative seems to have now been replaced by one driven relentlessly by mounting scientific evidence. With the very rare exception, we understand that our resources are finite and that the systems that support our societies are in continual need of monitoring, assistance and repair. This is a type of scientific and pragmatic repair. One whose success can be measured and applications gradually scaled up to include larger parts of our cities.

There is a series of projects that fit this 'type' with GoatLand being an excellent example.[5] They include landscape architecturally based urban interventions that use scientific terms and concepts and aim to deliver a series of pragmatic results, such as decontamination, waterway naturalisation and ecological rehabilitation. They look at an environmental repair and use terminology borrowed respectfully from geophysical engineering, biology and chemistry to explain their design and its purpose.

iredale pedersen hook, Walumba Elders Centre, Warmun, Western Australia, aerial view. Photograph, Peter Bennetts.

Often operating at a large scale and usually focussed on post-industrial sites they define a branch of urban design that revels in the gradual unfolding of the intended result. While they currently deal with parts of cities that could be described as 'post-architectural' they point to a way of repairing that could be applied simultaneously with building and habitation at a scale much larger than a single building.

Overt references aiming to appeal to a wider cultural intellect are generally interlaid into these schemes. They tell an intentionally simple story of how, through design, we can literally repair our damaged urban environments so that these once-forbidden places can be reoccupied. Such straightforward narratives presenting obvious solutions make it hard to believe we are not already repairing our cities

SueAnne Ware et al., GoatLand, Sydney.
Diagram of the phytoremediation process.
Image, SueAnne Ware.

in this way, and therefore have the potential to capture the imagination of the broader community. It is also perhaps another emerging area where our lexicon of design is developing conceptual and linguistic tools to better articulate how we repair our cities.

In short, if our urban renewal areas could be designed to rehabilitate the ground or reinstate a damaged ecology while supporting human habitation – living and working – we would be seeing genuine ecological repair. When this takes place at city scale, then we know we are making a difference that matters.

Given that we are a very recently urbanised country, all of our urban interventions, with few exceptions, have been roughly laid over the pre-existing landscape. The theoretic scheme for the regeneration of the low-lying, post-industrial Arden Macaulay precinct, titled, Arden Macaulay Island City, by Monash University's (MADA) Urban Laboratory, (6) poses an answer to this conundrum. It uses contemporary urban design techniques to overlay and then integrate an urban system into a highly damaged waterway.

Through projects such as this we have an opportunity to combine solutions for our cultural and ecological 'tears' and develop a method of repairing several systems in the one urban regeneration project. Fishermans Bend in Melbourne is one such location where development for over 80,000 new residences and almost as many workers will be built in the next fifteen years. The site of this significant rebuilding of the 'next CBD' is set on a very low-lying estuarine silt formation at the mouth of Melbourne's major river, the Yarra. Similarly to the Arden Macaulay project, this presents a real opportunity for significant repair on a large scale.

Both Fishermans Bend and nearby Arden Macaulay present two of the best opportunities that the Australian urban designer currently has to effect a large scale meaningful repair. They seek a large scale repair to the previous city making culture of Boyd's era that has created rips, tears and disjunctions in the city's relationship to the

systems that still exist under and within it. Over the past few decades, we have become very aware of what it is we need to repair; however, our next challenge is to convince ourselves that it is worth doing. It is only through a broader resolve amongst the urban design community – inclusive of architects, landscape architects, planners, engineers and public decision makers – that this will be achieved. We seem almost desperately in need of a defining approach to our cities, that fits our own cultural requirements and to stop referencing the ideas, politics and economic imperatives of others.

Emerging from the fog of our 'identity crisis'

Only very recently did Australian society stop continually reminding itself that we have an 'identity crisis'. Possibly spurred on by Boyd, one of our most characteristic Australian intellects, when he wrote in 1960 that, "Australia shuffles about in the middle, as she navigates the middle of the road, picking up disconnected ideas wherever she finds them." (7) Our country, it seemed to him, was an unedited scrap book of other people's ideas. Boyd appealed for a greater sense of responsibility to our nation's built environment and to essentially emerge fully and confidently from our colonial past.

Perhaps one of the best indications that we have progressed from Boyd's version of Australian 'cultural cringe' is the critical response to Rem Koolhaas' lecture on the work that he and David Gianotten have been developing on the concept of 'countryside'. (8) The work itself, as applied to the Netherlands, is not problematic; what is problematic, argues Jillian Walliss, (9) is Koolhaas' application of this concept to Australia. Walliss' article deserves a thorough read. Her response proves that Australia has developed the ability to immediately and almost effortlessly examine, critique and reject ideas that do not accurately resonate with our developed understanding of our Australian condition. Even if incorrect, the change here is that the confidence is now ours. It is almost ridiculous to point this out; however, it must be recognised that our culture of design, its maturity and level of self-awareness has developed so far beyond Boyd's Australia as to be almost unrecognisable.

Ironically, self-recognition has only led to a fresh anxiety that we are not acting with nearly enough gusto, conviction and commitment towards full repair of our urban condition and to reconcile it with the prevalent physical condition of our shared land.

As Walliss' article demonstrates, we have developed a culture where our thinkers and spokespeople for our cities' culture are able to respond so effectively to the lax application of external ideas. This could be mistaken for Antipodean parochialism; however, it is more simply a calling out of what appears to the Australian urban designer as a clear misreading of the Australian condition, with echoes of the past *terra nullius*. We recognise this blatant misreading as we, in Boyd's time became masters at it.

For all of our brilliant single-building responses to climate and context, for all the razor-sharp academic rebuttals of poorly constructed ideas, we still seem to have hit a crisis point. Like watching our disembodied selves in our own bad dream, we can see the flaws in our approach, and the damage being done; yet we feel almost helpless to change our course. This seems to be the burden of this generation of urban designers.

While our current approach to some buildings and single public realm projects is incredibly intelligent and sensitive, it is how we develop thousands of buildings – how we choose to create our cities – that really counts. These single reparative projects, we hope, can be held up as demonstrations of how our future cities need to be designed. Once again, there is little evidence that not enough of our decision-makers nor 'the market' are really paying attention.

Australia's urban repair, then, must seek: to develop well beyond the post-colonial angst of our Australian 'identity crisis'; to avoid the need to constantly import 'new ideas'; to be steadfastly focussed on the ability of our own society to develop a collection of places that best serve both our corporeal needs and nourish our collective spirit.

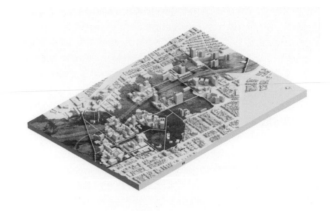

Monash University Urban Laboratory, Arden Macaulay Island City, Melbourne. Image, Monash University Urban Laboratory.

SueAnne Ware et al., GoatLand, Sydney. Contaminated sites around Sydney harbour. Image, SueAnne Ware.

It must also seek to push beyond the manufactured division between the identities of architects and landscape architects if it is to successfully translate this into a reparative urban design. The act of repairing the city and hinterland requires, as Boyd called for, a specific language that indexes the shift in philosophy about how we create and dwell in the Australian city.

Repair is a mechanism by which Australian design may develop its own, more specific lexicon of terms, accurately describing our relationship with our cities and hinterlands and how we inhabit them.

Repair: catalyst for a new urban design language

Within our western design culture, words, names and terms are like tools with which we articulate our proposals and direct their construction. So, given that neither architect nor landscape architect can act alone, that we must act within larger cultural and scientific systems than what has been considered as 'design, what is our lexicon?

Within the concept of repair are held many pragmatically useful synonyms: reconstruct; rehabilitate; reform; rebuild; readjust; and renovate. These are all terms that strongly suggest the requirement of a base condition that perhaps damage requires intellect and energy to be applied to it to elevate it once more to its proper working order.

To answer this, a break from the traditional terms used to describe static built systems is required. This evolved lexicon will need to include concepts and terms borrowed from fields that specialise in describing and interacting with continually changing complex systems. Landscape architects are familiar and regularly work with dynamic systems through their work. Modern ecological theory provides a deep and sophisticated method of understanding 'things that do not stay were you put them'. This interdisciplinary branch of science aims to describe how a series of interconnected systems affect each other in seemingly chaotic ways. Of particular interest is the concept of resilience, or the ability of a system to reorganise itself to accommodate a significant challenge to its existence. Recently, this term has found its way into the urban design lexicon; however, its meaning is often interchanged with sustainability. In fact, while related, they can often be diametrically opposed.

Simply put, when an ecosystem demonstrates resilience by rearranging itself it does not necessarily need to return to its pre-existing form when achieving equilibrium.

The ecosystem may have needed to purge no-longer-useful parts and may have developed new parts to compensate. The concept of repair is not so much a search for a return to a previous form, then, but rather more of a progression to a different arrangement that serves a changed condition more effectively. In this way, the urban response to the restoration of an inner-city waterway, for example, should not be to return the system to a duplicate of its pre-settlement form; rather, it could be to create an adapted hybrid that may have had to purge species or habitats that no longer serve a purpose.

Once again, the question of how to apply this to our dense urban areas remains. What place should the philosophy of modern ecology have in architectural and landscape architectural practice? With the benefit of hindsight, when we look at Boyd's world we can more clearly understand the role of mass production and the roots of 'globalisation'. But what Boyd most likely did not foresee was the impact that computing, and more specifically the 'digital' revolution that our world is really only just starting to come to grips with.

The general urban design community are just now beginning to realise that this 'digital thing' is far more than just a greater use of computers in everyday life; it is a change so profound that the cycles within which we communicate, organise and intervene in the real and virtual worlds become almost instantaneous. In other words, our reality will not be a fixed series of relationships and even our design studios will mimic a living ecosystem.

It may then be that the digital mindset will offer the answer to how we recast our design language. The concept of a digital city defies our traditional concept of our world as simply existing in Cartesian space. The connections between multiple communities and organisations are often driven by pragmatic needs, and when the relevance of a particular connection dissolves it is broken and remade to someone more relevant. In this way, our society is beginning to operate more like a true ecology, where only the 'useful' thrive and redundant aspects are purged, without a centralised governor making the decisions or setting out the 'master plan'.

Perhaps when looking for the lexicon to assist with repairing our current Australian condition, we need look no further than the incredibly intricate system of Australian Aboriginal languages. The *AIATSIS Map of Indigenous Australia*(10) is a snapshot of a mobile series of cultural systems frozen at the moment Europeans began to settle and detrimentally disrupt this rich and diverse cultural ecology. It depicts the map of the Australian continent overlaid with a series of coloured 'blobs', each attempting to signify the 'coverage' of a particular language group and therefore sub sets of the broader regional culture. Each blob or zone, as clumsy as they are, demonstrates a richer shading of Aboriginal culture, one that is as much influenced by the land as the land has been by this human culture, its rituals, processes and beliefs.

While geographically located, the languages merged and shifted position as their host cultures developed, thrived or died out. This connection between language, culture, and management of the land should form a basis for our design and operation of our evolving urban areas. In broadening our gaze to include more than just our European western heritage and current capitalist democratic beliefs we can add to our existing language and drive a new way of seeing and working with our cities.

Globally, many urban western designers have struggled to visualise these fluid relationships, often relying on drawings and concepts such as Bernhard Tschumi's 'transprogramming' and 'disprogramming'(11) to explain how differing programs or uses can coexist physically and temporally together, and yet remain distinctly independent. It is important to note, though, that these distinctly postmodern concepts retain a need for total control of the system it is describing. They never quite capture the mixture of immersion and lack of scale, chaos and the absence of an obvious central governing (human) intellect that a true ecosystem appears to have.

The truth is that over the past few decades our society has become far better informed about the role and workings of the broader set of ecosystems, and that we are in fact no less separate and reliant on them than any other living creature. The undeniable truth is that we are part of a changing ecosystem and that our cities, being an extension of us, are subject to the same cycles of purging and renewing. Tschumi, as many others have, developed terms to assist with dealing with the temporal shifting in the use of spaces; however, both architects and landscape architects seem to now need much more than this.

What next?

If our urban environments were simple objects or static systems that do not evolve nor change form and function continually, the act of designing a city to a preset 'ideal condition' would be simple. Things such as the jacket in need of repair, streets requiring reconstruction and the renovation of buildings all conform to a 'master plan' of some type, the ideal condition required by the designer.

It is the lack of a coordinating culture of repair that stifles our achievements when attempted through our smaller scale projects. The highly energy efficient office building, or house that works sensitively with its landscape would need to be replicated thousands of times to have a significant reparative effect. And then this is only the environmental and physical realm. Our deeper cultural repair, the one seeking to close gaps in our society created through the act of building our cities, is yet another frontier.

The absence of a broader understanding of what all designers are working towards and a language that articulates this is becoming more apparent as our cities become more densely populated. With some of the fastest growing urban centres in the world Australian cities have to respond to the infrastructural and cultural demands of a more compact way of living, and we are doing it with guess work.

Emerging however with the urban design discourse is a more scientific way of describing the intended outcome, providing a method by which its success can be measured and learning from failure in a specific and common language. Much like the medical profession when dealing with a complex system and attempting to repair just one part of it, it is critical to be able to measure the effect of repair in one area as on the broader organism. Urban designers, landscape architects, architects and planners do not have a concise method for measuring the effect their interventions have on the broader city, we just sort of guess. In this digital age it is time we develop one.

(1)   Boyd, R 1960, *The Australian Ugliness*, F W Cheshire, Melbourne, Victoria, Australia.
(2)   This approach by Boyd - his continuous inclination to 'spatial continuity' and forms of integration between built and open spaces - is the focus of a book by Mauro Baracco and Louise Wright: Baracco, M & Wright, L 2017, *Robin Boyd: Spatial Continuity*, Routledge, London, UK and New York, USA.
(3)   Boyd's critique of 'featurism' informs his book *The Australian Ugliness*, op. cit.
(4)   See Bélanger, P 2016, '1:1 Billion', descriptive text of *Extraction* exhibition at the Canada Pavilion, in *Reporting From the Front: Biennale Architettura 2016 - Participating Countries, Collateral Events*, catalogue of the 15th International Architecture Exhibition, La Biennale di Venezia, Marsilio, Venice, Italy, pp. 26-27.
(5)   These kinds of projects are very relevant to the concept of repair but were not included for exhibition in *Repair* because the Creative Directors wanted to provoke the role for architecture. GoatLand is a speculative project designed by a team including landscape architects SueAnne Ware (University of Newcastle, Australia), Chris Johnstone (Bosque Studio, Newcastle, Australia), Vanessa Sooprayen (University of Newcastle, Australia), Simon Kilbane (UTS Sydney), Katrina Simon (UNSW Sydney) and State government strategists Jake Nicol (Urban Growth NSW) and Nicole Campbell (Urban Growth NSW).
(6)   A description of this project is included in this catalogue/book.
(7)   Boyd, R 1960, op. cit.
(8)   MPavilion 2017 was designed by Rem Koolhaas and David Gianotten of OMA; these two architects gave an opening lecture at the University of Melbourne on 3 October 2017 in which they discussed these concepts.
(9)   Walliss, J 2017, 'A failed manifesto: OMA and the Australian countryside', *ArchitectureAU*, 12 October, viewed 10 December 2017, <https://architectureau.com/articles/the-antipodean-limits-of-a-manifesto-oma-and-the-australian-countryside-1/?utm_source=ArchitectureAU&utm_campaign=516ee136b0->.
(10) AIATSIS 1996, *The AIATSIS map of Indigenous Australia*, AIATSIS, viewed 5 December 2017, <https://aiatsis.gov.au/explore/articles/aiatsis-map-indigenous-australia>.
(11) See Tschumi B, 1996, *Architecture and Disjunction*, MIT Press, Cambridge, Massachusetts, USA, London, UK.

A CONVERSATION WITH THREE YOUNG PRACTITIONERS

LANCE VAN MAANEN AND JONATHAN WARE

Designed by landscape architect Kate Cullity (T.C.L.) for a garden
festival in Berlin, this garden installation seeks to educate visitors
about the unique and inseparable relationship between Australia's First
Nations peoples and Australian landscapes, highlighting the many plant
species that depend on fire for germination and the millennia-old
practice of fire stick farming. Image chosen by Ricky Ray Ricardo.
Photo, Lena Giovanazzi.

Conversation panel

Jonathan Ware (JW)
Architect
Lance van Maanen (LVM)
Architect
Ryan Moroney (RM)
Architect
Sarah Lynn Rees (SLR)
Architect
Ricky Ray Ricardo (RRR)
Landscape Architect

REPAIR:
A conversation with young
Australian practitioners

The idea of 'repair' is necessarily seen through a long lens, an expansion of traditional design thinking from years to generations. From our understanding, it is clear that an entrenched short-term view of the procurement, design and construction process is found wanting when faced with the complexities of our present condition. As a way of re-evaluating our role in the built environment, the following conversation explores the idea of repair through the viewpoint of three young practitioners in Australia.

Ryan Moroney, Ricky Ray Ricardo and Sarah Lynn Rees are each carving out unique pathways within landscape architecture and architecture that challenge the boundaries of a typical brief and project procurement method. Of particular interest is the way each choose to define their sites, or rather, leave the edges open, accepting cultural complexity and a broader ecology as critical contributors to a valuable design outcome.

The conversation seeks to position young architects and landscape architects within a larger generational shift in values that prioritise the loaded notions embedded in the term 'repair'.

Part 1: repair
(our collective understanding of repair).

JW/LVM: The term 'site' is a globally recognised architectural limit of control. How is the term 'site' unique to the Australian condition, how do you define site?

RM: I would like to start answering this question by quoting some words from the description of the story of Bábbarra, a sacred place in West Arnhem, Northern Territory:(1) "Listen Up – Bábbarra is my story! Everywhere we got Dreaming. Every outstation, all country. Bábbarra is that big billabong over airport way. You see that creek? That place. At the same time, Bábbarra means young girls, women." (2)
Bábbarra reflects a unique Indigenous Australian perspective of site as special places of great ancestral and cultural significance that should be valued, protected and cared for. The local women's centre under the same name, Bábbarra Women's Centre, is a source of great pride for the women of twelve different language groups who gather to share knowledge, ideas and create remarkable textiles. The works often explore life on the land which builds knowledge and reverence around specific sites and places. In return, the art practice provides opportunities for potential financial independence and better well-being outcomes.
This reciprocal and empathic connection between people and place ultimately governs aspects of daily life be it social, cultural, spiritual or territorial, and rightfully suggests we take a holistic view towards any site. 'Site' then I would define as the environment in which all living organisms have a relationship, both to each other and to the place. This environment has a nebulous edge spanning territorial networks – for example, from street to continent. Its juncture with neighbouring environments is defined by the relationships and value systems represented by local actors past and present.

RRR: Well I think we need to stop defining site, in the literal sense, and accept that there is no such thing as this 'blank canvas' that many architects and designers continue to refer to, and therefore embrace the complexities that come from that. When we work with land, we engage in systems – ecological, political, social and cultural – that we need to better understand if we are ever to repair our relationship with the external world and each other. So many of our country's largest ecological problems have arisen from landholders, developers and governments not considering what impacts their actions will have beyond their own limits of control. The Murray Darling Basin is a prime example.

Irreversible ecological damage has been inflicted on this fragile river system because of the tendency of landholders to take whatever water resources they could access in order to increase productivity, without any consideration or understanding of the wider system they were a part of. The rivers are being heavily depleted upstream while the river mouth often fails to meet the sea. But it's a false economy, because those undermining or exploiting the systems that underpin their lives, consciously or unconsciously, will be adversely affected in the long run, as aquifers empty, salinity spreads, dust storms increase and ultimately the climate changes.

SLR: It is important to know that many Indigenous people don't see land or 'site' as a commodity. We are responsible for the well-being of Country which not only includes the layers of land, but also the seas and the skies. The environment can only sustain us if we work with it rather than fight against it. Everything we construct as architects or landscape architects modifies that landscape and disrupts the ecosystem. We are responsible for the interventions and resulting damage we make when we don't consider the 'site' as a living entity. I think too often in architecture 'site' is seen as the extent of our impact, and from its boundary we look inward, rather than considering the social, cultural, political, ecological, economical, logistical and physical contribution we could be making to the street, the neighbourhood, the city, or the state.

JW/LVM: Why is the idea of 'repairing site' so relevant to young architects and landscape architects working in Australia? What have we inherited as an emerging generation that could benefit from repair through architecture?

RM:

Bábbarra Women's Centre at the Bábbarra billabong with Joy Garlbin (landowner for Bábbarra) in front.
Image chosen by Ryan Moroney.
Photograph, Ingrid Johanson.

As Jeremy Till describes "mess is the law".(3) There is a need to contest the apparent irrelevance and marginalisation of the profession by embracing the external forces architecture depends on. Investigating site uncovers these 'messy' everyday forces. Repairing site is then about collaborative efforts towards policy, social and spatial solutions that are generous, holistic and robust. I sense this is resonating with a generation witnessing the obvious effects of inequality, ignorance and a continual compensation of ethics for short-term gains of an influential few.

RRR: There is an incredible responsibility felt by young architects and designers to repair humanity's relationship with the natural world, and particular frustration with those who are currently in positions of power for not doing enough. Young people today are set to live through a period of unprecedented rapid change to our environment and climate, and in this context I think young architects and landscape architects are hungry to be a part of more substantial efforts towards repair than is currently taking place. On a more localised scale, there is also a desire to undo a lot of the damage that modernist and later neoliberal thinking has done to our cities. Whether it is restoring polluted waterways, increasing green space in the city or designing housing models that are more permanent and inclusive, young designers are passionate to affect change because our own futures look particularly unstable and concerning.

SLR: I'm sure this is the same for each generation but I think we have inherited a touch of disdain for the bureaucratic systems we work in and we see the implications this has on the built environment. We see designs we consider socially and culturally responsive being knocked back and a lot of developer driven giants that contribute nothing to the personality or community of their context. There is little transparency into this decision making process, so it is difficult to do anything other than speculate, however perhaps what we need is a system that equally values the qualitative and quantitative merits of a projects in a long term and meaningful way.

JW/LVM: The act of repairing site in Australia is inherently bound up with the notions of reconciliation. How can architecture/landscape architecture/urban design contribute to the building of trust and respect between the wider Australian community and Aboriginal and Torres Strait Islander peoples as Traditional Owners of the land?

John Mawurndjul, *Mardayin at Mumeka*.
Stringybark (*Eucalyptus Tetradonta*)
with ochre pigment and PVA fixative, 2016.
Image chosen by Ryan Moroney.
Image: Courtesy of Maningrida Arts & Culture and the
artist. ©John Mawurndjul/Copyright Agency, 2018.

RRR: It feels to me that there is greater interest and engagement with the idea that design can play a meaningful role in repairing the relationship between Indigenous and non Indigenous Australia. As a landscape architect, I think we have a way to go before we can claim to understand what post-colonial practice is as a profession. Whatever it is, it starts with listening. Seminal texts have emerged in recent years, such as Bill Gammage's *The Biggest Estate on Earth: How Aborigines Made Australia* (6) and Bruce Pascoe's *Dark Emu* (7) which have had a huge impact on our understanding of Indigenous Australian's long and complex relationship with the land. However, these stories were never lost, they lived on in stories but for a long time we just haven't been listening. So a vital first step is to reach out and listen, and work with Traditional Owners and benefit from the knowledge of this country that dates back tens of thousands of years.

SLR: In my opinion the term reconciliation is flawed; it implies that there is some moment in Australia's history we can return to that will restore relations. Even repair implies something is broken and can be restored to a previously known working condition. I know I am picking on language, but language is important. We need to build relationships; we need to take the time to get to know one another, learn how to communicate. Non-Indigenous Australia (apology for the generalisation) needs to overcome its fear of doing or saying the wrong thing, which seems to manifests in either denial, overcompensation or paralysation. I think 'repair' comes when we can establish common values to work towards. We can only do that when we establish and build relationships that are entered humbly, without ego and with open ears and minds. These relationships take time and last beyond project completion.

RM: I agree, trust is crucial. As a matter of universal example, the profession must advocate for strong Indigenous voice to "ensure community ownership of the decisions that affect the lives of Aboriginal and Torres Strait Islander peoples".(4)
The profession's contribution begins with advocating for a consciousness of Aboriginal and Torres Strait Islander issues within practice. Leading the way, organisations such as Indigenous Architecture and Design Victoria (IADV), Aboriginal Environments Research Centre (AERC) and the work of Bruce Pascoe and Bill Gammage offer new and accessible perspectives of Indigenous history, land management and economy.(5) Architects Without Frontiers Australia has been working with Bawinanga Aboriginal Corporation in Maningrida, West Arnhem Land on a new Maningrida Arts and Culture infrastructure project. Meaningful engagement founded on respect and listening, has allowed a shared and open dialogue of ideas to flourish. The remarkable work and passion of the staff and artists, particularly Kuninjku bark painter and sculptor John Mawurndjul, is shaping the values of the project and the enabling role architecture as a process and outcome plays in supporting these values of maintaining a deep connection to homelands and protecting culture.

**Part 2: education and early practice
(critique of institutional capacity to deliver content on current ecological and cultural repair challenges, and reliance on self-driven dialogue within colleagues and community over institution).**

JW/LVM: As a recent graduate of architecture/landscape architecture, how do you feel your education has prepared you for considering ideas of 'repair'? Where have you fed your interest?

RM: Studying architecture helped sharpen my critical thinking by encouraging deep observation, listening, compassion for landscape and integration of designed interventions within broader ecological systems – mechanisms key to repair.

However, I was uncomfortable with a prevailing culture of unconscious acceptance to detach propositions from reality. One particular studio I found productive challenged the role of the 'expert' in the design process by engaging the 'local' and revelling in the banal and vernacular of sites and places. We experimented with bottom-up approaches to interrogate site at a micro scale, revealing systems at a macro scale.

RRR: In landscape architectural education sure, in a way you could say that's a founding pillar of the discipline. But that said, I think the idea of 'repair' is inherently political, and the academy is conflicted in that space. I think becoming politicised is kind of essential to pursue an agenda of repair, and that often comes after graduating.

In the past five years I have worked as an editor and writer on topics of landscape architecture and urban design, and over that period I became more and more interested in how 'design thinking,' aka what we learn at design school, can contribute to mainstream conversations like housing affordability, resilience and cultural understanding and empathy. I feel like the design education I received taught me to always conduct vast amounts of research, to then test that research in many ways before progressing to any sort of proposed 'solution'. And even then, to understand that any solution was never complete and could always be improved upon by listening to and collaborating with others. Definitely a mode of thinking that many of our nation's political and media personalities could benefit from.

SLR: I think it's in both my education and perhaps more so the experiences around it that have fuelled my interests; conferences, public talks or client/consultant interactions. When you enter an educational institution, you are buying into their values and for me it has been the diversity and often contrast of opinion of external influence that allows for a constant deconstruction and reconstruction of ideas. Critical discussion on values and motivations constantly feed our personal architectural ethos. Both my undergraduate and post graduate were conducted during the infancy of each degree, which resulted in a sense the courses trying to 'find themselves' and establish their position. As a result, there was an element of uncertainty which created space for questioning, probably much to my various tutors' and lecturers' dismay, but for me personally I feel the culture of questioning why we do the things we do is value I gained from those circumstances. Obviously, I am interested in establishing and promoting alternative forms of practice that collaborate with Indigenous Communities. This is

not something I learnt in Australia. My UK education was unique in that we spent two years on one self-directed project, exploring its social, political, economic, cultural and physical realities. I wrote my thesis on Indigenous housing in remote Australian communities and spent six months conducting fieldwork in Yuendumu.(8) While I am Indigenous, I am from Tasmania, which is

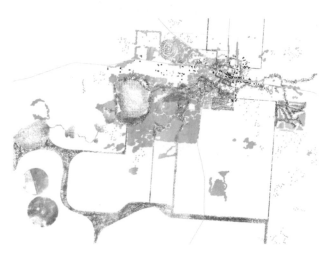

Jonathan Ware, Banksia farming for nectar and flower production + community archive, integrated with existing hotel/pub, Apsley, Victoria, view and urban scale plan including existing indigenous Banksia parklands. This project investigates forms of cross-programming and integration of built and open space for the economic and ecological repair of Australian rural towns. From: *Regenerated Towns in Regenerated Nature* laboratory, d___Lab.,School of Architecture and Urban Design, RMIT University. Images, Jonathan Ware.

a culturally different place to Central Australia so my time in Yuendumu taught me more about communication, patience and listening than any other aspect of my degree. But again, that is an unplanned consequence.

So, in response to the question I feel no, the intended learning outcomes of my degrees have not been geared towards repair, it is more the self-driven interest that facilitated this learning. Maybe that was the point all along, who knows!

JW/LVM: As a young practitioner engaging with acts of repair, what are the limitations and opportunities for agency you have encountered within the profession?

RM: An opportunity lies in the facilitation and enabling of the agency of the 'local'. In late 2016, the State Government of Queensland released a draft 2050 regional plan for South East Queensland asking for community feedback – the response from 17-25 year olds was an alarming whisper. To address this, I was part of a team at CoDesign Studio that designed and delivered a 'Youth Summit' involving over 100 young leaders from town, coast and country settings. Groups participated in various interactive activities which interrogated key regional plan areas of transport, agriculture, land conservation, housing and energy. The responses were proudly presented by the group to the Deputy Premier, Jackie Trad in the full view of passers-by in the central mall. As a result, the regional plan was revised incorporating a shared vision for the future shaped by the demographic that mattered most.

RRR: To begin on limitations, I was dismayed to learn a couple of years ago that the professional institution I was a member of had entered into a corporate partnership arrangement with two companies that were known for positions that clashed with the ethics of our discipline. One company for instance had played a key role in the fight to repeal the carbon pollution reduction scheme in Australia, yet their logo absurdly adorned every piece of printed or digital collateral that our institution issued in the period of their sponsorship agreement. How can we take ourselves seriously and expect others to take us so if we publicly contradict our core values? On the opportunities front, in my previous role as the editor of a national landscape architecture publication I had a privileged platform to pursue agendas that I believed deserved greater exposure. One of these was to challenge the Australian landscape architecture profession to address gender equity, achieved through commissioning two provocative articles; one on the gender pay gap and one profile of a practice that promoted flexible work models. Both of these widely-read articles pressured the institute to establish a working group on the topic. Another article I commissioned authored by Dr. Jillian Walliss, delivered a spectacular take-down of the colonial sentiments within a public lecture given by Rem Koolhaas and David Gianotten of OMA on 'the countryside.(9) This lecture, which disturbingly echoed ideas of *terra nullius*, was attended by over 600 people in 2017.

(10) Jillian's critique was easily the most read article on the website for a number of months, remarkable for a lecture review, and was republished twice. And finally, I will mention two further articles that I commissioned on the topic of regenerative agriculture and the potential for landscape architectural practice to expand into this territory, as has been done in the USA and New Zealand. One article was by farmer David Marsh who wrote about his experience switching from a mechanical mindset in the 1970s to a more organic approach over several decades and the phenomenal changes he has witnessed on his property in terms of ecological repair.(11) The second was a review by Jock Gilbert of the book *Call of the Reed Warbler* by agricultural scientist and farmer Charles Massy,(12) whose central concern is the repair and regeneration of this continent.(13)

SLR: I think one of the most fundamental limitations is that architects are seldom involved in the brief development stage. We are handed the parameters without the nuanced knowledge of how they were arrived at or the potential alternatives that were explored prior to receiving a quantified list. How can we have agency in the design process when we are not involved in the generation of project values? As young practitioners, we need to build the skills to interrogate briefs and market ourselves as valuable to the development process.
We also need to insert ourselves more in public debate and institutions with frameworks to facilitate change. We shouldn't just passively engage, we should find ways to drive the agenda.

Part 3: opportunities in a collective momentum?

JW/LVM: It would seem that *Repair* may suggest an approach that pushes architects to act beyond the traditional roles of the profession. Where do you see opportunities to pursue a practice that contributes to a broad sense of repair?

RM: Architecture is stuck between pursuing social, political and environmental ideals and delivering a building within capitalist frameworks. To break the bind and remain relevant, architects can play, as Mel Dodd suggests, a 'double agent' shifting back and forth between 'expert' and adopting the position of the 'local' by enabling community agency. (14) This approach to repair through localisation and engagement can apply to architects willing to recalibrate their skills to work collaboratively in cross-disciplinary teams across broader humanitarian, community development, post-disaster, research and political settings.

RRR: Over 50% of Australia's landmass is grazing land. In terms of landscape architectural practice, I believe there is a huge, largely untapped market for management plans geared towards farming and large scale landholdings that balance agricultural output with ecological repair. This kind of approach can increase productivity over time by providing grazing security and long-term ecological stability of large environments through the use of indigenous grass and grain species. The consequence of this would be long-term and invaluable including higher soil carbon retention, less reliance on irrigation and fertilisers, and a reduction in erosion of topsoil (to name a few).

SLR: I don't believe any form of practice is static, in the same way that we aren't, and the landscapes we impact aren't. Before we can seek opportunities to pursue change in the profession in any sense, we need to understand how we as individuals currently operate. We should record our own development, define and continually redefine our ethos and be conscious of when we are doing so. Recognising the

Completed in 2012, the Winton Wetlands project repaired a large wetland system in northern Victoria that was previously dammed for irrigation purposes. The masterplan for the restoration was prepared by Taylor Cullity Lethlean (T.C.L.) and is a rare example of an Australian landscape architecture practice working at a territorial scale in the Murray Darling Basin, Australia's most important and ecologically degraded river basin. Image chosen by Ricky Ray Ricardo.
Photo, Scott Hartvigsen.

moments in life that change our perspective and not get stuck in a single mindset. This is why exposure to a diversity of opinion and developing the capacity to critically analyse is invaluable. At the moment, I'm particularly interested in process and protocol on projects involving Indigenous clients, stakeholders or end users. How we can effectively bridge the communication divide and move from a situation where we (we, being those who contribute to the built environment process, governments included) are telling communities what is happening with

a surface level of engagement, to a robust engagement process where communities feel are integral to the process.

JW/LVM: Do you feel there is a sense of momentum within young architects building towards an understanding and consideration of repair, a way of re-evaluating how we approach our collective work? What platforms exist/are required in order to progress this shift in design culture?

RM: I think there is a prevailing critique of architecture's relevancy that resonates with most emerging practitioners in Australia. To progress this culture shift we can contextualise platforms within known mechanisms of change: discovery, diffusion and innovation. First, we can nurture our exposure to new ideas through self paced discovery across a broad spectrum of outlets. Secondly, continual collaboration of leaders across multiple disciplines is key for divergent thinking and for cultures of other practices to be mutually valued and have influence on each other. New procurement models and social platforms could help this sharing and diffusion of practice cultures. Finally, these are critical for social or cultural change. Open source investment platforms, crowdsourcing and grant programs offer vital resources to develop ideas along the innovation curve.

SLR: There is certainly a momentum in the Indigenous sphere. When I left Australia five years ago it was barely a conversation and it certainly wasn't an area we covered at university. As far as I am aware there is currently only one purpose-built core subject on Indigenous cultural intelligence in all of the twenty architecture schools in Australia. I've been back from the UK for just over nine months and in that time I've been humbled by how many people are consciously thinking about engaging with Indigenous communities. Now we need to increase the action. Every site in Australia is on Aboriginal Land and every project interfaces with Aboriginal cultures, living memories and continuing living histories. They don't all do it well, in fact most turn their backs, but there is an optimism and growing social responsibility which will drive action, precedent and normalisation.

JW/LVM: How can the traditional mode of practice learn from the type of work which is being explored through this way of thinking? What is the relevance to and impact on the profession at large?

RM: The architectural profession is being questioned at every level. Education is incredibly expensive,

Jonathan Ware, Catalytic Acupuncture,
RMIT Architecture Masters final thesis project for
residential accommodation and infrastructure/ecological
remediation, Melbourne. This project approaches urban
and ecological repair through remediation of contaminated
ex-industrial areas in sensitive sites (creeks, wetlands,
green easements, etc.), residential densification and
application of renewable energies in towers spread out
throughout Melbourne's west areas.
Image, Jonathan Ware.

the labour force is often stressed, and practices are forced to race to the bottom to secure a job only to then relinquish influence to design-build procurement models. Projects are arrested by the realities of delivering built outcomes within narrow and predetermined project success measures. This I fear is leading to a devastating omission of any meaningful connection of the built environment with urban ecology, landscape and social-cultural networks. 'Repair' calls for contextualising design decisions within larger ecosystems and networks. It calls for greater collaboration with multi-disciplinary teams. It calls for greater transparency and accountability of impact. Ultimately, 'repair' calls for empathy to be the new normal in practice.

SLR: Where do you draw the line and say this is the definition of the traditional mode of practice? Modes of practice are constantly changing, we should take joy in that fact rather than feel oppressed by the machine we have inherited. It is our responsibility to evolve the profession to suit the times, or ideally be ahead of them. We shouldn't forget the momentum of change we have inherited including, women in practice, working towards income parity (slowly), flexible working arrangements, the list goes on. The question is what momentum will you perpetuate and/or start as a legacy for future generations? I intend to have a part in the normalisation of Indigenous collaboration in the built environment.

(1) "The West Arnhem Regional Council is a local government area of the Northern Territory, Australia." See Wikipedia n.d., *West Arnhem Region*, Wikipedia, viewed 2 February 2018, <https://en.wikipedia.org/wiki/West_Arnhem_Region>.
(2) Djabibba, L djungkay (mother's country and ceremonial manager of Bábbarra) & Garlbin, J (landowner for Bábbarra) n.d., *Bábbarra story*, Bábbarra Women's Centre, viewed 2 February 2018, <https://babbarra.com/about/babbarra-story/>.
(3) Till, J 2009, *Architecture Depends*, MIT Press, Cambridge, Massachusetts, USA, London, UK.
(4) Australian Institute of Architects 2017 (May), *Indigenous Housing Policy*, Australian Institute of Architects, viewed 19 February 2018, <http://sitefinity.architecture.com.au/docs/default-source/national-policy/indigenous-housing-policy-2017.pdf?sfvrsn=2>.
(5) "Bruce Pascoe…is an Australian Indigenous writer, from the Bunurong clan, of the Kulin nation. He has worked as a teacher, farmer, a fisherman and an Aboriginal language researcher." See Wikipedia n.d., *Bruce Pascoe*, Wikipedia, viewed 17 February 2018, <https://en.wikipedia.org/wiki/Bruce_Pascoe>; "William Leonard 'Bill' Gammage AM, FASSA…is an Australian academic historian, Adjunct Professor and Senior Research Fellow at the Humanities Research Centre of the Australian National University (ANU)… In 1998, Gammage joined the Humanities Research Centre at the ANU as a senior research fellow for the Australian Research Council, working on the history of Aboriginal land management". See Wikipedia n.d., *Bill Gammage*, Wikipedia, viewed 17 February 2018, <https://en.wikipedia.org/wiki/Bill_Gammage>.
(6) Gammage, B 2012, *The Biggest Estate on Earth: How Aborigines made Australia*, Allen & Unwin, Crows Nest, NSW, Australia.
(7) Pascoe, B 2014, *Dark Emu: Black Seeds Agriculture Or Accident?*, Magabala Books, Broome, Western Australia, Australia.
(8) Yuendumu is a town in the Northern Territory of Australia.
(9) Walliss, J 2017, 'The Antipodean limits of a manifesto: OMA and the Australian countryside', *Landscape Australia*, 10 October, viewed 11 October 2017, <https://landscapeaustralia.com/articles/the-antipodean-limits-of-a-manifesto-oma-and-the-australian-countryside/>.
(10) The lecture was delivered at the University of Melbourne on 3 October 2017.
(11) Marsh, D 2017, 'An ecological approach to grazing', *Landscape Australia*, 9 November, viewed 10 November 2017, <https://landscapeaustralia.com/articles/an-ecological-approach-to-grazing/>.
(12) Gilbert, J 2018, 'Call of the Reed Warbler: A manifesto for regeneration', *Landscape Australia*, 19 January, viewed 20 January 2018, <https://landscapeaustralia.com/articles/call-of-the-reed-warbler-charles-massys-call-to-action/>.
(13) Massy, C 2017, *Call of the Reed Warbler: A New Agriculture - a New Earth*, University of Queensland Press, St Lucia, Queensland, Australia.
(14) Dodd, M 2013, 'The Double Agent', in R. Hyde, *Future Practice: Conversations from the Edge of Architecture*, Routledge, New York, USA and London, UK, pp. 72-84.

IN CONVERSATION WITH LINDA TEGG

INTERVIEW BY CAROLINE PICARD

Linda Tegg, *One World Rice Pilaf*, 2016,
Chickpea Detail.
Production still.

THE CONVERSATION BETWEEN CAROLINE PICARD AND LINDA TEGG TOOK PLACE IN FEBRUARY 2018, DURING THE PREPARATION OF *REPAIR* EXHIBITION.

CP: How does one identify what needs repair?

LT: One way to start lies in identifying where an injury has been sustained, but sensing the injury is the hard part. Witnessing a rapid transformation, say the felling of a tree or concreting of a creek is easy to identify but violence inflicted on the environment often plays out along time scales beyond our perception – they occur over life times. Working with grasslands was part of overcoming my own lack of awareness that was symptomatic of a kind of cultural amnesia. My generation didn't grow up learning much about either our colonial history or what was lost in the building of the city.

CP: The notion of repair reminds me of Joseph Beuys' sculpture, *Tallow. The sculpture that will not become cold* (1977).(1) He took a dead corner in an underground pedestrian walkway and filled it with twenty tons of animal fat. After it hardened,

Joseph Beuys, *Tallow*, 1977,
20 tons of tallow fat.
Installation view, Hamburger Bahnhof, 2016.
Photograph, Linda Tegg.

he cut the fat out and claimed the process healed the passageway, transforming negative space into positive form. I love the idea but doubt it's real ability to perform any applied repair, or transformation. The beauty of the piece remains abstract... Part of what's interesting about your intersection with architecture is that architecture actually has the skill set, material, and engineering degrees to have direct and literal impact.

LT: It's true, the knowledges in art take time to filter into the broader culture. Whereas architects are making decisions in the here and now that have wide ranging material effect on the shared environment, their thinking directly influences how our cities develop. It's exciting to think that discussions surrounding 'repair' might influence policy, might shift what is considered valuable and what is not. There is a longstanding legacy capturing how architects have worked in relation to the Australian environment. Our team is taking a step towards articulating that legacy in a new way, for this moment.

CP: Do the power dynamics between human and nature change when identifying the earth as a 'client'?

LT: For the *Repair* team we are learning through a number of projects across Australia that show how architects, through their many and various decisions, can facilitate the repair of natural ecosystems. We are seeing moments of decentring the human or architectural object in favor of a more holistic approach to land and culture. This can be anything from noticing when a plant community is showing signs of life and finding ways to support that, to designing buildings that give generously to a multitude of publics. I like how the client-earth can provide and withdraw resources/life. Throughout the Biennale, I imagine each pavilion will seek answers to Farrell and McNamara's proposition.

Their call for architects to provide for the "well-being and dignity of each citizen of this fragile planet"(2) also reminds me of conversations about more-than-human persons. Drawing ecosystems into the legal system raises their visibility. I'm also curious about the more established corporate personhood, and how this system allows the human to disappear, and detach from their rights and responsibilities. Still, *[laughs]* I don't know how clients are understood in architecture.

CP: That's a good point.

LT: Sometimes I imagine it's like, "the client wants xyz, they're out of their minds." Or, "the clients have the purse strings but they don't know what they need."

CP: They insist on including the ugly light fixture for sentimental reasons that override architectural vision...

LT: *[laughs]* I don't know. But I like thinking with this idea of Earth as client. How do you manage client expectations?

CP: When did you produce the first iteration of *Grasslands*?

LT: I came to grasslands through a fellowship at the State Library of Victoria. I was interested in what was living on the site prior to the Library. The pictures collection offered only three images from which we could infer what the library had replaced; pictures of the subdivision of Melbourne; a cottage, and the back of the Melbourne gaol. There were thousands of images of the building itself. This felt like a blind spot so I decided to work with what was known to bring the grasses back onto the site. I learned a lot about what stays and what goes. I see this new work as a physical dialogue between the building and the plants. The Australian Pavilion is well designed for the appreciation of certain cultural objects. The team and I believe that this plant community is of enormous cultural importance so we are working to engineer a lighting system that allows the plants to live and be represented on this stage.

CP: Do you think of *Grasslands* as a kind of institutional intervention?

LT: I never set out to make an institutional intervention. I wasn't bound by an established political position, I just wanted to see what would happen if I brought the grassland back to the site.

CP: You mentioned there is one window only in the Australian Pavilion; how did you develop the lighting design?

LT: My first impulse was to see if it was possible to remove the roof – it wasn't. We decided (as best we could) to artificially supply the light required by the plants into the exhibition space. I understand that it comes at a cost, and I'm interested in tracing that too. Where is all this energy coming from? We could ask this of any aspect of the process, but the lights make it highly visible. In terms of carbon emissions we have learned that *Skylight*(3) is equivalent to about eight people's return flight from Melbourne to Venice.

CP: Do you have to think about different kinds of light to serve the plants and humans?

LT: Absolutely. In meetings with our lighting designer Nic Burnham(4) there has been an interesting dynamic where Nic and Louise are concerned about the human viewing experience (these lights could give you a headache) and I am always pushing for more lux, thinking of the Australian summer sun that the grasses are accustomed to. We have been testing at Baracco+Wright's Studio. Our plants have been living well for nearly two months.

CP: I'm interested in *Grasslands'* conceptual portability. I have seen a few different iterations in Chicago and feel like each time the significance of the work is directly influenced by its varying contexts. This brings out an interesting conceptual adaptability in the grasses you work with.

LT: Looking back, both bodies of work, *Grasslands* in Melbourne, and *One World Rice Pilaf* in Chicago were really driven by a need to make a connection.

Linda Tegg, *Breath*, 2015.
Process image.

The gap came before the plants. *One World Rice Pilaf* began as a homespun experiment; I had read an article that described how when we burn fat it is exhaled as carbon dioxide and water. Abstractly, I understand that breath would manifest in the bodies of plants. To make this visible, I grew wheat berries (the seeds most convenient to me in Chicago) inside a series of terrariums: one sealed off, one open, and one that I breathed into daily. It was surprising to not only see my breath materialise in the bodies of the plants but also witness how something from the supermarket could actually grow. From there, I decided to grow everything I could from the bulk section of the supermarket – to spoil the grains as food and understand them as plants. They lived indoors under grow lights in the Chicago winter.

Linda Tegg, *Wolf on Display*, 2012.
Archival inkjet print,
100 x 120cm.

CP: That process of undermining their value as food, highlights something consistent throughout these iterations, namely that you keep the grasses in focus for the viewer – they maintain a presence otherwise denied or diminished when relegated to the background or 'site' upon which a structure is built.

LT: The persistence in the perception of the grassland as ground for human use is challenging to shift. Across all the installations I have made, multiple

dynamics are in play: the image of the rolling green hill, the complexity of the plants, the artificiality of the construction, displacement, caretaking, the pressure on the plants, and the plant's pressure on the building.

CP: Jasmin Stephens described how your work with animals, handlers, and trained human performers explores "ideas of display and performance in staged scenarios."(5) This plays with the idea of charismatic animal subjects and the way they perform to fulfill our conceptions of nature.

LT: It's true, I've worked with a lot of charismatic animals – pedigree dogs bred to fulfill a certain image, and animal actors trained to perform naturalistic behavior for the camera. A lot of these works were made in parallel with videos of dancers and bodybuilders who were striving to attain an image and visibility for themselves. Across both bodies of work I was thinking through this sense that we are all performing. Everyone was already thoroughly affected by images. I became interested with what happens when you bring those you almost only see in representation directly into the gallery.

CP: But grasslands seem essentially non-charismatic and yet they perform in the contexts you create...

LT: By drawing a living grassland into an artwork, culturally, we are removing its human use value. It's no longer ground to exploit, it's a cultural artifact to be contemplated and conserved. Those who do not subscribe to the history of western art may still use it as food or habitat.

Simon Starling, *Kakteenhaus*, 2002.
Volvo 240 estate, Cereus cactus, piping, cables, text,
dimensions variable.
Production photograph at Texas Hollywood.
Film Studios in Tabernas, Almeria, Spain.
© Simon Starling, photograph by Simon Starling.
Courtesy the artist and neugerriemschneider, Berlin.

CP: What happens to our conceived value of grasslands once it is in a gallery? Does it gather cultural capital?

LT: In one sense we are using the grassland, providing a platform for the plants to perform, drawing them into an exhibition and making art out of them. But I also see how the plants resist that structure. It would be wonderful if the grassland at the Biennale attains cultural capital for the grasslands currently under threat on the outskirts of Melbourne and other threatened ecosystems more generally. Because there are so many plants, however, I'm not sure what kind of cultural value they will maintain beyond the space they occupy in the Biennale. This is significant but I don't see it as equivalent to artworks that would enter an art market. Even a singular plant would be different. To create *Kakteenhaus* (2002), Simon Starling drove a cactus from Spain to northern Europe – it's a single cactus with an epic story. (6) Our plants live within the anthropocentric structure of an artwork; they have a transformative story of being collected as seeds from Victoria, transported by an architect to Italy in a suitcase (an alarming gesture for an Australian, as we live with stringent bio-security laws), and coming to life in an international biennale, but their quantity might undercut their capital. In an art-object sense, our plants are 1 of 10,000. Their value to us is in their massing, in their presence together. This 1 of 10,000 thought makes me think of how the process of articulating how endangered a species is also creates a sense of value. I'm interested in how things come in and out of our view.

CP: I love this idea of visibility – particularly within an architectural dialogue where it's the single building that is often funded. People recognise the building because it's singular, it breaks the skyline. The grasslands push against that paradigm, even simply emphasising that the ground is alive. It has presence.

LT: Yes. *[laughs]* I completely agree that it's interesting to see what happens when you are tuned into something that really shifts between a very simplistic overview and an extremely complex community or environment. It's suddenly challenging to contend with one's own presence and what one's impact might be… I want to create a space where you can actually see the grassland without artificial focal points, just to contemplate the plant.

CP: By entering the Pavilion, one commits to paying attention. You demand the audience be open to not only the grasslands, but also the relationship between grasslands and the buildings.

Ground. Photograph, Linda Tegg.
NMBW Architecture Studio, Kullurk/Coolart:
Somers Farm and Wetlands, Victoria.

LT: The grasses are enough. *[laughs]* But, if we include video projections, could the grass just become a background or accouterment to a diorama experience? That's really not what I'm going for at all. I hope for a phenomenal experience where we can consider our physical presences in space. Perhaps we can contemplate where the plants had come from, how they got there, why they are there. I want that presence to be in balance with the other forms of representation captured by the films.

CP: Is there a relationship for you between the site of a building and the frame of a camera?

LT: I see a relationship in terms of what is included or excluded from view. Generally speaking, the site of a building is located in space, but there are infinite ways that space can be understood and related. In the most rigid Cartesian sense the site of a building as defined by a property boundary or street address could be easily correlated to the frame of the camera, they both put up artificial hard edges. I love the idea of grasses as spies, they are certainly migratory bodies. Our boundaries are meaningless to them. They advance and recede as conditions allow.

CP: That's amazing! It illustrates how a certain invisibility would be beneficial, allowing grasses to cross borders, cross-pollinate, and ostensibly transform ecosystems.

LT: It sounds great, and touches on how problematic our sense of order in the environment can be – what constitutes a weed? What should remain invisible?

But as I see it today, most people are quite blind, or not caring, as to what value a grassland might have. In a suburban setting it's not a stretch to say that most people would be concerned that native grasslands are unkempt habitats for snakes etc. In that environment, humans have so much power to erase what they don't understand that I think it's worthwhile to attune them to the value and beauty of indigenous species. Grasslands are (in one sense) fast moving migratory bodies and could themselves be considered colonising.

CP: I want to talk a bit about the architectural videos you're shooting as your technique is contrastingly air born. What's it like to work with the frame of a drone camera?

LT: It's completely ungrounded. Up, down, it's like scuba diving. You can coast over the ocean floor or the ground. I'm working within a two-channel framework. At least two points of view running simultaneously, and then, when I can, I'm visiting the sites ahead of time and seeing what makes sense to me. Every site is different. I might go and shoot a number of different perspectives and then chip away at the result to create a final moving portrait of a structure within an environment. I begin the process with an idea about what I think is going to work because I'm researching the site beforehand, and talking the projects through with the team. But then often, on the ground, things change.

CP: So much is improvised but you always have to think in two frames at once, is that right?

LT: Yes. You think of a certain shot and have to hold a second one in your mind at the same time. I do think the shot through ahead of time, and how they'll work in aggregate, but plans change on the ground. Thinking and discovery continues throughout the making process. And these sites are often quite different from how you encounter them on Google Maps. Google uses an algorithm to assemble images into a specific relation. My interest in each place goes beyond that. As an image-maker (and almost all of us are now) I'm interested in how things pass back and forth through the picture plane – where do images come from? And how do they then inscribe themselves on the rest of the world?

CP: What you are describing almost parallels the migratory grasses – for example, the way a seed might pass through space, eventually landing and influencing. It sounds like images do the same...

LT: Absolutely, I often think in terms of an ecology of images. It's fascinating to trace images as they disconnect from one context and drift into another set of conditions. To see how they then influence other images, and affect how we shape our worlds. Like images, grasses are fast.

CP: Let's talk about presenting the grasses in Venice. What is even considered 'indigenous' there? Venice has so much historic Middle Eastern influence from historic trade routes and, as I understand, eventually sacking the Ottoman Empire. Those factors participate in a larger conversation of authenticity because Venetian culture feels so distinct and unique, even if it's a weird product of overlapping influences. You play with that by insisting that the grasses are native to Melbourne even as they are transported to another country.

LT: Absolutely. There's also a certain kind of thinking – this idea of a purist landscape, natural, indigenous, all those things lead people to act. Thinking of the decision to pull out a weed. You have to be certain that it's out of place. I've witnessed arguments over whether a gorse shrub hosting a bird's nest should be cut out of a grassland. One aspect that has made me feel okay with participating in shipping the seeds abroad is that I feel like I can give something over to the plants. I think maybe this is part of – this sounds pretty weird – their agenda. The plant community's agenda to gain prominence, or to gain visibility, or to extend their own territory. Maybe they want to emigrate.

CP: They have been plotting to cross the ocean for thousands of years, probably.

LT: It's easier for us to understand the human side of how something like that might occur.

CP: Especially given the larger discussion about migration in Europe at the moment. We've been talking about how grasses migrate, but you've also talked about how they connect to food and prosperity.

LT: In some sense images of grasslands are interchangeable, this might have something to do with the inadaptability of works we talked about earlier. I've read studies that suggest that simply looking at an image of open grasslands can make you feel good, no reference to a place required. It's the out of placeness of this living grassland (in the pavilion) that might prompt the viewer to think through its connections to actual places and actions. Explorer accounts of Australia always described grasslands with such emotive language, promoting them as a means to expansion and prosperity.

CP: You see lush grass and you think, "This place can support me".

LT: Yes. It reminds me of how rolling green hills are used in sci-fi – as an escape from some kind of post-apocalyptic world.

CP: *Battlestar Galactica*(7) ends on a rolling green meadow of some kind.

LT: I think of the first *Blade Runner* – not the director's cut(8) – rolling green hills came in.

CP: That's wild. Do you think that conception still has traction? For some reason, I want to compare it to something like a swamp and see how the two measure up. For instance, I've heard some of the flooding in Houston has been attributed to city's extensive development, particularly how it paves over swamp, diminishing the swamp's natural ability to handle large influxes of water. Swampland doesn't have the same appeal as a grassy meadow yet in both cases, I think, there is a desire to pave over both and build skyscrapers and roads. Where does that impulse come from? Does that impulse touch on what you all are working on with regards to reframing architecture as an act of repair?

LT: I am sure it has something to do with our dependency on the land, and desire to control the terms of that relationship. In Melbourne's founding both swamplands and grassy plains were subdivided and paved over. But it was the promise of grasslands that drove the development.(9) It's been argued that the settlement of Melbourne catalysed an uncontrolled land-grab across the continent that caused the disintegration of Aboriginal sovereignty, and ingrained a land-as-resource mentality that settler Australians still maintain. I'm talking about Melbourne because that is where I am from, but know there are many parallel stories. Perhaps during our time in Venice we'll find ways to learn about the swamp below. Some systems treat land like a blank sheet of paper. That abstraction denies the histories, ecologies and stories of the country. With *Repair* we are asking what decisions can architects make to repair those connections.

(1) See description of this work in the context of a later exhibition of Joseph Beuys' art work: Sokhan, A 2013, 'Exhibition // Germany in Felt and Fat: the Works of Joseph Beuys', *Berlin Art Link*, 24 September, viewed 10 February 2018, <berlinartlink.com/2013/09/24/exhibition-germany-in-felt-and-fat-the-works-of-joseph-beuys/>.

(2) Farrell, Y & McNamara, S 2017, '16th International Architecture Exhibition, Biennale Architettura 2018, Freespace', *La Biennale di Venezia*, viewed 20 November 2017, <labiennale.org/en/architecture/2018/16th-international-architecture-exhibition>.

(3) For a further description of *Skylight* installation see Baracco, M, Wright, L & Tegg, L, '*Grasslands Repair, Skylight, Ground*' in this catalogue/book.

(4) Nic Burnham, NDYLIGHT Lighting Design, Melbourne, Australia.

(5) See Stephens, J 2013, 'Samstag Scholars 2014, Linda Tegg', *Samstag Museum*, viewed 14 February 2018, <unisa.edu.au/Business-community/Samstag-Museum/Samstag-Scholarships/The-Samstag-alumni/2014/Linda-Tegg/>.

(6) See Vanderbilt, T 2002, 'A Thousand Words: Simon Starling Talks about Kakteenhaus', *Magazine Article ArtForum International*, *Questia: Trusted online research*, viewed 14 February 2018, <questia.com/magazine/ 1G1-101779189/a-thousand-words-simon-starling-talks-about-kakteenhaus>.

(7) "Battlestar Galactica (BSG) is an American military science fiction television series", from *Battlestar Galactica (2004 TV series)*, Wikipedia, <en.wikipedia.org/wiki/Battlestar_Galactica_(2004_TV_series)>.

(8) *Blade Runner*: original version, 1982; Director's Cut, 1992.

(9) These ideas are mostly discussed by Australian writer James Boyce in Boyce, J 2011, *1835: The Founding of Melbourne & the Conquest of Australia*, Black Inc., Collingwood, Victoria, Australia.

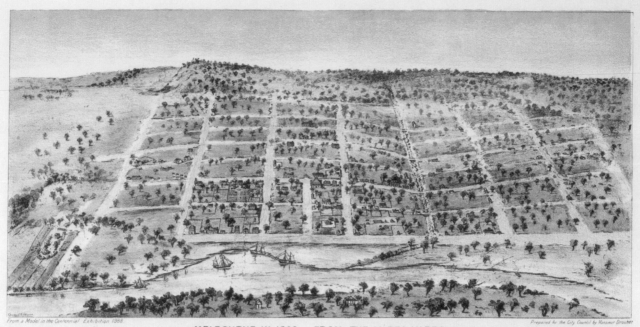

From a Model in the Centennial Exhibition 1888.   MELBOURNE IN 1838,   FROM THE YARRA YARRA.   Prepared for the City Council by Monsieur Drouhet

LINDA TEGG: SPACES AND OTHERNESS IN THE ANTHROPOCENE

GIOVANNI ALOI

Spaces always are charged environments – physical dimensions defined by material boundaries which in turn shape what we can see and say about the bodies that are encountered in them. It is between boundaries that knowledge develops out of complex relationships in which seeing is power and the world is formed.[1] Post-structuralist philosopher Michel Foucault paid particular attention to architectural spaces and how these function as delimitations in which the gaze engages in complex power/knowledge dynamics; where the dichotomy between object and subject is problematised; and most importantly, through which political identities take shape. From the cell in the panoptic prison or the edge of the page in a natural history treaty to the cage perimeter in royal menageries or the white walls of an art gallery, spatial delimitations constitute the prerequisite for the production of knowledge.[2]

These conceptions of the architecture of knowledge are also extremely important to artistic media. The material and cultural place-markers that define the idiom of a medium, its specific qualities, and competencies, provide the implicit parameters through which artists and viewers negotiate pressing cultural conundrums.

George Stubbs, *Whistlejacket*, 1762.
Oil on canvas, 292 x 246.4cm.
Courtesy, The National Gallery of Art, London.

Jannis Kounellis, *Untitled (12 Horses)*,
L'Attico di via Beccaria, January 1969.
Courtesy, The Estate of Jannis Kounellis and
Gavin Brown's Enterprise, New York/Rome.
Photograph, Claudio Abate.

Linda Tegg's photographs, videos, installations, and performances, thus, make the viewer acutely aware of these coordinates through a witty play of reconfigurations that reveal the power structures underlining our relationship with space and otherness in contemporary art.

Tegg's early series of 'animal studies',[3] for instance, is a particularly cunning example of the artist's ability to subvert the power dynamics that most regularly prevent us from seeing animals beyond pre-established cultural norms, and most certainly from seeing them beyond the objectifying and symbolic enmeshing of classical art and patriarchal

Linda Tegg, *Horse on Display*, 2009.
Archival inkjet print,
100 x 120cm.

norms. It is in this sense that Tegg's series engage with the current philosophical discourses of posthumanism and human-animal studies, and at the same time confront the implications of previous artistic statements about animals, nature, and humans.

Tegg's *Horse Study*, the first in her longstanding inquiry involving animals and representation, re-situates an Andalusian mare from the stables to the stately interior of the Alliance Française of Melbourne. This transposition results in an uncanny conflation of George Stubb's famous painting *Whistlejacket* (1762) and Jannis Kounellis' Arte Povera statement *Untitled (12 Horses)* from 1969. *Whistlejacket's* psychological depth is, in Tegg's work, coupled to the awkward material presence of Kounellis' live horses in the gallery space. The tension inscribed in the video and photographic images comprising *Horse*

Study is palpable – the horse appears suspended between the ineluctability of its animal self and the distinctly anthropocentric architecture that constricts its animal-essence beneath layers of domesticating demands. Here, the architecture becomes a metaphor of human social status and rationality, while the animal is instead exposed in its enigmatic constructedness: no longer wild, yet not quite human, but akin enough to race and work in complicity with the human. Domestication is thus essentially revealed as a *de-animalisation* process of both humans and animals. Architecture rationalises humans in ways similar to how humans rationalise certain animals. The elegance of the architecture and the elegance of the animal, both the result of extensive processes of amelioration, is the result of millennia of practices and cultural approaches that reciprocally shape us and animals.

Linda Tegg, *Goat Study Part 3 B*, 2011.
Archival inkjet print,
62 x 42cm.

Linda Tegg, *Sheep Gallery*, 2010.
Archival inkjet print,
60 x 40cm.

Linda Tegg, *Tortoise (Adelaide)*, 2016.
HD video, 11:47 minutes.

Subsequent 'animal studies' series have seen Tegg working with sheep and goats, domesticated animals riddled with contradictory symbolic meanings. The 220 references to sheep included in the Bible have cast the animal as the quintessential incarnation of the faithful responding to the pastor's voice.(4) Goats however, bear a different symbolic lineage that originates from Greek and Roman mythology.(5) The animal was entrusted with the responsibility to suckle infant gods and was associated with sexual drive, fertility, and unruliness. Tegg's staged encounters with sheep and goats in the gallery space break down the power relations inscribed in the classical representational tradition, strip layers of symbolism, and challenge the purity of the gallery space itself – representational regimes of power are made to collapse and the world-forming ability of film and photography are also exposed. As postmodern, or more aptly posthuman beings, we think through the architectures of media that in turn shape the architecture of our thinking – animals appear irresolubly defined by the idioms of these interfaces, always existing as already encoded representational figures. Tegg, therefore, explores the possibilities of conceiving animality as it emerges at the boundaries of language and signification, beyond the cultural apparatuses that oversimplify animals and reduce their otherness.

In this sense, Tegg's work is directly connected to the 'animal-turn' in art and philosophy that has characterised the past twenty years. However, her projects aim to reach beyond conventional inquiry and always take a 360 degree speculative approach – everything is up for questioning. And most importantly, Tegg is not looking to replace an old certainty with a new one. Her practice situates itself at the intersection of multidisciplinary discourses in which negotiations are key to envisioning representations that might index a *real* concealed behind the facades constructed by metaphors – true experimentation knows no certainties.

This, for instance, is the essence of *Tortoise*, a performance piece in which a crew of dancers constantly shifts and reorganises a number of differently sized circular mirrors. In its fluid and pseudo-organic state of reconfiguration, *Tortoise* bypasses the entrapments of symbolic representation, gesturing towards an irredeemable state of fragmentation that characterises the essence of being. It inscribes Lacanian denominations of the 'mirror stage'; encompasses the impossibility of attaining a true and cohesive sense of identity; explores the von Uexküll-informed consideration of multiple perspectives and points of view within one being and amongst different species;(6) mistrusts the illusion of space as a cohesive entity;

Jan van Huysum,
Still Life with Flowers and Fruit, c. 1715.
Oil on panel, 78.7 x 61.3cm.
Source, The National Gallery of Art, USA.

acknowledges the fallibility of perception, alluding to the tragic proclivity of we humans to see reflections of ourselves in everything around us.

Tegg's *Tortoise* thus perfectly summarises the very essence of the artist's speculative approach to reality, architecture, and the knowledge that can be produced within the parameters they impose on our human condition. The piece pushes the viewer to the very edges of prescribed cultural codings where opportunities to rethink our certainty might indeed arise. What is underneath, what is behind, what is beyond?

Staying at the forefront of recent speculative aesthetics and always envisioning original approaches to the non-human in art, Tegg has more recently focussed her attention on the enigmatic otherness of the vegetal world.(7) Like animals, the wealth, vitality, and alterity of plants in art have been reduced to anthropocentric metaphorical functions. Still-life paintings from the Dutch Baroque era are the quintessential manifestation of the ways in which we have co-opted plants as vehicles for human concerns.

Flowers, leaves, fruits, and seeds have always ventriloquised religious meanings, romantic messages, and most regularly, have incarnated the ineluctable absent-presence of death. It would be incorrect to claim that the presence of animals and plants in classical art has not been conspicuous. However, in classical art, complex syntaxes articulate the transcendental at the expenses of the living. Seeing something means to think by symbols, and therefore to actually see something else in the place of that

Linda Tegg, *Grasslands*, 2014.
Installation view.
Photograph, Matthew Stanton.

Linda Tegg, *Grasslands*, 2014.
Installation view.
Photograph, Linda Tegg.

something. Carnations represent Jesus; a fly, death; jasmine incarnates the sweetness of the Madonna; and apples always are Eve's ultimate temptation. So how can we see plants beyond classical symbolic tropes?

If in 1980 art historian John Berger thought it worthwhile to ask 'Why Look at Animals?' – this was the title of his seminal essay in which he critiqued fundamental aspects of our limited ability to look at animals through different media, spaces, theoretical contexts, and historical milieus – we are now certainly ready to ask 'why look at plants?'[8] From an aesthetic perspective, moving beyond the symbolic power-entrapments entails the possibility to consider new modes of attention and to craft novel models of perception. Both opportunities can bear substantial productivities in our relationship with the current challenges impacting our planet – the ramifications are substantial. At stake is the possibility to understand plants as integral, coexisting actants who play defining roles in the functioning of ecosystems. Thus, what we look at and how we look constitute essential parameters in the recovery of 'alternative gazes' and the crafting of new ones – modalities of engagement entailing more than the ocular spectrum; modalities that can lead to a substantial rethinking of our relationship with the living in the spaces we share.

In 2014, Tegg's *Grasslands*, a large scale installation project at the State Library of Victoria, provided an actual and poetic layering between past and present, architecture and vegetation, urban environment, and nature. For this project, the artist worked across institutions. Through her residency, the artist became aware of a blindspot in The State Library's archives and thus researched a wealth of visual and textual documentation about the vegetation which once thrived on the building's site. In collaboration with John Delpratt, a horticulturalist at the University of Melbourne, Tegg was thereafter able to grow 15,000 plants of sixty indigenous species which were once situated where the Library now stands. As in her work with animals, Tegg capitalised on the uncanny tension caused by the repositioning of bodies in space. Here, audiences of passers-by and library users were encountered a multi-layered vegetal-ghost of sort. In an operation harnessed by important political overtones, vegetal, indigenous representatives were able to temporarily reclaim their land – to rewind history – thus engaging in a decolonising aesthetic maneuver underpinned by a biological flourish. The many varieties included in the installation, which featured many flowering species, brought birds and insects back to the library grounds, where they are typically rarely seen. Testament to the importance of this project and the relevance that this type of speculative interaction in art is capable of mobilising was Melbournians' repeated request to make *Grasslands* permanent.

Furthering her research into the transhistorical co-evolutions between humans and plants, Tegg's *One World Rice Pilaf* aimed to reconnect us with the embryonic plant-life we systematically consume and simultaneously ignore in our supermarket shopping. As the artist admits:

"For someone who has eaten as much hummus as I, the difficulty of visualising a chickpea plant is astonishing. Naturally, the legumes and cereals contained in slick clear acrylic should be full of potential, not only as food but also plants, so I decided to grow what I could."[9] Germinating the seeds in shallow plastic trays, and deliberately disrupting the capitalist economies that prevent these plants from seeing the light of day, Tegg brought to the gallery space the opportunity to rethink the concept of nature as a consumable and to focus on the essence of plant-being. This work is a valuable contribution to the growing momentum around the importance of plants in the contemporary philosophical spectrum. Michael Marder, a leader in the field of critical plant studies has theorised the potentialities involved in attuning ourselves to plant-life and therefore approaching a dimension he calls "Plant-thinking":

" 'Plant-thinking' refers, in the same breath, to (1) the non-cognitive, non-ideational, and non-imagistic mode of thinking proper to plants (hence, what I call 'thinking without the head'); (2) our thinking about plants; (3) how human thinking is, to some extent, de-humanized and rendered plantlike, altered by its encounter with the vegetal world; and finally, (4) the ongoing symbiotic relation between this transfigured thinking and the existence of plants."[10]

These ideas came to problematise Tegg's original iteration of *One World Rice Pilaf* into a collaborative project with video and installation artists Joshi Radin and Brian M. John. A Program for Plants harnessed the essentially de-objectifying strategies already deployed in Tegg's work through a speculative approach capable of inducing an empathic connection with the non-human. In the project's first phase, Radin, John, and Tegg measured the Photosynthetically Active Radiation (light) emitted by the Video Data Bank's 50 most watched videos. They subsequently screened the videos to a spectrometer and took measurements of the light levels emitted to assess which would be more suited to a plant audience. They then pared the selection down to the top five films with the largest matching outputs. With the plants' preference in mind, they then produced a film festival, projecting the films on a loop directly onto the plants, thus nourishing them with light frequencies they presumably liked.

The plants were so enabled to choose their favourite: a 1966 black and white filmed performance of *Trio A* by choreographer and filmmaker Yvonne Rainer. *Trio A* is a 5 minute piece which essentially poses radical questions about the nature of dance, movement, and performance. Rather in keeping with the scope of the project, *Trio A*'s main aim is to undermine the classical representational value of dance in order to reach deeper, beyond pre-encoded aesthetics for the purpose of renegotiating the presence of bodies in space. According to *Trio A*'s philosophy, simply

Linda Tegg, *One World Rice Pilaf*, 2016.
Plants sprouted from the bulk section of Wholefoods,
growing media, recycled PET bags, lights.

moving is indeed 'dancing'.(11) *Trio A*, therefore, deploys
a seemingly untrained and non-virtuosic movement
vocabulary to resituate human experience of architecture
and the body in space. That *Trio A* should be the 'plants'
favourite video' turned out to be incidentally in alignment
with the overall conceptual scope of A Program for Plants.
The project thus concluded with a series of live renditions of
Trio A performed by the artists and specially conceived for
selected live plant audiences.

These performances well encapsulate the speculative
nature of our current desire to overcome the inherited
utilitarianism of capitalist structures; the given-for-granted
relational modes that alienate us from other non-human
beings; the economies of power and subjugation that
relentlessly produce unfulfilling urban environments around
the globe; and the lack of commitment towards life on
this planet. Much of Tegg's work ultimately points in this
direction, providing many opportunities to rethink what we
already thought we knew. But most importantly, much of the
innovative strength in her vision lies in the determination to
develop new multidisciplinary registers of empathy and to
craft new aesthetic strategies designed to critically appraise,
expand, and diversify our knowledge at a point of deep crisis
in our troubled relationship with the rest of the planet.

Yvonne Rainer, *Trio A*.
Still from 1978 16mm film produced by Sally Banes.

A Program for Plants
(Brian M. John, Joshi Radin and Linda Tegg),
Trio A Pressured: Horticultural Fragment, Chicago, 2016.
Video stills, top to bottom: Lincoln Park Conservatory,
Lake Michigan, Home Depot.

(1) Foucault, M 1976, 'Questions of Geography', in C Gordon (ed.) 1980, *Power/Knowledge: Selected Interviews and Other Writings, 1972-1977*, Harvester Press, Brighton, UK.
(2) Foucault, M 1966, *The Order of Things: An Archaeology of The Human Science*, Routledge (1970, 2003), London and New York; Foucault, M 1975, *Discipline and Punish: The Birth of the Prison*, Penguin (1991), London, UK; Foucault, M 1973, 'The force of flight', in JW Crampton & S Elden (eds) 2007, *Space, Knowledge and Power: Foucault and Geography*, Ashgate, New York, USA, pp. 169-173.
(3) Since 2009, Linda Tegg has been exploring issues of animal representation in site-specific installations as well as through photography and video. *Horse Study*, 2009; *Sheep Studies*, 2010; *Goat Studies*, 2011; *Wolf Studies*, 2012.
(4) "Truly, truly, I say to you, he who does not enter the sheepfold by the door but climbs in by another way, that man is a thief and a robber. But he who enters by the door is the shepherd of the sheep. To him the gatekeeper opens. The sheep hear his voice, and he calls his own sheep by name and leads them out. When he has brought out all his own, he goes before them, and the sheep follow him, for they know his voice. A stranger they will not follow, but they will flee from him, for they do not know the voice of strangers." John 10:1-16; John 10:27; John 10:16; John 10:4; John 10:3; John 10:1-42; John 10:5; John 10:3-4.
(5) Hansen, W 2017, *The Book of Greek & Roman Folktales, Legends & Myths*, Princeton University Press, Princeton, New Jersey, USA. Also, *NIV, Matthew 25:31-33* "When the Son of Man comes in his glory, and all the angels with him, he will sit on his glorious throne. All the nations will be gathered before him, and he will separate the people one from another as a shepherd separates the sheep from the goats. He will put the sheep on his right and the goats on his left".
(6) Baltic German biologist Jacob von Uexküll (1864-1944) "was interested in how living beings perceive their environment(s). Uexküll argued that organisms perceived the experience of living in terms of species-specific, spatio-temporal, 'self-in-world' subjective reference frames that he called *Umwelt* (translated as *milieu, situation, embedding*-lit. German for *environment*)." See von Uexküll, J 1940, *A Foray Into the Worlds of Animals and Humans*, Minnesota University Press, Minneapolis, USA (2010).
(7) Robin MacKay, Luke Pendrell, and James Trafford, authors of *Speculative Aesthetics*, have identified the emergence of this awareness as a condition in which "contemporary art vigilantly exposes its own compromises with the aesthetic, in an on-going mission of failure and culpability". MacKay, R, Pendrell, L & Trafford, J (eds) 2014, *Speculative Aesthetics*, Lulu Press, Morrisville, North Carolina, USA, p. 3.
(8) Berger, J 1980, 'Why Look at Animals?', in *About Looking*, Vintage, London, UK (1993). A book titled *Why Look at Plants? Vegetal Revolutions in Contemporary Art* (including a contribution by Linda Tegg) edited and co-authored by Giovanni Aloi is in the process of being published in 2018 by Brill, Leiden, the Netherlands.
(9) Tegg, L 2018, 'One World Rice Pilaf', in G Aloi (ed.), *Why Look at Plants? Vegetal Revolutions in Contemporary Art*, op. cit.
(10) Marder, M 2013, 'What is Plant Thinking?', *Klesis – Revue Philosophique, Philosophies de la Nature*, vol. 25, pp. 124-143. *One World Rice Pilaf* encapsulates many of the aspects of plant-thinking theorised by Marder. Tegg's installation presents plants in an anti-aesthetic way, which contradicts the tradition of botanical representation, and even popular culture conception of how plants should be represented. The trays of *One World Rice Pilaf* prevent the viewer from focussing on one specific plant, thus suggesting a collective being and shared network of sensing that reaches beyond traditional notions of identity. It is in this way that the work alters our thinking about plants and also proposes alternative blue prints over which new human-plant cognitive dimensions can be explored.
(11) MoMALearning, n.d., *Trio A, Yvonne Rainer*, MoMALearning, viewed 17 February 2018, <moma.org/learn/moma_learning/yvonne-rainer-trio-a-1978>.

The artist, the editors, and the author would like to thank the Estate of Jannis Kounellis and Gavin Brown's enterprise, Yvonne Rainer and A Program for Plants for sharing their images.

WESTERN PLAINS GRASSLANDS

LOUISE WRIGHT

"... at first glance (temperate grasslands) look like ill-kempt paddocks, until, on hands and knees the diversity of a micro-landscape is revealed...(A challenge is to) convey the natural and Indigenous cultural importance of these landscapes in the face of the demand for urban growth. Our still embryonic understanding of the complex interplay of plants, animals and microorganisms continues to challenge us. What we do know is that it is essential to retain the existing threads of native vegetation in our landscapes and that these areas need to be linked together with wide habitat corridors and buffered from surrounding land uses."(1)

Western Plains Grasslands are an ecological community.(2) They are located across the Victorian Volcanic Plains (VVP), which is recognised as one of Australia's fifteen national biodiversity hotspots. It is a large, flat to undulating plain punctuated by scattered volcanic cones and stony rises.

Grasslands of south-western Victoria were central to the culture and sustenance of the local Aboriginal people, who managed them for tens of thousands of years. They were also important for the grazing of native animals, supporting the agriculture and grazing of the European settlers from the early nineteenth century, and up until this day the urbanisation of Melbourne continues to spread into these flat areas, due in part to their suitability for construction.

Temperate grasslands are recognised nationally as among the most threatened vegetation types and represent some of Victoria's most threatened and fragmented ecosystems.(3) Formerly extensive on the Victorian Volcanic Plains, they are now reduced to mostly small, highly fragmented remnants in a landscape that has been largely cleared for agriculture. Remnants also occur in and around Melbourne and other regional towns and cities, so and as such are subject to ongoing clearance and other threats from urbanisation.

The Natural Temperate Grasslands are usually dominated by one or more of the following native tussock-forming grasses: Kangaroo Grass (*Themeda*

triandra), Wallaby Grass (*Austrodanthonia spp.*), Spear Grass (*Austrostipa spp.*) and/or Tussock Grass (*Poa spp.*). A variety of native herbs, including wildflowers, may be interspersed among the native grass tussocks. In some circumstances, the native grasses may be sparse and the other native herbs are dominant, for instance after some fire regimes, and so these native herb fields are included as part of the national ecological community. Trees and large woody shrubs are absent to sparse. Good examples can be seen in Victoria at

Map of Australia showing major cities and south east Victoria grasslands (grey).

Craigieburn Reserve, Laverton North Grassland Reserve and Mortlake Common Flora Reserve.(4)

Patches of grasslands in good condition are likely to constitute less than 1%. Research, however, is providing new ways to manage grasslands, and techniques for restoration are advancing.(5) The importance of ongoing stewardship also means it is vital to develop new strategies to encourage a broader cross-section of society to understand and appreciate native grasslands and their ecology.(6)

Grasslands Repair at the Australian Pavilion

When we compiled our plant list we referenced the Environment Vegetation Class (EVC) '132 Plains Grassland'. We reviewed and built this list with the assistance of horticulturalist Susan Murphy and John Delpratt. The final list of what is exhibited reflects the seed we were able to acquire, and what germinated and grew successfully.

Searching for seed of Western Plains Grassland plants, it became evident that there was not a lot of this plant community left to get seed from, and when we started to grow it, just how little is known about these plants in terms of how to get them to germinate and grow. Leading horticulturalists', ecologists' and reference publications revealed that the study of temperate native grasslands is a relatively young field and it is unclear how to reliably get many of the species to germinate. Some of the seed we sourced demonstrates the continuation of land clearing; as an example, Flora Victoria, a native grass farm in outer western Melbourne, collects seed from areas about to be bulldozed – while describing some Wallaby Grasses they state:

"...this mix of Wallaby Grasses was originally harvested from Sydenham Park and contains five species that naturally occur there...Since harvesting this seed, half this site was destroyed when a road interchange was constructed for the Calder Freeway."[7]

In the *Repair* exhibition there are approximately sixty-five species of grassland community plants, which are a representative but not necessarily a scientifically perfect list. They have mixed provenance from over thirty sites, stretching even to Western Australia (where some of these species grow, albeit with different genetic makeup). This unusual mix of provenance makes the *Repair* grassland a novel grassland.

Several of the species exhibited are listed as endangered: Basalt Pepper Cress (*Lepidium hyssopifolium*), Hoary Sunray (*Leuchochrysum albicans var. tricolor*) and Button Wrinklewort (*Rutidosis leptorrhynchoides*).[8]

The effort and difficulty of acquiring seeds, germinating them, and keeping them alive inside the pavilion reveals the significance of clearing these plants for farming roads, housing and so on, something that could be done in an hour with a bulldozer. We don't confidently know what we are removing and it's really hard, in fact impossible, to put it back.

(1) Macmillan, L 2011, 'Merri Creek', in M Baracco (ed.), *Tree Sprawl*, School of Architecture and Design, RMIT University, Melbourne, Victoria, Australia, p. 12.
(2) An ecological community is a naturally occurring group of plants, animals and other organisms that are living together and interacting in a unique habitat. Its structure, composition and distribution are determined by environmental factors such as soil type, position in the landscape, climate and water availability. See Australian Government, Department of Sustainability, Environment, Water, Population and Communities 2011, *Nationally Threatened Ecological Communities of the Victorian Volcanic Plain: Natural Temperate Grassland & Grassy Eucalypt Woodland*, Commonwealth of Australia, Barton, ACT, Australia, viewed 29 January 2018, <http://www.environment.gov.au/system/files/resources/e97c2d51-08f2-45e0-9d2f-f0d277c836fa/files/grasslands-victoria.pdf>.
(3) Ibid.
(4) Ibid.
(5) See Williams, N, Marshall A & Morgan JW (eds) 2015, *Land of sweeping plains: managing and restoring the native grasslands of south-eastern Australia*, CSIRO Publishing, Clayton South, Victoria, Australia.
(6) For example projects such as Wootten Road Reserve in Tarneit, Melbourne, Victoria by Glas Landscape Architecture establishing five grassland ecologies as a public park. See Ricardo R R 2017, 'Grassland: A provocation', *Landscape Architecture Australia*, no. 156, November, pp. 50-55.
(7) Flora Victoria: The Grassland Experts n.d., *Products*, Flora Victoria: The Grassland Experts, viewed 2 January 2018, <https://chris-findlay.squarespace.com/species-and-prices/>.
(8) These are species showing an extremely high risk of extinction in the wild in the immediate future.

GLAS Landscape Architecture, Wootten Reserve, Melbourne.
A park of grassland planting.
Photograph, Drew Echberg.

GRASSLANDS REPAIR:
INDIGENOUS NAMES AND USES

Species	Common Name	Indigenous Name	Indigenous Group	Indigenous Use	Flowering Fruit Season	Form	Flower Col.
Acacia implexa	Lightwood	*Muyang Toolayowa, Yawan*	Wathawurrung (Blake 1998) Gunai (VACL 2001)	Fish poison, implements/artefacts, medicinal, seeds/fruits eaten (Florabank.org)		tree	
Acacia Mearnsii	Black Wattle	*Garrong Garrong Warrarakk Currong Ngelitj*	Wurungjeri (Monash 2010) Woi wurrung (De Angelis 2005) Djab wurrung (De Angelis 2005) Lake Condah (De Angelis 2005) Wathawurrung (Barry 1998)	Gum oozes from trunk where tree is damaged - water-soluble, made into drinks. Gum used as adhesive; bark used for string, containers; also medicine (Gott, 1995) Gum exuding from branches is eaten as a treat in the bush (Wreck Bay Community & Renwick, 2000:33) wood used for implements, The bark was used for medicine, applied to wounds and sores (Monash, 2010)	Flowers in spring; seeds in summer	tree	
Acacia melanoxylon	Blackwood	*Muyang Mootchung Burn-na-look Mooiung* (young state) *Moéang*	Wathawurrung (Blake 1998) Djab wurrung (De Angelis 2005) Yarra (De Angelis 2005) Coranderrk (Smyth 1878) Coranderrk (Smyth 1878)	The inner bark of this wattle-tree was used to make coarse string, and was heated to apply as a medicine for rheumatism. The wood was used for spear-throwers and shields. (Monash Uni 2010)		tree	
Allocasuarina Verticillata	Drooping She Oak	*Wayetuck Gneering Ngarri*	Woiwurrung (De Angelis 2005) Wunditjmara (De Angelis 2005) Wathawurrung (Barry 1998)	The soft young cones were eaten. Mature cones were powdered up for medicine for sores and rheumatism, and bark and wood extracts were also used medicinally. Boomerangs and clubs were made from the wood, and the smoke from cones put into a fire was said to blind a man. Boomerangs, 10,000 years old, made from this tree were found in a swamp in South Australia a few years ago. (Monash, 2010)	Winter-spring	tree	
Arthropodium fimbriatum	Nodding Chocolate-lily			Tubers eaten (Gott, 1995)	January - February	perennial herb	purple
Arthropodium milleflorum	Pale Vanilla-lily			Grows abundantly and has many root tubers branching out from each plant. The tubers which are white inside were roasted before they were eaten.' (Zola & Gott, 1992:42)	Late summer (Flood, 1980:93)	perennial herb	purple
Arthropodium minus	Small Vanilla-lily	*Karrap-karrap?*	Wathawurrung (Barry 1998)	Grows abundantly and has many root tubers branching out from each plant. The tubers which are white inside were roasted before they were eaten.' (Zola & Gott, 1992:42)	Late summer (Flood, 1980:93)	perennial herb	purple
Arthropodium strictum	Chocolate-lily	*Buyang ka(a)l?*	Wathawurrung (Barry 1998) could be any Arthuropodium	Edible tubers (De Angelis 2005)		perennial herb	purple
Banksia Marginata	Silver Banksia	*Woorike*	Wurundjeri (Monash, 2010)	The flower-cones were soaked in water to make a sweet drink, and the dry cones were used as strainers. (monash Uni 2010)	Flowers spring-summer (Flood, 1980:94)	Tree	
Bulbine bulbosa	Bulbine Lily	*Parm Puewan Pike Mulatarui-wel?*	Gunditjmara Djab wurrung Coranderrk (Zola & Gott, 1992) Wathawurrung (Barry 1998)	The corm, which can be eaten all year was probably cooked first; ... one of the sweetest of lily roots (Zola & Gott, 1992:43)	October - November; late summer on high mountain ridges (Flood, 1980:94)	perennial herb	yellow
Burchardia umbellata	Milkmaids	*Popoto*	Lake Condah (Zola & Gott, 1992)	Roots cooked before eating. (De Angelis 2005)	September	perennial herb	white
Bursaria spinosa	Sweet Bursaria/ Australian Blackthorn	*Warrewarral Karron*	Wiradjuri (Gott 1995) Wathawurrung (Barry 1998)	Food, technology. Honey can be sucked out of numerous flowers (Flood, 1980:95) Wood used for 'waddy' (short stick) (Gott, 1995)	Flowering late summer (Burbidge & Gray,1976:191)		
Caesia calliantha	Blue Grass-lily			Perennial plants which produce a clump of finger-shaped tubers, sweet tasting but not starchy ... crisp texture and are quite good to eat fresh. Available all year round.' (Zola & Gott, 1992:44)	Flowers in spring - summer	perennial herb	blue
Chamaescilla corymbosa	Blue Squill	*Mudrurt*	Lake Condah (Zola & Gott 1992)			perennial herb	blue
Convolvulus remotus	Pink Bindweed	*Taaruuk (root)* *Yowanduk*	Gunditijmara; Djab wurrong (Monash Uni 2010) Lake Hindmarsh (Monash Uni 2010)	The root is tough and starchy; it was cooked and kneaded into a dough. The flowers are pink.	October - December (Fraser & McJannett, 1993:78)	perennial herb	pink
Convolvulus remotus	Grassy Bindweed	*Darruk* (potato: generic)	Wathawurrung (Barry 1998)			perennial herb	pink
Dianella abrevicaulis/ revoluta	Black-anther Flax-lily	*Murmbal* *Murmbal*	Lake Hindmarsh (Zola & Gott 1992) Gunditjmara (De Angelis 2005)	Leaf fibres used, fruits eaten raw and the roots pounded and cooked on hot rocks (Fraser & McJannett, 1993:70) '... blue fruits and shiny black seeds of most Dianella species are eaten raw. They have a sweet flavour, which becomes nutty once the seed is chewed. (Stewart & Percival, 1997:17) 'The leaf was split into two down the midrib and rolled in the manner of string to make a tie.' (Zola & Gott, 1992:59)	October - December		
Dianella spp. (various)	Black-anther Flax-lily			Dianella caerulea leaves are used to make a high-pitched whistle .'(Wreck Bay Community & Renwick, 2000:45) 'Roots boiled and drunk as tea as medicine for colds (D. longifolia)' (Gott, 1995)	October - December	perennial herb	blue

Scientific name	Common name	Indigenous names	Language group (source)	Uses	Season	Form	Colour
Enchylaena tomentosa	Ruby Saltbush	*Gurgudj* *Kurrkuty*	Wemba Wemba (De Angelis 2005) Wemba Wemba (Monash 2010)	Red button-shaped berries picked and eaten. (De Angelis 2005) A dry-country ground cover plant bearing tiny edible red fruits which were shaken off onto a sheet of bark. (Monash, 2010)		shrub	green
Eucalyptus camaldulensis	River Red Gum	*Be-al* *Peeal* *Ta'art* *Dharnya* *Moolerr* *Biel* *Bial* *Beeul*	Woi wurrung Djab wurrung Gunditjmara Yorta Yorta Wimmera Wemba Wemba Gunditjmara Lake Boga (all Zola & Gott 1992)	Canoes made from large sheets of bark. Bark also used to makeshelters, shields and containers. Sap used to seal burns and mixed with water to treat diarrhoea. Leaves were used in aromatic steam baths as a remedy for a range of ailments. (De Angelis 2005)		Tree	
Eucalyptus melliodora	Yellow Box	*Urah, Uaredry* *Dagan*	Wiradjuri (VACL 2001) Gunai (VACL 2001)			Tree	
Exocarpus cupressiformis	Native Cherry	*Baloyt* *Ballee* *Wombariga* *Palatt, Ballot* *Pul-loitch* *Nyora*	Wathawurrung (Barry 1998) Wurundjeri (Monash Uni 2010) Wiradjuri (VACL 2001) Lake Condah (Zola & Gott 1992) Jajowerong (Zola & Gott 1992) Boon wurrung (VACL 2001)	Fleshy pedicels of fruit were eaten (raw) (Flood, 1980:94) 'Each small, green, hard fruit is supported on a larger, swollen, fleshy stalk which was eaten in winter. When fruits are yellow, they are bitter but when they turn deep red, they are quite sweet and palatable.' (Oates & Seeman, 1979:7) Wood used for spearthrowers and bullroarers. (Zola & Gott, 1992:48) sap for snakebite (Monash, 2010)	Summer fruiting (Flood, 1980:94)		
Geranium solanderi	Austral Crane's Bill	*Terrat* *Kullumkulkeetch* *Kawurn Kallumbarrant*	Coranderrk Djab wurrung Gunditjmara (all Zola & Gott 1992)	Large fleshy roots were roasted (Flood, 1980:95) Plants with tough roots - need to be pounded; contain nutritious starch and can be eaten after cooking; some contain tannin - unpalatable (Zola & Gott, 1992:47)	October tuber available (summer-autumn) (Flood, 1980:95)	perennial herb	pink
Glycine clandestina	Variable Glycine	*Nanggert*	Coranderrk (Smyth 1878)			perennial herb	blue
Glycine tabacina	Small-leaf Glycine			G. tabacina were reportedly roasted, pounded, chewed and the fibre spat out by Aborigines in NW Queensland; liquorice flavour (Gott, 1995)	Spring - summer	perennial herb	blue
Hardenbergia violaceae	Purple Coral-pea			The leaves were boiled by Aboriginal people to obtain a sweet drink.' (Fraser & McJannett, 1993:59) [Source not cited; possibly refers to Smilax glyciphylla, Native Sarsaparilla instead, as I have found no other reference to Aboriginal use of H. violacea.] 'We have tried boiling the leaves, and find that the drink produced is slightly sweet and reasonably pleasant' (Cribb & Cribb, 1987:207)	September - October		
Hypoxis hygrometrica	Golden Weather-grass	*Nyulami dja?, Korro-wort-wort?*	Wathawurrung (Barry 1998)	Root roasted in ashes (Gott, 1995)	November - January	perennial herb	yellow
Juncus pallidus	Pale Rush	*Kurung bûwitch*	Lake Hindmarsh (Smyth 1878)				
Kennedia prostrata	Running Postman	*Nall* *Kabin*	Gunditjmara (De Angelis 2005) Coranderrk (Smyth 1878)	Nectar sucked from red pea flowers. Trailing stems used as ties. (De Angelis 2005)		perennial herb	red
Linum marginale	Native Flax			The numerous small seeds were eaten (Flood, 1980:95) Seed used, stem soaked, stripped beaten for string (Gott, 1995)	Available late summer (Flood, 1980:95)	perennial herb	blue
Lomandra spp. (various)	Scented Mat-rush	*Karawun* *Ballan-cowat (String bag)* *wirrana*	Wurundjeri (Zola & Gott 1992) Wathawurrung (Barry 1998)	Leaf bases edible (Flood, 1980:94) Mat rush leaves were used for making baskets. The method followed in the baskets made by Mrs Thelma Carter - the leaves once picked are split down the centre into two and left to dry for 3 or more days. Before being worked they are dampened with water for 24 hrs to render them pliable (Zola & Gott, 1992:59) Leaf bases and flowers eaten; leaves 'woven into mats and baskets and into bands around an aching limb to relieve pain.' (Fraser & McJannett, 1993:51)		perennial herb	yellow
Microlaena stipoides	Weeping Grass			Grass seed was an important food source for desert tribes but not for Victorian Plain area (Monash 2010)			
Microseris spp. (various)	Yam Daisy	*Minngar* *Murnong* *Muurang, Keerong* *Munja* *Pun'yin* *Bam-mùnya* *Murnang*	Wiradjuri (Gott 1995) Wurunjeri (Zola & Gott 1992) Gunditjmara (Zola & Gott 1992) Malee area (Monash Uni 2010) Djab wurrung (Monash Uni 2010) Like Hindmarsh (Smyth 1878) Wathawurrung (Barry 1998)	Tubers can be eaten raw but were most often cooked in baskets (Zola & Gott, 1992:8) A staple food in S. Uplands; sweet milky tubers were roasted (Flood, 1980:96) M. scapigera Alpine Murnong - more fibrous but still edible root; Murnong was gathered by women using digging sticks (Zola & Gott, 1992:8) Murnong was once very plentiful, but it was rapidly eaten out by the settlers' sheep, thus depriving people of one of their most important foods. It has several different forms and is difficult to cultivate. (Monash Uni 2010)	Summer - autumn flowering	perennial herb	yellow
Oxalis exilis	Shady Wood-sorrel			Oxalis Corniculata was eaten			
Pelargonium rodneyanum	Magenta Stork's-bill	*Mirrak?*	Wathawurrung (Barry 1998)			perennial herb	
Pimelea spp. (various)	Curved Rice-flower	*Wikerich (p. humilis)*	Lake Condah (Smyth 1878)	1830s account of extraction of Pimelea fibres to make string for nets (Zola & Gott, 1992:33) P. axiflora is called "Bootlace Bush" because of the strength of string Bark stripped, dried, soaked in water, beaten with sticks or stone, nets used to catch Bogong moths (Gott, 1995)	September - November	shrub	white
Plantago gaudichaudii	Narrow-leaf Plantain	*Nhulam-I djiina*	Wathawurrung (Barry 1998)			perennial herb	green
Plantago varia	Variable Plantain	*Nhulam-I djiina*	Wathawurrung (Barry 1998)			perennial herb	green

Latin name	English name	Aboriginal name	Language group	Use	Season	Type	Category
Poa spp. (various)	Common Tussock-grass	Bowat (p. labillardieri) Bobat (P. labillardieri)	Wurundjeri (Monash, 2010) Woi Wurung (De Angelis 2005)	Stems and leaves of large tussock grasses were twisted and used to make baskets, mats and net-bags. (monash 2010)		C3 grass	grass
Podolepis spp. (various)	Podolepis	Tamburn	Wathawurrung (Barry 1998)	The thick taproot was eaten. Alpine Podolepis, P. robusta and Long Podolepis, P. hieracioides were probably also eaten. (Monash, 2010)		perennial herb	yellow
Pteridium esculentum	Bracken	Moo-laa Makkitch Geewan Mukine/Mawkum	Djab wurrung (Monash, 2010) Gunditjmara (Angelis 2005) Gippsland (Angelis 2005) Lake Condah (Angelis 2005)	Thin starchy roots (rhizomes) eaten raw or roasted; rhizomes available late summer to autumn (Flood, 1980) Rhizomes of P. esculentum harvested in late summer can be chewed to extract the starch but they must be roasted first to destroy the toxins, (Cherikoff & Isaacs in Stewart & Percival, 1997:29) Bracken roots were gathered as a staple food, roasted and beaten into a paste (Zola & Gott, 1992:37) 'Young juicy stems … were rubbed on to relieve the stinging and itching of insect bites.' (Zola & Gott, 1992:56) 'Curled tips of young fronds have a nutty flavour and may be eaten.' (Wreck Bay Community & Renwick, 2000:18) Starchy roots gathered and roasted in hot ashes before being beaten into a paste with water and baked. Roots must be treated in this way before being eaten. (Angelis 2005)	all year		
Pterostylis nutans	Nodding Greenhood			Root eaten raw or cooked; roots (tubers paired) often abundant - 439 plants/sq.m recorded (Gott, 1995)	September on Black Mountain (FOAB, 1997:72)		
Rytidosperma spp. (various)	Wallaby-grass			Grass seed an important food source for desert tribes but not in the Victorian Plains (Monash, 2010)		C3 grass	grass
Schoenus apogon	Common Bog-sedge	Bourt-bourt?	Wathawurrung (Barry 1998)				
Stylidium spp. (various)	Trigger Plant	Pinnong (S. graminifolium)	Lake Condah (Smyth 1878)			perennial herb	pink
Themeda triandra	Kangaroo Grass	Worronkai(t) Wuulot Wuuloitch Karn	Wathawurrung (Barry 1998) Gunditjmara (Monash, 2010) Djab wurrung (De Angelis 2005) Lake Tyers (Zola & Gott 1992)	String was made from the leaves and stems, especially in Gippsland, but other plants made stronger string; an important food for desert tribes but not for plains tribes (Monash, 2010) Seeds could be ground and baked (Flood, 1980: 93) Themeda avanacea ground and made into cakes in western NSW & NT (Gott, 1995) Fibre extracted from leaf & stem - used for making fishing net at Yelta, Murray River (Gott, 1995)	December - March (FOAB, 1997:83) Kangaroo Grass	C4 grass	grass
Thysanotus patersonii	Twining Fringe-lily			… cluster of white watery tubers at the base of the plant stem. … would probably have been cooked before being eaten.' (Zola & Gott, 1992:44) Root eaten, 'sometimes roasted but usually raw.' (Cribb & Cribb, 1987:175)	Spring and Summer	perennial herb	purple
Thysanotus tuberosus	Common Fringe-lily	Buyang ka(a)l?	Wathawurrung (Barry 1998) could also be arthuopodium	… cluster of white watery tubers at the base of the plant stem. … would probably have been cooked before being eaten.' (Zola & Gott, 1992:44) Root eaten, 'sometimes roasted but usually raw.' (Cribb & Cribb, 1987:175)		perennial herb	purple
Viola betonicifolia	Showy Violet			Flowers can be eaten raw. No confirmed use by Victorian Aborigines. (De Angelis 2005)		perennial herb	blue
Wahlenbergia communis	Tufted Bluebell			Flowers eaten (Fraser & McJannett, 1993:65)	November - January	perennial herb	blue
Wahlenbergia gracilis	Sprawling Bluebell			Flowers eaten (Fraser & McJannett, 1993:65)	November - January	perennial herb	blue
Wahlenbergia luteola	Yellowish Bluebell			Flowers eaten (Fraser & McJannett, 1993:65)	November - January	perennial herb	blue
Wahlenbergia stricta	Tall Bluebell			Flowers eaten (Fraser & McJannett, 1993:65)	November - January	perennial herb	blue
Wurmbea dioica	Early Nancy			One of the first flowers each spring! 'The tubers are small, round and very starchy.' (Zola & Gott, 1992:44) This lily has a very small starchy bulb with a black covering. The white flowers are banded with purple, and appear very early in the spring. (Monash 2010)	Spring	perennial herb	white
Xerochrysum bracteatum	Golden Everlasting	Borrom-borrom? Word for any everlasting	Wathawurrung (Barry 1998)	Decoration of houses (Barry (1998)	March - November	perennial herb	yellow

Plant List of Victorian Volcanic Plains
with Aboriginal, English and Latin names

Prepared by Jessica Kane, Aboriginal Environments Research Centre, University of Queensland, Australia. The Victorian Volcanic Plains Bioregion extends across south-western Victoria through the traditional lands of the Kulin and Warnambool greater language groups. The Kulin greater language group encompasses most of central and western Victoria and extends into southern New South Wales. This language group contains four sub-groups: Eastern Kulin, Western Kulin, Colac language and Watha Wurrung, that incorporate individual languages (VCAA n.d.). Some languages have recorded local dialects. For example the Warnambool language group contains dialects such as Peek Wurrung and Keerray Wurrung (Dawson 1881). The spelling (or orthography) of language names and words varies based on sources. The accompanying table does not change the spellings used in the source materials.

Note by Author

We have taken the words given by Blake (1998) to be of the Wathawurrung dialect as this was the title of his monograph. However, there may be contention regarding inclusion of some words. Please refer to this source for more precise information regarding dialect names and divisions. In Gunn et al. (n.d.) it is stated, "The information provided relating to the Aboriginal use of plants for food, items or medicinal purposes has been approved by the Wathaurung People."

(Overpage) Grassland in flower, clustered everlasting (*Chrysocephalum semipapposum*). Photograph, Linda Tegg.

GRASSLANDS REPAIR: SPECIES LIST

Species	Common name
Trees	
Acacia implexa	Lightwood
Acacia mearnsii	Black Wattle
Acacia melanoxylon	Blackwood
Allocasuarina verticillata	Drooping She Oak
Banksia marginata	Silver Banksia
Bursaria spinosa	Sweet Bursaria
Eucalyptus camaldulensis	River Red Gum
Eucalyptus melliodora	Yellow Box
Grasses	
Amphibromus acheri	Pointed Wallaby-grass
Anthosachne scabra (syn. Elymus)	Common Wheat-grass
Austrostipa spp. (various)	Spear-grass
Bothriochloa macra	Red-leg Grass
Chloris truncate	Windmill Grass
Dichanthium sericeum	Silky Blue-grass
Dichelachne crinita	Long-hair Plume-grass
Microlaena stipoides	Weeping Grass
Pentapogon quadrifidus	Five-awned Spear-grass
Poa spp. (various)	Common Tussock-grass
Rytidosperma spp. (various)/Austodanthonia	Wallaby-grass
Themeda triandra	Kangaroo Grass
Acaena agnipila	Downy Sheep's Burr
Acaena echinata	Sheep's Burr
Acaena novae-zelandiae	Bidgee-widgee
Allittia cardiocarpa	Heart-fruit Daisy
Arthropodium fimbriatum	Nodding Chocolate-lily
Arthropodium milleflorum	Pale Vanilla-lily
Arthropodium minus	Small Vanilla-lily
Arthropodium strictum	Chocolate-lily
Asperula conferta	Common Woodruff
Asperula scoparia subsp. scoparia	Prickly Woodruff
Brachyscome basaltica var. gracilis	Basalt Daisy
Brachyscome dentata	Lobed-seed Daisy
Brachysome chrysoglossa	Yellow-tongue daisy
Bracteantha Viscosa	Sticky Everlasting
Brachyscome diversifolia	Tall Daisy
Brunonia australis	Blue Pincushion
Bulbine bulbosa	Bulbine Lily
Burchardia umbellata	Milkmaids
Caesia calliantha	Blue Grass-lily
Calocephalus citreus	Lemon Beauty-heads
Calocephalus lacteus	Milky Beauty-heads
Calotis spp. (various)	Yellow Burr-daisy
Chamaescilla corymbosa	Blue Squill
Chrysocephalum apiculatum	Common Everlasting
Chrysocephalum semipapposum	Clustered Everlasting
Convolvulus angustissimus	Pink Bindweed
Coronidium gunnianum	Pale Everlasting
Coronidium scorpioides	Button Everlasting
Craspedia paludicola	Swamp Billy-buttons
Craspedia variabilis	Variable Billy-buttons
Crassula sieberiana	Australian Stonecrop
Cullen tenax	Tough Scurf-pea
Cynoglossum suaveolens	Sweet Hound's-tounge
Dianella spp. (various)	Black-anther Flax-lily
Dichondra repens	Kidney Weed
Drosera aberrans	Scented Sundew
Drosera auriculata	Tall Sundew
Drosera hookeri (syn. D. peltata)	Pale Sundew
Eryngium ovinum	Blue Devil
Eryngium vesiculosum	Prickfoot
Geranium solanderi	Austral Crane's Bill
Geranium potentilloides	Cinquefoil cudweed
Geranium retrorsum	Grassland Crane's Bill
Glycine clandestina	Variable Glycine
Glycine latrobeana	Twining Glycine
Glycine microphylla	Clover Glycine
Glycine tabacina	Small-leaf Glycine
Gonocarpus elatus	Tall Raspwort
Gonocarpus tetragynus	Common Raspwort
Goodenia spp. (various)	Goodenia
Goodenia Pinnatifida	Cut-leaved Goodenia
Haloragis heterophylla	Variable Raspwort
Hydrocotyle spp. (various)	Pennywort
Hypericum gramineum	Small St John's Wort
Hypoxis hygrometrica	Golden Weather-grass
Kennedia prostrata	Running Postman
Lagenophora stipitata	Blue Bottle-daisy
Lagenophora huegelii	Coarse Bottle-daisy
Leiocarpa panaetioides	Woolly Buttons
Lepidium hyssopifiolium	Basalt Cress
Leptorhynchos squamatus	Scaly Buttons
Leptorhynchos tenuifolius	Wiry Buttons
Leucochrysum albicans subsp. albicans	Hoary Sunray (yellow)
Leucochrysum albicans subsp. tricolor	Hoary Sunray (white)
Linum marginale	Native Flax
Lobelia pratioides (syn. Pratia)	Poison Lobelia
Lobelia purpurascens (syn. Pratia)	Whiteroot
Lomandra spp. (various)	Scented Mat-rush
Microseris spp. (various)	Yam Daisy
Oxalis perennans	Grassland Wood-sorrel
Pauridia glabella (syn. Hypoxis)	Tiny Star
Pelargonium rodneyanum	Magenta Stork's-bill
Plantago gaudichaudii	Narrow-leaf Plantain
Plantago varia	Variable Plantain
Podolepis spp. (various)	Podolepis
Ptilotus spathulatus	Pussy-tails
Ptilotus spp. (various)	Ptilotus
Pycnosorus chrysanthes	Golden Billy Buttons
Pycnosorus globosus	Drumsticks
Ranunculus lappaceus	Austral Buttercup
Rumex brownii	Slender Dock
Rumex drumosus	Wiry Dock
Rutidosis leptorhynchoides	Button Wrinklewort
Scaevola spp. (various)	Pale Fan-flower
Senecio spp. (various)	Erect Groundsel
Solenogyne dominii	Solenogyne
Solenogyne gunnii	Hairy Solenogyne
Stackhousia subterranea	Creamy Candles
Stylidium spp. (various)	Trigger Plant
Stypandra glauca	Nodding Blue Lily
Swainsona procumbens	Broughton Pea
Thysanotus patersonii	Twining Fringe-lily
Thysanotus tuberosus	Common Fringe-lily
Tricoryne elatior	Yellow Rush-lily
Triptilodiscus pygmaeus	Common Sunray
Velleia paradoxa	Spur Velleia
Veronica gracilis	Slender Speedwell
Viola betonicifolia	Showy Violet
Viola hederacea	Ivy-leaf Violet
Vittadinia gracilis	Wooly New Holland Daisy
Wahlenbergia communis	Tufted Bluebell
Wahlenbergia gracilis	Sprawling Bluebell
Wahlenbergia luteola	Yellowish Bluebell
Wahlenbergia stricta	Tall Bluebell
Wurmbea dioica	Early Nancy
Xerochrysum bracteatum	Golden Everlasting
Xerochrysum viscosum	Sticky Everlasting
Rutidosis leptorhynchoides	Button Wrinklewort
Bossiaea prostrata	Creeping Bossiaea
Einadia nutans	Nodding Saltbush
Enchylaena tomentosa	Ruby Saltbush
Eutaxia microphylla	Small-leaved Eutaxia
Pimelea spp. (various)	Curved Rice-flower
Vittadinia cuneata	Common New Holland Daisy
Vittadinia gracilis	Woolly New Holland Daisy
Hardenbergia violaceae	Purple Coral Pea
Microtis parviflora	Slender Onion-orchid
Microtis uniflora	Common Onion-orchid
Pterostylis spp. (various)	Greenhood orchid
Cheilanthes spp. (various)	Rock Fern
Pteridium esculentum	Bracken
Juncus paliddus	Pale Rush
Juncus subsencundus	Finger Rush

MORE THAN A HUMAN POWER,
JOHN DELPRATT

"Jane Williams (nee Reid) arrived in Tasmania as a child on 1 March 1822 (Brown 1941). Reminiscing in 1840, following her return to Scotland, on her observations of the impact of settlement and grazing on native vegetation, she wrote:

'The plains of Van Diemen's land presented at the period I speak of as beautiful a floral sight as the imagination can conceive. The spring and summer still offer much to please the eye, but since the large flocks and herds which have been the real sources of wealth were introduced, the flowers have become comparatively rare; for there as elsewhere beauty is sacrificed to utility – a more than human power alone can combine both. In the new colonies of Port Phillip and Adelaide the country now presents the same lovely scene which I have alluded to in Van Diemen's Land for some years after our arrival' (Brown 1941).

Jane Williams was acutely aware of the rapid impact of European pastoral settlement on the grasslands of her colonial home. Her nostalgia for the seasonal displays of wildflowers she recalled from her childhood, less than two decades earlier, provides an insight into the rate at which these diverse plant communities were altered under European pastoral systems. Her conviction that to combine beauty and utility would take 'a more than human power alone' issues a powerful challenge to those in the late twentieth century who work to understand, preserve and even reconstruct such complex biological communities."[1]

(1) Brown, PL (ed.) 1941, *Clyde Company papers – 1 Prologue 1821-1835*, Oxford University Press, London, UK (1956) as referenced in Delpratt CJ 1999, 'Investigations of seed production potential of indigenous grassland forbs', Masters thesis, the University of Melbourne, p. 8.

GRASSLANDS REPAIR, GROUND, SKYLIGHT

MAURO BARACCO
LOUISE WRIGHT
LINDA TEGG

The exhibition has been driven by three key artworks
– *Grasslands Repair, Skylight*, and *Ground*. Each work
has acted as a provocation, a unique set of material
and representational challenges through which we have
developed our collective and individual ideas around the
concept of 'repair'.

At the intersection of art and architecture, these works
have been developed through varied modes of collaboration.
Our work together began with the proposition of adapting
a previous artwork, *Grasslands,* 2014,(1) for the Australian
Pavilion. Together we have been navigating the pragmatics,
and poetics of this gesture. In this mode we have also
designed *Skylight* that both supports *Grasslands Repair*
and presents its own dilemmas.

The third element is *Ground,* a series of experimental
videos that seek to visually conflate the architectural
object with its environment. *Ground* focuses on Australian
architectural projects that we have identified as exemplifying
varied approaches to repair. Collectively we have devised
frameworks and carved a space for video art within an
exhibition showcasing Australian architecture.

Through each work we hope to disrupt how we usually
conceive of and view architecture as an object, to reveal a
dynamic of how it is (back, front, inside, outside, connected,
large scale, small scale) to provoke a rethinking of how we
value and make our built environment.

(Overpage) Packet of seed used to make *Grasslands Repair*.
Photograph, Linda Tegg.

Baracco+Wright Architects in collaboration with Linda Tegg,
Grasslands Repair at the Australian Pavilion,
Biennale Architettura 2018, plan.
Image, Baracco+Wright Architects.

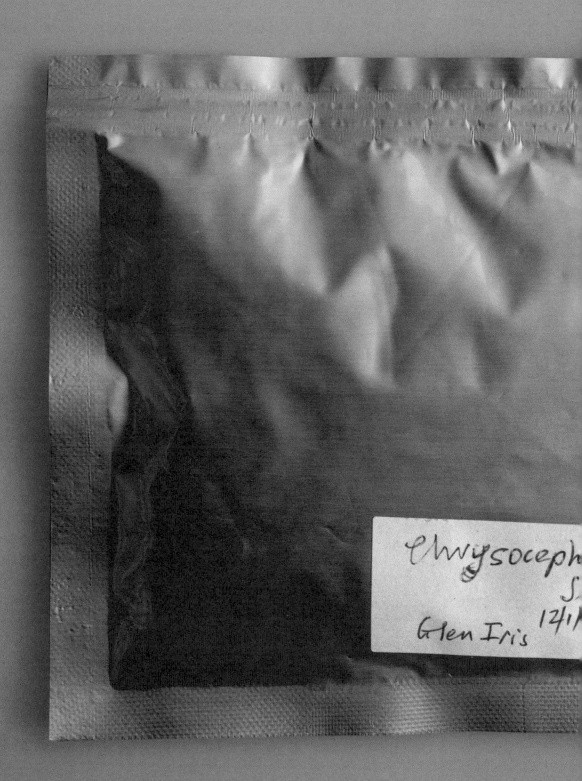

5038

~pupposum

4gms

GRASSLANDS REPAIR (2018)
LINDA TEGG WITH
BARACCO+WRIGHT ARCHITECTS

Victorian western plains grassland plants, growing media, recycled pet grow bags, support systems

Grasslands Repair presents over sixty species from the Victorian Western Plains Grasslands. Only 1% of this plant community remains from pre-European settlement times,[2] having been removed through urbanisation, agriculture, grazing and industrial land use. *Grasslands Repair* aims to reveal what is at stake when we occupy land.

The area of plants exhibited is similar to that taken up by the pavilion. It is also a smaller area to that of an average Australian family house.[3] Such an area takes around an hour to bulldoze.

The plants are arranged inside and out, 'through' the corner of the pavilion, at the only moment where the gallery meets the ground plane. The ground itself is an artificial hill, made from Venetian landfill in the time before the Giardini operated on this site and exaggerated in the new landscaping to meet the fire exit. We imagine this hill being completed by the installation rather than 'cut' by the building.

The fire exit remains open, in recognition of this moment of connection, and an invitation to enter through this less celebrated, less framed, alternative doorway. Similarly, the other two openings in the gallery walls, the window and entry proscenium, are altered to be the same size, changing the hierarchy of back, front and framed view. A provocation to notice the ways we 'see' and relate to the 'outside' world – the 'natural' world.

Grasslands Repair continues the themes of Tegg's 2014 *Grasslands* installation that attempted to recreate the pre-European settlement grassy plains woodland that once occupied the site on which the State Library of Victoria now stands. Each installation is a unique set of relations between plants and place. Living plants destabilise spaces that have been designed for the preservation of cultural objects. Through these acts of reclamation and displacement the plants also undergo a categorical shift – from ground for human use, to inhabitants of Australia's cultural institutions.

These relations are manifested through the process of making *Grasslands Repair*. From sourcing seed, learning how to germinate them, transporting them to Italy, growing them with the Italian partners, and bringing them into view for an audience. *Grasslands Repair* has provoked alternate ways of knowing and thinking of the Victorian Western Plains Grasslands. It needed to be inside.

A language of modularity and reconfiguration is in play with the life of the plants. The artificiality of producing a grassland this way is acknowledged by using component bags, laying bare the means of construction.

It is further emphasised through the work *Skylight*. However, a shift has taken place through this collaboration where now the work actively engages with the architecture in ways that comment on the way architecture occupies land and separates human and non-human life, and generally does not support plant life.

(1) Linda Tegg, *Grasslands*, State Library of Victoria, Melbourne, 2014.
(2) See Greening Australia n.d., *Great Southern Landscapes: Victorian Volcanic Plains*, Greening Australia, viewed 20 January 2018, <greeningaustralia.org.au/ project/Victorian-volcanic-plains>.
(3) Currently 189.8m², as stated in James, C & Felsman, R 2017, 'Australian home size hits 20-year low, CommSec Home Size Trends Report', *Economic Insights*, *CommSec*, 17 November, viewed 7 February 2018, <commsec.com.au/content/dam/EN/ResearchNews/ECOReport.20.11.17_Biggest%20homes_size-fall.pdf>.

GROUND (2018)
LINDA TEGG AND DAVID FOX WITH BARACCO+WRIGHT ARCHITECTS

Series of two-channel videos

Ground is a series of two-channel videos made at different sites across Australia. They resist easy classification: they are multi-purpose and multi-perspective. The title *Ground* challenges us to reorient ourselves in relation to what we might consider the world-around-us, or world-for-us. The ground is also what connects everything to everything else.

Like *Grasslands Repair*, *Ground* is motivated by a desire to foreground what usually goes unnoticed and underfoot. Across our collective disciplines, our practices pay attention to what is commonly considered ground. This awareness has prompted us to document architecture through a series of connections between sites, histories, and kinds.

Ground takes on multiple viewpoints. It resists the linear perspective that has dominated the representation of architecture since the Renaissance and provided the framework for mass human expansion. It joins the multitude of image-makers who have sought to disrupt the certainty provided by the horizon, who have problematised subject-object relations, and sought alternate ways of seeing and relating to an ever-changing world. The convention of how architecture is usually communicated, through the still and object based image, has influenced how it is made.

Each video is made at a site of architectural thought. Some projects have been established for many years, some transformed, some remain unrealised. Through the videos we hope to make visible the moments where architecture has recognised its embeddedness within worlds and has sought to 'make good' the relationship.

SKYLIGHT (2018)
BARACCO+WRIGHT ARCHITECTS WITH LINDA TEGG

LED light fixtures suspended

Skylight is a life support system. Suspended between the ceiling above and the grassland below, it is engaged in an unlikely act of transference. It channels energy from the Italian electricity grid – 64% Fossil, 21% Hydro, 9% Wind and Solar, 5% Nuclear, and 1% Geothermal – into the bodies of plants.

To emulate the sun for the benefit of the plants is a precarious proposition. At first thought it stinks of folly and hubris. However, in this situation, it is necessary as the building fabric denies light, and therefore the possibility of sustaining plant life. With the gesture of bringing the grassland into the pavilion comes an imperative to provide for it. The pavilion can no longer act as an object separated from its environment, it now hosts *Grasslands Repair* and is revealed as a conduit for the systems that sustain it.

We questioned whether it will work? What it would cost? Will it be bearable for a human audience? The struggle to maintain life within such an artificial environment becomes real. The fittings themselves are standard industrial fittings designed to illuminate large warehouses. Here they no longer illuminate the distribution of goods but provide nourishment for plants.

Skylight is a powerful actant within the assemblage. From its constrained position, *Skylight* mediates the dialogue between the grassland, videos, and the pavilion. Each by their very nature would otherwise overpower and erase the other.

Ground. Video still, Linda Tegg.
Bower Studio, Wave Hill Walk-off Pavilion, Junani.

(Overpage)
Ground. Video still, Linda Tegg.
Robin Boyd, Featherston House.

MAKING *REPAIR*

INTERVIEW BY
CATHERINE MURPHY

Sowing the seeds for *Grasslands Repair*,
Istituto 'D.Aicardi', Sanremo, Italy.
Photograph, Louise Wright.

CATHERINE MURPHY TALKS TO LOUISE, MAURO AND LINDA ABOUT THE MAKING OF THE EXHIBITION

CM Catherine Murphy
LW Louise Wright
MB Mauro Baracco
LT Linda Tegg

CM: Catherine: Why were you drawn to making an exhibition in the Australian Pavilion at the Venice Biennale?

LW: It was really that we had an idea for an exhibition that was meaningful to us, rather than the dream to be at Venice.

MB: We have been working on these ideas for a number of years now, so the exhibition transpires from many things – from the book about Robin Boyd on spatial continuity,(1) from the studies on the landscape of the Wimmera in Victoria(2) as well our projects which consider landscapes and buildings(3) – we wanted to put this forward at the high level of the Biennale.

CM: You have a strong connection to Italy through Mauro's Italian heritage, and you have been to many Biennales; this must have meant it was easier to imagine that you make an exhibition for that place?

LW: Yes, when we were living in Italy in 2016 we went to Venice a few times so it was fresh in our minds. As well, for us as architects, the Biennale has always been a big thing – Mauro brought that into our office as in Italy the Biennale is a household name. That hasn't always been the case in Australia but there is certainly a growing knowledge of the event and engagement with it.

CM: So you had this initial idea, which came out of your practice and work, so how did the collaboration with Linda arise?

LW: The original idea was a little bit different than what it ended up being in the final proposal and it has also evolved since then. Initially we were going to propose an abstract installation of our project Garden House as a building with plants inside the gallery.(4) We wanted to collaborate with somebody on the plants. I had seen Linda's grassland installation in 2014 outside the front of the Victorian State Library(5) and I went to her talk there and I knew that she was interested in what was on the site before the building was there. Because of this, I thought that she would be a good fit so we met and chatted, and then invited Linda into the project right from the start.

CM: It seems to me that this project has blurred the line between architecture and art. Did you frame the collaboration from the start or has it just evolved?

LT: We never went into it thinking it was a traditional commission or another iteration of a work. We understood that we were going to make the work together, in a very material sense. I could see that Louise and Mauro had a lived practice of tending and enabling the revegetation of a block of land. So we all brought to the projects slightly different perspectives that we had gained from longstanding engagement with plants.

LW: Why wouldn't you collaborate if you weren't trying to do something that was expanded from how you would normally think? Part of the aim of our exhibition is to present architecture in a non-traditional, non-conventional way – architecture in relationship to its context rather than an object. A lot of Linda's work presents you with something from a different perspective. So what's been really great from the word go about the collaboration is that we will have an idea, but then Linda will present it back to us in a different way. I feel like this process has really enriched the project. A great moment in the project for me was when Linda and I went together to Venice for the first time, and we walked around the Australian Pavilion and all the other pavilions and the way we looked at them together was different than if it had just been me; that for me was when things started to come together in a really conceptual way. There seems to be much crossover at the moment in the worlds of art and architecture and there are some interesting overlaps in responding to space and buildings.

CM: Mauro and Louise you have already a history of exhibiting work, curating exhibitions and publishing. Has this collaboration extended this practice?

LW: Yes it has. It's always difficult to exhibit architecture because so much is lost. I suppose for an educated architectural audience drawings are fine, but they don't transmit that fourth dimension. In this exhibition, the shift has been made in framing things conceptually, whereas on our own we probably would have made an exhibition that might have still been compelling, but it probably wouldn't have had that breadth of thinking that has come about through the collaboration.

CM: Did it feel like a natural extension of your work Linda?

LT: Yes it does. Architects often make exhibitions but not necessarily art. We use different languages, have different end points. I think often about representations of architecture as referring to something somewhere else but here together it's about this place and moment.

CM: There is also an expanded creative team that comes in and out, but nonetheless are playing a role. So the idea of having this expanded team proposes that the concept of repair means that architects can't act alone for this to happen?

A meeting of the Creative Team
at the studio of Baracco+Wright Architects, Melbourne, 2017.
Photograph, Louise Wright.

MB: That idea that architects can't work alone by themselves is obviously a key message of this project, yet at the same time we are advocating a role for architects that they have the capability to be strategic thinkers working with teams of different disciplines. Architects by nature are generalists rather than particularists – on each job we deal with completely different issues, budgets and briefs, so we like to think that the future for architects is much more in this integrative role, across issues and keeping teams together and negotiating between many voices.

LW: So yes we wanted to have an expanded creative team to support the project. The team has worked well and we have enjoyed many interesting dialogues both individually and with the team. This has certainly helped shape the exhibition focus and content.

CM: Let's talk about the most risky component of the exhibition, which is the grassland installation. Can you tell me how you have gone about making this?

LT: This was a big challenge. We made the decision early on that it was going to be an attempted recreation of a western plains grassland, as we're interested in that plant community for various reasons. Then we had to work out how to grow it – do we grow it in Australia and send the whole grassland over to Venice, or do we grow it overseas? We quickly established that quarantine regulations would be very difficult and shipping it would be very expensive and very risky, so we decided the best approach was to take seed over and grow it in Italy.

MB: The climatic conditions in parts of Italy are quite similar to Australia, so we hoped that growing the grasses there would work.

LW: We needed lots of grass seed and needed it quickly. We got seed from lots of sources – there are indigenous nurseries and seed banks across Victoria from which we either bought seed at a very cheap price, or we were given seed. There is a native grass grower out of Melbourne, Flora Victoria, which farms local grasses to collect the seed. There is a sad side to how this comes about – the original seed they sow in their plantation is collected from sites that are going to be cleared for housing estates and train lines. Greening Australia also gave us seed from their seed bank, the Burnley Campus of the University of Melbourne gave us some, and we also got some from a company called Nindethana and Seed Shed in the south-west corner of Western Australia where certain grass species grow in the temperate climate and soil conditions that are similar to Victoria. In all we collected around sixty-four different species of grasses – it is a pretty mixed provenance and this is interesting to us. It highlights the difficulty of recreating something that we are hastily removing.

Grassland seeds sown, Istituto 'D.Aicardi', Sanremo, Italy.
Photograph, Louise Wright.

Around one month after sowing.
Photograph, Louise Wright.

CM: So then you took it over to Italy to grow?

LW: Yes, but first we had to go through a number of processes of getting it inspected and certified to take it overseas. After we got all of the approvals, I took these large plastic bags of seed in my luggage, somewhat terrified of course, but actually I didn't have any problems at all. Arriving in Italy and passing through customs was a great moment!

MB: The irony wasn't lost on us that we were doing in taking these seeds over to Italy what has been done to Australia in reverse. Some of the species could be invasive, we don't know in those conditions. That has been something that has troubled us a bit – that Italy does have some intact ecologies, but these are usually out in the Alps and the possibility of contamination is quite low.

CM: So what happened once the seeds got to Italy?

MB: We organised with an agricultural school in Sanremo in Italy to take on the project of germinating the seed and growing the plants until they were ready for transport to Venice, so we worked with students at the school to plant the seed.

LW: One of the major issues we faced was germinating the seed. We were very fortunate to have experts Susan Murphy from Burnley and ecologist John Delpratt who were particularly generous with their knowledge about how to grow and germinate the first batch of seed we took over to Italy. Much of this knowledge can't be looked up in a book and it is a complex and varied process that can involve three or four different methods that may or may not be successful. There was soaking, smoking, scratching the seed coat, and applying gibberellic acid. We tried a range of these treatments and we found that even the leading experts in this field don't know everything. What came home to me and what I found confronting, is that we are busy destroying our grasslands and we don't even know how to grow it.

LT: I think we sowed about 30,000 seeds. Of that, over 17,000 grew successfully and then we took over and planted another 8,000 seeds, which increased the plant diversity so we ended up with about sixty-four species growing.

CM: How will they be moved to Venice?

MB: A professional plant moving company moves the grasses on a truck from Sanremo to Tronchetto, in a one-day trip. You can fit 9,000 plants in 14 centimetre pots to fill one truck. The rest of the plants will stay in Sanremo in case we need them during the exhibition.

CM: There was obviously a degree of risk in this project, for example, the plants could die in transit. Was there a Plan B if something happened to the plants?

LW: A lot of work has gone into ensuring the plants stayed alive. This whole project is very hands on – the level of risk requires somebody to take responsibility for all of the details. And besides, we know these plants – they are tough. And we had double the number of plants that we needed to have on show at any one time.

MB: We had the ideal team in terms of temperament; we have Louise who is relatively positive, we have Linda who is so conceptual that she would embrace the death of the plants as it would show how fragile they

Linda Tegg making *Ground (Glebe4)*.
Photograph, David Fox.

are, and then there is me, who was advocating that failure would be a disaster!

LT: I think there is a real poetic in having the grasses live inside the Pavilion in Venice for six months. We are giving them our best effort – we have good lighting, people are caring for them and rotating them around. So it won't appear effortless as if by magic; it will be evident that it's artificial, and I think in a performative sense, that this care and making it all visible is important. The space is about the size of a house block and we want people to think about how much is going on artificially to keep them alive, and when, within one hour, you could just bulldoze them away.

CM: So how are the grasses arranged within the space?

LT: The grasses are contained in circular fabric root pouches that are made out of recycled PET. These are a horticultural product designed to promote healthy root growth in large scale agricultural contexts. They are modular and can be stacked and arranged as we wish, and can be carried by one or two people, so the grassland will be able to move around.

CM: Are the pouches a strong part of the exhibition or will they recede?

LT: If the grasses are really verdant and healthy you won't see the pouches very much but if the grasses start to decline and shrink away, these structures will come forward as stronger element in the exhibition.

Conceptually, we are happy for the pouches to be visible as it shows that grassland has been brought in through a man made structure.

LT: And then the work *Skylight* hovers above the grasses, which aims to provide enough light to the plants to keep them alive. This is made of LED pendant lights and like the root pouches, these are an off the shelf product so there is nothing to customise. We worked with lighting designer Nic Burnham(6) on the specifications, as an enormous amount of light is needed to replicate even a shady day. This dynamic between the lights, and the grass is really exciting, because we are not really sure how it is going to play out.

CM: So then there are the architecture projects that are represented through videos in an artwork entitled *Ground*. What was the process for finding and selecting the projects?

MB: We prepared a brief that asked people to present their ideas of 'repair' at multiple scales from the very tiny, insect-like scale through to large systemic scale. The focus was as much on the context and process, as it was on the built outcome. The Australian Institute of Architects put out a call for submissions that needed to respond to the brief.

CM: Did you get the range of projects that you were expecting or hoping for?

LW: Yes we did and then some. We were really humbled by the submissions – maybe there wasn't a clear group that just shone through, but upon examination a lot of them were really rich and presented the theme of repair in ways we hadn't thought of.

CM: How did you select the final ones for inclusion?

MB: The selection was done in conjunction with the larger team. This was a very productive process and it was very useful having a range of both architectural and non-architectural reflections. We were generally in broad agreement and Louise and I did the final cut. These included unbuilt, historical, and built works ranging from landscapes to buildings around Australia.

CM: And then Linda has made video artworks of each of these projects? Did you plan that from the start?

LW: At first, it was undefined who would make the videos. It is the nature of how we went along with making the exhibition that every step was so involved, that we turned our minds to things as they come along.

I knew that Linda was also a video artist and one day when I was visiting her studio, she showed me a video she was working on from a recent trip to East Timor and I was so impressed and I knew that she was the natural choice, and then we talked about a few ideas and decided that she would make the videos. We decided to proceed in this way because it has something that enriches the process. Everyone is listening to each other and that is why we wanted to collaborate – it would have been a very different path to commission someone to do a script that we would write.

CM: So the videos are artworks and representations of architecture?

LT: Yes they are both. I didn't choose the individual projects, rather they were presented to me as a carefully curated group. In this sense I am working with them in a collective sense. I have looked to strike a chord between my thinking as an artist and the needs to represent the architecture.

LW: We certainly collaborated on the conceptual approach for the project representation and I think it was very helpful for Linda to hear us talk about why we chose those projects. The submissions did not always reveal all aspects of the project, or sometimes we saw them a bit differently in our own interpretation, so it was important for Linda to hear us speak about the project in that way in order to clarify some approaches.

LT: I was fortunate to be travelling around Australia to spend time with and document the projects. I remember I had a couple of days in the Featherston house(7) with dancers, Deanne Butterworth, Sarah Aitken, Shian Law, and Luke Fryer. It was quite a privilege to have the time to be in the house, to understand it through the lens and by way of the dancers. To begin to really register what Boyd had created. Louise and Mauro have been drawing my attention to aspects of the projects that are exciting to them.

CM: How has the building impacted on the concept and the way that the project has developed?

LT: We couldn't ask for a building that was in greater contrast to the needs of our artwork, as a living thing. This is a building that has evolved for a certain aesthetic appreciation, which is not about accommodating living things. So the response that I had to the building is that I am always thinking on behalf of the plants, worrying about access to sunlight.

LW: Ironically, most of the pavilions in the Giardini have skylighted roofs and they would have been perfect for our exhibition, as they are incredibly bright spaces. But the Australian Pavilion is dark with limited light. So we had to bring in light so that the plants could survive, and we called the light artwork *Skylight* in response to the broader Giardini. The arrangement of the plant installation was also derived from the response to the building. For instance, we hadn't considered having the plants outside until we went to the space, now we have the plants extending from inside to outside as if the wall wasn't there.

MB: There is one spot where the interior meets the ground and that's through the fire exit, so we are keeping that open in recognition of that threshold.

LW: The arrangement in plan is an egg shape with the wide part of the egg being inside the gallery, and the pointy bit being outside the gallery. That came about from where you enter as we were trying to get a sense of density within the gallery. Very early on we had a different shape of an opening in the middle of the space and you were surrounded by plants like a crater, but now when you enter into the space, it is a mass collection and there are narrow tracks within it, but it presents as a mass.

LT: There are multiple ways that you can move through the space and I hope that people will slow down and see the complexity of the grasses, not just see it as a grassy mound. We hope some people will sit down and feel immersed within it.

LW: Also, because we are keeping the fire door open people can come in through that door and there is a circuit that gives people a space to move through. We are not celebrating a big entry. We are reducing the size of that main window and the main opening to the same dimension as the fire exit so they are all the same size.

CM: How is the space programmed?

LT: The space is programmed so that when the lights are on there is time for exploring the grassland, and then the lights dim and the films are screened. We have a program where the timing for the screening of each of the projects is advertised.

LW: It's quite cinematic and you will be able to sit and have a similarly relaxing experience to the Pool exhibit at the last architecture Biennale.(8) Some people will choose to stay for a while and others won't. That is always the way of exhibitions.

MB: There is also a large format newspaper that includes comprehensive information about each of the exhibited projects that people can take away. This is a very important part of the exhibition, as very few people will stay long enough to see more than one or two of the projects being screened.

CM: The last thing I wanted to talk about is the broader engagement and context of the exhibition beyond the work itself, how you get the ideas out beyond the exhibition.

MB: Well importantly there is the catalogue which is a book that has been published by Actar which is something new for the Australian Pavilion and very important for broader distribution of the ideas.(9) This captures all aspects of the project and includes a number of articles from the expanded creative team. We also have worked with graphic designer, Studio Round,(10) on the brand identity for the exhibition, and there is some merchandising being produced with Australian fashion designer P.A.M.,(11) and so you will see tote bags and t-shirts around for a while! There will also be events in Venice and Australia organised by the Institute of Architects and us at the pavilion and as part of the official calendar.

LW: The theme lends itself to extension in the profession. We have been invited to write an environment design guide paper for the Institute of Architects, which is sort of like a white paper to effect broader policy. The Institute has also talked about getting some of these ideas into a number of their own policies. And we have been invited to be the editors of a monographic issue of *Landscape Architecture Australia*, to be released around the same time as the Biennale.

MB: And in a way this exhibition has been about building new and enduring relationships whether that be with ecologists, landscape architects, Indigenous people or students. And these relationships create new opportunities. Like our relationship with the school at Sanremo. Those students have learned how to sow seeds and grow these plants and then come to Venice to replant them in situ. This is a unique opportunity for them. Another spin off is that the school in Sanremo introduced us to a plant horticulture research institute, which services the local horticultural industry, finding new species that they can grow commercially. They are now interested in some of the species that we are growing for flower production. To me that's a really fantastic outcome that we could somehow contribute to an extended life for these threatened species, even if in Italy!

CM: And a final thing, what is going to happen with the grasses when the exhibition finishes?

LW: There could be a range of things that could happen – some will go to the Istituto Regionale per la Floricoltura in Sanremo that was mentioned before. We are also interested in the idea of collecting the seed from the plants and bringing them back to Australia for planting, and we could also plant some of the grasses around the Australian Pavilion in Venice – but we would need to get permission from the Giardini and there is some concern about the climate, as it is not perfect. That's the thing with the grasses and with all aspects of this exhibition, it's a dynamic process.

(1) Baracco, M & Wright, L 2017, *Robin Boyd: Spatial Continuity*, Routledge, London, UK and New York, USA.
(2) See Baracco, M with Ware, J 2015, *Regenerated Towns in Regenerated Nature*, d___Lab., School of Architecture and Urban Design, RMIT University, viewed 17 February 2018, <http://www.dlabresearch.com.au/projects/regenerated-towns-in-regenerated-nature-2/>. See also Ricardo, RR 2015, 'Regenerated Towns in Regenerated Nature: an interview with Mauro Baracco', *Landscape Architecture Australia*, no. 146, May, pp. 30-32.
(3) See Baracco+Wright Architects n.d., *Projects*, Baracco+Wright Architects, <http://www.baraccowright.com/work/>.
(4) A description of this project is included in this catalogue/book.
(5) Linda Tegg 2014, *Grasslands*.
(6) Nic Burnham, NDYLIGHT Lighting Design, Melbourne, Australia.
(7) A description of this project is included in this catalogue/book.
(8) Visitors enjoyed spending time and standing by the pool at *The Pool* exhibition in the Australian Pavilion at the Biennale.Architettura 2016. The exhibition was described as "an immersive multi sensory experience…(to) transport visitors poolside". See Aileen Toland, I, Sage Holliday, A (Aileen Sage) & Tabet M n.d., *Statement by the Creative Directors of The Pool, Australia's Exhibition at the 2016 Venice Architecture Biennale*, Australian Institute of Architects, viewed 18 February 2018, <http://wp.architecture.com.au/venicebiennale2016/australian-exhibitions/>.
(9) International publishing company Actar is mostly focused on "books on Architecture, Landscape and Urbanism", <http://actar.com/>.
(10) Studio Round, <https://www.round.com.au/>.
(11) P.A.M. Melbourne, <https://perksandmini.com/>.

LED lighting test at Baracco+Wright Architects' studio, Melbourne.
Photograph, Linda Tegg.

(Overpage)
Linda Tegg, Tim Walsh, and Michael Fairbairn
making *Ground* (Prince Alfred Park and Pool).
Photograph, David Fox.

PROJECTS

PROJECTS OF REPAIR

MAURO BARACCO AND LOUISE WRIGHT

As we had hoped, the broad selection of projects submitted for *Repair* revealed that there are many architects thinking about how to repair the environment, address social issues and catalyse cultural repair. This was demonstrated in the 126 entries that responded to a nationwide call for submissions to teams of architects working with landscape architects and urban designers. The submissions reveal that repair can be approached in many ways, from a small piece of furniture, to a football stadium, to a landscape region. Some of the submissions received have been referred to elsewhere in this catalogue/book as offering ways into the complex issues of repair.

To effect repair in the ways we have conceived it requires a coming together of the multiple disciplines of architecture, landscape architecture and urban design. Given the environmental focus of the exhibition, we were sensitive to the risk of framing landscape architecture as architecture, and not surprisingly there were many excellent landscape architecture projects that could have been exhibited as compelling examples. But as our primary aim is to provoke the role of architecture, we sought projects where the distinction between these disciplines was not always clear but did involve architects – some are more landscape-based, some less. In the final selections, the disciplinary boundaries are often blurred, collaborative, intertwined.

The submissions were made up of about 25% of unbuilt projects. These were impressive in their reach and hope. Many built and unbuilt projects demonstrated skill in a technological approach to repair through sophisticated solutions to such issues as contaminated and degraded land and power generation, and architectural skill was often associated with aims of social and urban fabric repair to address such issues. And, with around 20% of the submissions working in indigenous communities we are reminded of this deep need.

There were some consistent as well as emergent themes across the projects that signify what is in need of repair: remediation of land and waterway contamination; land erosion; creation of fauna, invertebrate and insect habitat; revegetation, restoration and reinstatement of natural systems such as wetlands and creeks; flood resilience; memorialisation of indigenous culture; provision of health care services for indigenous communities and spatially appropriate arrangements according to indigenous culture; buildings for communities in trauma; and links between small and large scale systems, among others.

When we selected projects for exhibition, we came back to our initial aims for *Repair*: architecture that integrates built and natural systems to effect repair of the environment, and in so doing, repair of other conditions; and to expand the point of view from the 'object of architecture' to the way it operates in its context.

We have leaned more towards projects within mixed and complex urban and suburban fabrics than dense urban ones. The important contribution urban density can make to repair of the environment through the concentration of population, decreasing the need to expand at the fringes of our cities, is well established.

In our final selection, we chose projects that represent a geographic, scale and project-type mix that illustrate different design processes and identify challenges. Some of the selections may seem modest or perhaps not as effective as others at repairing. However, they all show a trajectory we are keen to provoke and strengthen, one that can be meaningful for the architecture profession, where the 'thing' to be repaired pushes back on how the architecture or built form and its relationship to context is conceived and made.

This is a way of approaching architecture that is at the heart of the theme *Repair*.

Consistent and emergent themes of repair

In addition to those exhibited, we have named some other submissions here to provide an overview and record, and invite the reader to pursue further interrogation.

Where architecture was paired rather than integrated with environmental repair, a stewardship of the site catalyses the repair. This is one important approach reflected in exhibited project Kullurk/Coolart: Somers Farm and Wetlands [1] and can also be found in submissions such as Back to the Future Garden,(2) Edithvale Seaford Wetlands Masterplan and Discovery Centre,(3) Lake Connewarre Residence,(4) Cape Otway House(5)and Lune De Sang residence (and various buildings)(6) which plans this stewardship over hundreds of years.

The integration of vegetation in their response to connect fragmented vegetated space in difficult urban and peri-urban contexts was demonstrated in the exhibited projects Prince Alfred Park Pool and Park upgrade,(7)Weave Youth and Community Services building(8) and Garden House,(9) as well as the submission Arthur & Yvonne Boyd Creative Learning Centre(10) where the building is conceived as a bridge, facilitating the restoration of a water course. These are examples of approaches that work with the (otherwise) in between space or actually integrate their forms with the repair strategy identified earlier as a key challenge in shifting how buildings operate in their context. Spatial (open) and ecological sensitivity effects the form which is spatially, and sometimes ecologically, connected to large revegetated areas and the urban fabric, crossing disciplinary boundaries between building/landscape and urban design.

Submissions that compellingly privileged vegetated open space over built form include the Gunyama Park competition design(11) that sets an aquatic centre amidst a recreated indigenous wetland landscape that is part of the water filtration strategy, and Rosemaur Gallery proposal(12) that sites the buildings to work with revegetated ex-agricultural land. A concept proposed for Orchard Manufacturing Facility(13) involves adjacent indigenous vegetation to envelope and be encouraged to grow through the building.

These projects also represent a greater awareness of the role of urban ecologies, where increased biodiversity of vegetated open space is now acknowledged for its contribution to biodiversity, beyond say concrete or mown grass. Indicative of this approach are submissions such as Native Tracks(14) – the vegetation of railway buffer zones with indigenous species pursued this possibility – and the Museum of Native Ecology(15) which proposes the revegetation of a 5 kilometre corridor linking Sydney Harbour to Cooks River as a living and performative museum.

Projects connecting cities spatially back to their waterways by repairing sites of former industrial uses were strongly represented. It seems almost every headland or bay in Sydney's harbour was used industrially and the same could be said for much of our urbanised waterways. The Foreshore Walk of the Glebe4 project(16) is exhibited particularly for how the edge condition of the land and water have been designed to connect the linear spaces back into the adjoining suburbs, filter water, provide habitat and register the site's archaeology.

The remediation of White Bay Power Station on Sydney Harbour to phytoremediation gardens, performances and event spaces in the project GoatLand(17) uses phytoremediation techniques and (in later stages) goat communities to consume the final garden breaking down PH imbalances through bio-agents found within their bodies. Ballast Point Park(18) involves an extensive use of recycled materials from the site in the creation of a public park, providing optimism that spectacular sites can sometimes be returned to the public. We hope that less spectacular sites might someday also be recognised for their environmental role above a commercial one.

Sites on waterways undergoing more urbanised regeneration were also represented. The in construction Perth Stadium Park(19) is a large urban regeneration project that will potentially revitalise the eastern end of the city. This area, Whadjuk land, traditionally used for birthing, welcoming, fishing, hunting as well as burials and ceremonies, was then used as a golf course and then landfill – clearly a site in need of cultural repair.

Elizabeth Quay in Perth(20) also makes a connection between the city and the Swan River and infrastructural sites such as Yagan Square(21) also in Perth, are being upgraded. These urban regeneration projects will continue to reshape our cities and their interaction with their settings. They have a lot to offer in their wide-ranging potential impacts on local businesses and real estate, as well as awareness of Indigenous presence on the site, site remediation, stormwater treatment and densification, that might mean cities don't expand elsewhere.

The contamination of water was also reflected in some projects that sought to repair water quality through built intervention, or removal. The River Derwent Heavy Metal Project(22) constructed a floating island, similar to a barge, for repairing seagrass habitat by removing heavy metals within the Derwent River in Tasmania. Through the mapping of turbidity (which smothers seagrass and signals disturbance of heavy metals) using satellite imagery, a floating island is located and actively removes heavy metals (zinc solids) by means of a chemical process within the floating structure. Its platform structure means it can be used recreationally.

Reinstatement of natural systems was understandably the realm of more landscape-based projects. Big Plans for Small Creek(23) reinstates 1.6 kilometres of the channelised Small Creek on the traditional land of the Jagera, Daranbirrin and Ugarapul in Ipswich, Queensland, providing diverse community benefits. By re-engaging the floodplain and vegetating the corridor, flood velocities have significantly decreased across all modelled scenarios, with additional water quality benefits. Small Creek eventually enters Moreton Bay. This project repairs through the removal of built form.

Proposals involving a hybrid of reinstatement of natural systems with urban densification are visionary but also a viable middle ground, embracing a mutually beneficial realignment of natural systems and urban environments. Submissions such as The City of the Clear Night Sky(24) imagines that at the heart of Melbourne's future growth to the west is a 'dark patch', an exclusion zone that allows a new engagement with the reality of Greater Melbourne's ecological territory and Indigenous presence. The exhibited Arden Macaulay Island City,(25) a speculative and visionary project for the Arden Macaulay precinct on the western edge of the CBD in Melbourne, proposes the regeneration of the low-lying, post-industrial Arden Macaulay precinct where dynamic natural and human-made environments coexist in a dense urban setting. Along the widened floodplain of Moonee Ponds Creek, braided watercourses and wetlands spread between artificially raised islands. Further upstream, the natural chain of ponds formation is nurtured back into existence, with the channelised drain broken down and meanders reinstated to slow down the velocity of floodwaters.

Another type of approach positions the architect as a strategic thinker, often now referred to as 'design thinking'. The exhibited Triabunna Gatehouse project(26) in the main street of Triabunna on the east coast of Tasmania is one of a series of planned small scale interventions intended to effect large scale urban revitalisation and economic stimulus after the effect of a highway bypass and decline from change of economic activity of the town. Similarly, the exhibited project the The Globe(27) in the western Queensland town of Barcaldine, approaches repair of the decline of regional towns through regeneration of public space and gateway buildings transformative of the public realm and connected to a series of small interventions. Both projects integrate Indigenous presence.

Projects that we might call 'Indigenous' were either for indigenous communities and/or somehow memorial of or advocating cultural awareness. Organisations such as IADV (Indigenous Architecture and Design Victoria) and the Aboriginal Environments Research Centre at the University of Queensland advocate for careful consideration of (and/or the revelation of) Indigenous occupation and meaning in urban environments. To this end, we acknowledge the important work carried out by Kevin O'Brien and colleagues through *Finding Country* exhibited at the Venice Biennale in 2012, which showed the response of fifty designers and architects who were asked to take a piece of the Brisbane city grid and remove 50% of its built environment. It was described as "a speculative exercise in extracting something of what has been lost since European settlement".(28)

Signs of this approach were varied but evident. A research project called Permanent Trace(29) aimed to reveal and value Indigenous origins in an urbanised landscape within an institutional campus at Trinity College, Melbourne, through a planting design referencing a pre-settlement vegetation class and sites of cultural significance within it. Greenaway Architects' important project at RMIT University, the exhibited Ngarara Place, (30) serves to create an Indigenous presence and cultural awareness, also within an institutional campus and urban setting, and is used to perform ceremonies becoming part of contemporary Indigenous life.

The exhibited project Wave Hill Walk-off Pavilions(31)

at Jinbarak, Junani and Kalkarindji (Gurindji community), Northern Territory, aims at cultural repair through process, infrastructure and the memorialisation of the 'walk-off' protests of 1966. (32) Small scale shelters connect and are part of a culturally significant large scale 20 kilometre walking trail; the shelters' forms are derived to retain the continuous ground plane and positioned to acknowledge cultural cues in the landscape. The process involved the engagement of the Gurindji Indigenous community in inception and construction. There was also a representation of projects that sought to create or address memorialisation of the First Nations peoples, such as Over Obelisk(33) which proposes a series of architectural interventions that physically reframe historical narratives put forth by urban monuments.

New Natives(34) aims for an agency for biodiversity within built environments that are not necessarily indigenous. Proposing an alternative guide book to the native 'Flora & Fauna of Western Australia', the New Natives Guide is a book documenting the new 'natives' of Western Australia we might usually consider pests or weeds. This argument is well made by Alistair Kirkpatrick in his article 'The Emperor's New Clothes: Questioning The War On Weeds in Urban Streetscapes'(35) where he argues that the war on weeds in Australia is a well-intentioned, and in most cases a very valuable, environmental movement, but that its pursuit sometimes has adverse effects in the urban landscapes.

Reuse of existing buildings, and already cleared land, is an important approach represented. The exhibited project Main Assembly Building, Tonsley Innovation District(36) in Adelaide, South Australia converts the ex-Mitsubishi car assembly building for reuse, keeping the concrete slab and saw tooth truss roof structure, opening the remaining building to create a new world underneath a single roof. The as yet unbuilt Spring Bay Mill, (37) involves the reuse of a once economically viable but now disused woodchip mill on forty hectares of waterfront land close to Triabunna on the east coast of Tasmania. Interventions are made to reuse almost all the existing mill buildings and industrial structures for accommodation and a restaurant. The planting of the site is allowed to enter the remnant structures. As well as reuse, densification of already developed land is a meaningful way to offset the destruction of uncleared land. The submission Alternative Infill(38) explores the important role of small to medium scale infill in densification in a site-responsive way, while In My Backyard(39) proposes small careful adjustments of fenced land and title boundaries adjacent to public open space in suburban fabrics to redefine connected open space. The exhibited Grassland Common(40) contemplates starting with the grassland to concentrate denser forms of work and living along already disturbed sites adjacent to road networks as an alternative to the laying of a suburban grid over the landscape. A filament footprint is located along a proposed new highway at the edges of a fragmented grassland.

The project proposes that development and ecological restoration can coexist, where the rehabilitated open vegetated space is transformed into a large scale lightly infrastructured public parkland, a 'common' also including community, sport and leisure activities as well as pedestrian and bike circulation to nearby transport facilities buffered by landscaped areas surrounding the new housing.

Buildings for communities in trauma was a topic of repair well represented by several projects including the Flowerdale Community House(41) in Flowerdale, Victoria, a project that rebuilds a site on the Silver Creek destroyed by the 2008 bush fires, and gives a new home to a wide range of local events in this community. The as yet unbuilt Aboriginal Males Healing Centre(42) on Nyiyaparli/Martu land is strategically located on a significant men's ceremonial path which forms the spine of the proposed development in amongst a number of significant cultural sites that will be protected, conserved and repaired as part of the Healing Centre's programs. The exhibited Walumba Elders Centre(43) for the Warrmarn Community, Gija Country in the east Kimberley, physically repairs facilities after a flood event and provides health services so that elderly can stay on Country. The new buildings respond to the flood prone site and the spatial arrangement seeks to address and manage complex and critical factors inherent in Aboriginal culture. The National Arboretum(44) in Canberra involves the planting of thousands of trees, a project instigated after the bushfires of 2001 and 2003.

The effect of mining and quarries on the environment but also communities and the need for repair was reflected in the conceptual proposal to repurpose and revegetate Ravenhall(45) (quarry and landfill), also considered for its connections to the waterways across metropolitan Melbourne, and the Jabiru Rejuvenate project(46) for the rehabilitation of not only the Ranger Uranium mine but also Jabiru, a purpose-built mining township created to house the estimated 3,000 persons who would support the mine in Kakadu National Park (on traditional lands) – here the infrastructure is being harnessed and turned to support new purposes.

The Creative Directors' choice to include the Featherston House, 1967-69,(47) was in recognition of a shift in Australian architecture that began to respond to the places it was a part of, in this case allowing the natural ground plane to continue through the building.(48)

(1) NMBW Architecture Studio with William Goodsir and RMIT Architecture.
(2) Cooper Scaife Architects.
(3) MvS Architects.
(4) Kerstin Thompson Architects.
(5) Bild Architecture.
(6) CHROFI with DW Knox & Partners.
(7) Neeson Murcutt Architects with sue barnsley design landscape architecture.
(8) Collins and Turner.
(9) Baracco+Wright Architects.
(10) Kerstin Thompson Architects.
(11) CHROFI in association with McGregor Coxall.
(12) Architecture Associates.
(13) BENT Architecture.
(14) Gretel Stent, Emilia Fabris and Hannah Wexler.
(15) Eleanor Peres and Casey Bryant.
(16) James Mather Delaney design, Lacoste Stevenson Architects, TGZ-Tonkin Zulaikha Greer Architects.
(17) SueAnne Ware (University of Newcastle, Australia), Chris Johnstone (Bosque Studio, Newcastle, Australia), Vanessa Sooprayen (University of Newcastle, Australia), Simon Kilbane (UTS Sydney), Katrina Simon (UNSW Sydney), Jake Nicol (Urban Growth NSW) and Nicole Campbell (Urban Growth NSW).
(18) McGregor Coxall and CHROFI.
(19) HASSELL.
(20) ARM Architecture with T.C.M.-Taylor Cullity Lethlean.
(21) Lyons in collaboration with iredale pedersen hook architects, ASPECT Studios and material thinking.
(22) Office of Other Spaces.
(23) Landscapology and Bligh Tanner, with Ipswich City Council and Streamology.
(24) Peter Brew (RMIT University), Reg Abrahams (Indigenous Protected Areas Project Coordinator, Wathaurong Aboriginal Co-operative) and Ben Akerman (Wyndham City Council).
(25) Monash University Urban Laboratory (MADA).
(26) Gilby + Brewin Architecture.
(27) m3architecture in association with Brian Hooper Architect.
(28) See Grace, R 2013, 'Finding Country', ArchitectureAU, 28 October, viewed 15 February 2018, <https://architectureau.com/articles/finding-country/>. Finding Country was originally proposed and awarded for exhibition at the 2008 Australian pavilion but unfortunately did not go ahead; it was subsequently exhibited in 2012 at the Spiazzi Gallery (Associazione Culturale Spiazzi) in Venice in the context of the 13th International Architecture Exhibition of La Biennale di Venezia: Common Ground directed by David Chipperfield.
(29) Hayball, Openwork, Greenaway Architects, IADV-Indigenous Architecture and Design Victoria, MGS Architects.
(30) Greenaway Architects.
(31) Bower Studio, University of Melbourne.
(32) In August 1966 the Gurindji walked off the Wave Hill Cattle Station and went on strike over the mistreatment of their people and their land. Their defiance attracted increasing levels of support until their claims were recognised in a ceremony in 1975. For a further description of this event see essays by Paul Memmott and Carroll Go-Sam in this catalogue/book.
(33) Sibling Architecture.
(34) Gertjan Groen, Valerie Schoenjahn, Anika Kalotay & Serena Pangestu.
(35) Kirkpatrick, A 2017, 'The Emperor's New Clothes: Questioning The War On Weeds in Urban Streetscapes', Landscape Architecture Australia, no. 154, May, pp. 26-27.
(36) Woods Bagot with Tridente Architects and Oxigen.
(37) Neeson Murcutt Architects.
(38) Damian Madigan.
(39) Anna Fairbank.
(40) d___Lab., RMIT University.
(41) Antarctica Architects.
(42) PM+D Architects.
(43) iredale pedersen hook.
(44) T.C.M.-Taylor Cullity Lethlean.
(45) MUIR Architecture and Openwork.
(46) dB(A) Decibel Architecture.
(47) Robin Boyd (1919-1971).
(48) A discussion of Robin Boyd's work (also including the Featherston House) as anticipatory of integration between built environment and natural systems is advanced by Baracco, M & Wright, L 2017, Robin Boyd: Spatial Continuity, Routledge, London, UK and New York, USA.

A note by the authors:
the texts for the following project descriptions were sourced from the submissons, with editing and additional writing by Mauro Baracco and Louise Wright.

Ground.
Video still, Linda Tegg.

With this small building the architects aimed to explore a semi-permanent structure that was conceived through the inclusion of the house in the site's ecosystem.

The site is part of a leftover heavily vegetated corridor in between cleared grazing land. A historical anomaly, it gives a glimpse into what used to be there, although it too now is mostly altered through domestic gardens, human and (non native) animal activity. Small patches of the endemic vegetation remain, mainly tea tree heath, among mown grass, introduced species and plants considered invasive weeds. Half of the street is trying to support these patches through seed collection and dispersal, weeding and connecting. The other half of the street routinely chop down trees and mow down any emergent endemic species that might pop up in their lawn.

The site connects to its neighbouring vegetation and Westernport – a large tidal bay. The road now occupies the position of an ephemeral creek, and being downhill, the area can be seasonally wet and dry, and can flood. It acts as a compromised wildlife corridor for animals travelling from nearby Gurdies and Grantville Nature Conservation Reserves to the coast, and perhaps most successfully supports birds.

On this site the existence of endemic terrestrial orchids indicated that the soil had not been altered, and that, embedded in the soil and under the introduced grass were the bones of a plant community that once grew there. With an aim to support the strength of the remnant indigenous vegetation present on the site, weeding was carried out using the Bradley method – which works from 'good' outward, so that slowly the vegetation can re-establish.[1] What occurred is a new type of balance. Isolated from the overall web of relationships and systems, it is difficult to know if you are strengthening a plant community or if it will now always depend on you. However, as mentioned elsewhere in this catalogue/book, the presence of Greenhood Orchids (*Pterostylis Nutans*) are evidence of the presence of *Mycorrhiza* (required at the germination stage) and often a symbiotic relationship with certain trees. *Mycorrhiza fungi* is a crucial foundation for healthy soils and have recently been credited with the network used by trees to communicate with each other.[2] Continued mowing and fertilisation of the (non native) grass on the site when it was bought, a hasty positioning of the house on their location, potential changes to the hydrology of the site such as water penetration/overland flow/microclimate, and symbiotic tree removal among others would have meant these orchids would have disappeared in the near future.

By observing and supporting the expansion of small remnant patches of endemic vegetation, a shape of the site emerged that revealed an area where no regeneration was occurring, and as it turned out had been the site of imported fill, effectively smothering the seed stock and altering the soil.

The house was situated on this 'clearing', raised above the ground to allow for overland flow and so as not to 'cut' the site. Apart from a small utilities area, no ground is sealed. This supports the expansion of the vegetation inside the house. Now part of this ecosystem, this house supports life. The disturbance generated by the construction was quite minimal,[3] but nonetheless enough to generate the expansion of tea trees (which respond to disturbance). Tea trees now regularly grow inside.

The decision to make a building that admitted a lot of light, was in order to sustain plant life. Extremes are controlled through summer use of shadecloth, and also the strategic planting of the endemic trees that will in time further shade the house.

As a holiday, and experimental house, it is conceived as just a little more than a tent: a deck and raised platform, covered by a transparent 'shed', the interior perimeter 'verandah' is garden space and living areas are dynamic yet subtly spatially defined; up, down, under, above. The soil and natural ground line are maintained and carried through.

(1) See Australian Association of Bush Regenerators (AABR) n.d., *Working with natural processes: the Bradley method*, Australian Association of Bush Regenerators, viewed 10 February 2018, <http://www.aabr.org.au/learn/what-i-bush-regeneration/general-principles/the-bradley-method/>.
(2) See Wohlleben, P 2016, *The Hidden Life of Trees: What They Feel, How They Communicate - Discoveries from a Secret World*, Blanc Inc., Carlton, Victoria, Australia.
(3) Through an unusual application of garage kit construction technology, very little disturbance or waste was created (around one cubic metre of waste, the majority of which was recyclable).

1

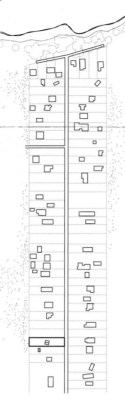

2

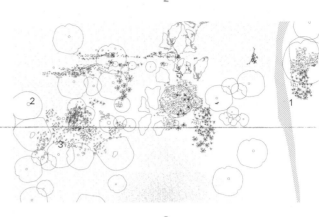

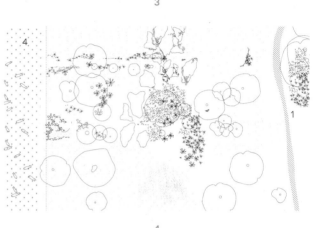

3

4

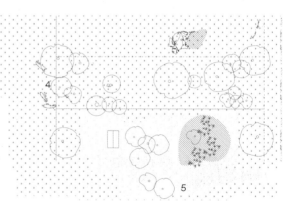

5

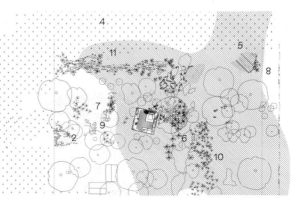

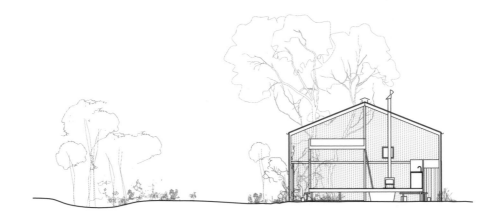

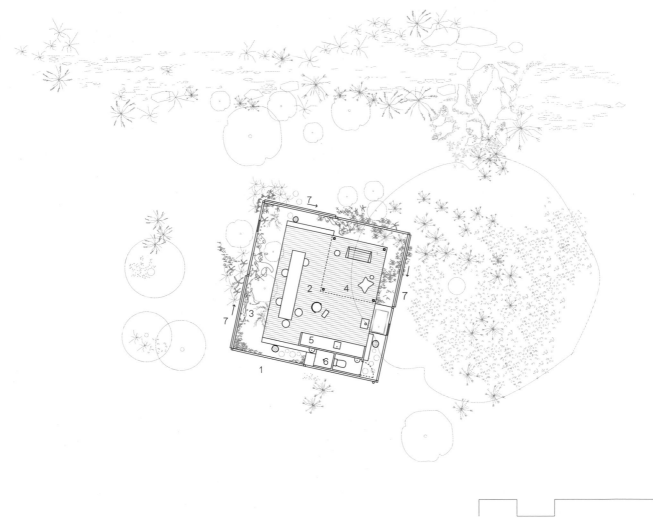

3

1-2 *Ground*. Video still,
     Linda Tegg.
3-4 *Ground*.
     Photographs, Linda Tegg.
5   (Overpage) *Ground*.
     Photograph, Linda Tegg.

WAVE HILL
WALK-OFF PAVILIONS

BOWER STUDIO,
UNIVERSITY OF MELBOURNE

Ground.
Photograph, Linda Tegg.

The indigenous Gurindji people pioneered the Australian land rights movement, protesting against their exploitation by an international grazing company that had stolen their land and forced its people to work for low pay and in terrible conditions. In August 1966 the Gurindji walked off the Wave Hill Cattle Station and went on strike over the mistreatment of their people and their land. Their defiance attracted increasing levels of support until their claims were recognised in a ceremony in 1975. Bower Studio was invited by the Gurindji to help commemorate the 50th anniversary of the 'Wave Hill Walk-off' by helping design and construct three pavilions along the heritage-listed trail. In 2016 a team of students and community members assembled a giant 'meccano set' of prefabricated steel ribs and panels, seating and landscaping elements that interprets the Gurindji's stories and attachment to their land. Each of the shelters uses the same architectural language but is unique to the landscape and stories at each site. They importantly allow the ground to pass through the structure. The pavilions act as a focal point for visitors and the Gurindji alike and help maintain the 'track mob' 's legacy as pioneers of the land rights movement. They are memorials, shelters and places for the transmission of knowledge.

The Walk-off story has become a powerful narrative both nationally and internationally and the Walk-off pavilions are the first physical representation of this event. The pavilions reflect the Gurindji's stories as told to the design team which were then reinterpreted. The first pavilion, located at Jinbarak, focuses on the direction taken by the Gurindji as they began their 22 kilometre journey via Junani (second pavilion) to their settlement at Wattie Creek and Kalkarindji (third pavilion). Curved sheets of corten steel and corrugated iron placed through the landscape mark the pathways from, through and to the pavilions and reveal the path taken by the Gurindji fifty years ago. The three pavilions track only one portion of the Gurindji's stories but highlight their struggle and journey to repair their lands and spirit in the face of the dislocation and disruption of European colonists.

As the discussions of a strike and walk-off gained momentum the Gurindji moved from the Wave Hill Cattle Station and walked to their ceremonial lands on the banks of the Wattie Creek near Kalkarindji. Here, away from the control of the cattle station owners and the cattle that was destroying watercourses and grasslands that had sustained them for over 65,000 years, they were free to reconnect with their traditional ways of living and make plans for an autonomous future. Moving from Jinbarak (Wave Hill) the Gurindji repaired connections with traditional lands and the ceremonies attached with their lands. However, they had been forced to make significant compromises as the loss of tribal lands at Jinbarak had severely curtailed their capacity for traditional hunting and gathering ways and the practising of ceremonies upon that land. Furthermore, many families became refugees on another tribe's land.

Maintaining deep connections to the land is of paramount importance to Australia's Indigenous people and has both pragmatic and spiritual dimensions. Whilst the Gurindji's brave stand for land rights and an independent homeland was recognised in 1975 it was impossible to rewind the clock and erase the physical effects of European settlement upon the land. Nowadays cattle grazing continues at Jinbarak but not at Kalkarindji – where the land is spared, the waterholes remain clean and the land rejuvenated. Spiritual repair is another dimension to the healing process and recognition of the Gurindji's resilience has been formalised with the construction of the three Walk-off Pavilions. These pavilions are used to celebrate the Gurindji's role as pioneers of the land rights movement in Australia and as a sign of the healing process. The pavilions emerge from both the landscapes as well as the Gurindji's narratives regarding place making and story telling.

The Walk-off Pavilions are one part of a larger project to help repair and rejuvenate the lands of the Gurindji people. The introduction of cattle nearly 100 years ago led to the loss of significant ecosystems and biological diversity. Cattle and horses devoured much of the delicate plant life – particularly along the watercourses. Introduced dogs and foxes wiped out many native species of fauna. Once the Gurindji highlighted their dispossession and were ultimately successful in their land claims, efforts have been made to restore their place as recognised owners of the land. The acclaimed Indigenous Rangers Program employs Gurindji people as both custodians of the land and as teachers who share their knowledge with the younger generations and with visitors. The Rangers and Elders use the Walk-off Pavilions as an informal classroom space where this knowledge can be shared.

This project and the Bower Studio implement 'design make' processes (as does the Kullark/Coolart project – included in this book – for the bird hide building), where architectural students are involved in the design project learning, and often design project making. The exposure of the students to the process improves cultural awareness where Indigenous people are consistently involved in the Studio prior to students heading out on field projects. And they are exposed to remote community partnerships, as well as complex issues of land relationships, desert ecology, economic enterprises and Indigenous cultural sustainability in remote Australia.

The reader may like to watch the documentary of the Wave Hill Walk-off story: *Ripples from Wave Hill*, directed by Elton Rosas and Jeremy Boylen.

1

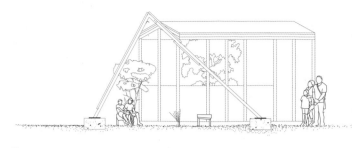

2

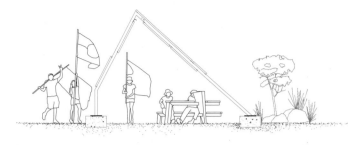

3

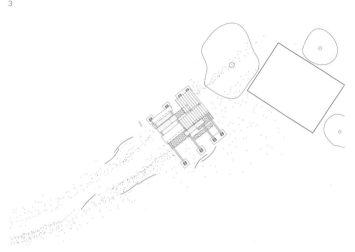

4

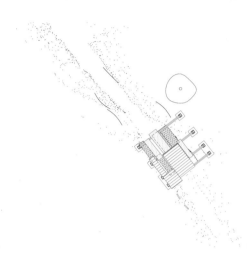

5

6

7

1   Jinbarak section.
2   Kalkarindji section.
3   Jinbarak roof plan.
4   Kalkarindji roof plan.
5   Jinbarak site section.
6   Kalkarindji site section.
7   Context plan.
8   Junani section.
9   Junani roof plan.
10   Junani site section.
11   Junani ground plan.

Context plan key

1   Jinbarak
     (old Wave Hill Homestead).
2   Junani (Gordy Creek).
3   Kalkarindji.
4   Daguragu (first camp
     and handover sites).
5   National Heritage
     Wave Hill Walk-off route.

8

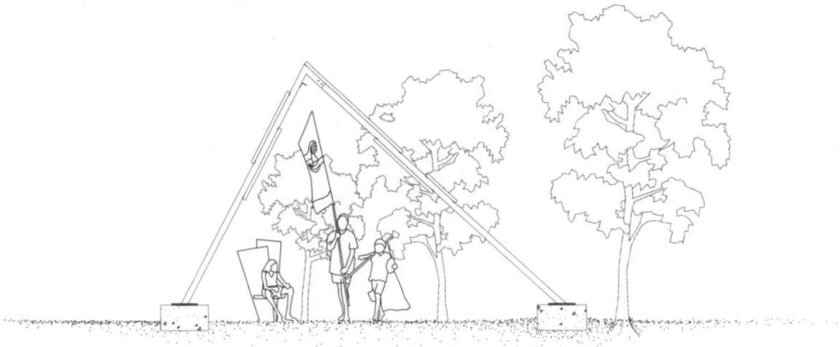

9

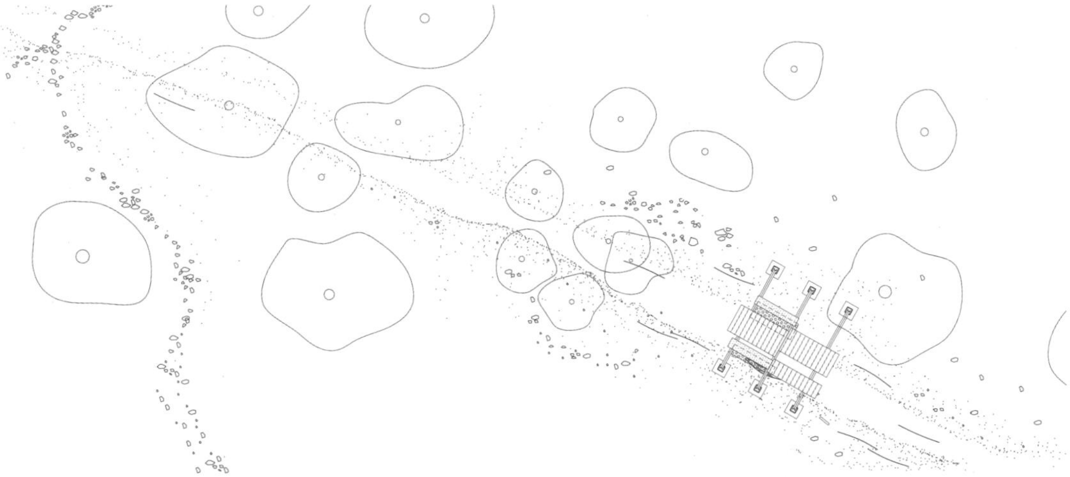

10

11

0   5

1-4 *Ground*.
   Photographs, Linda Tegg
   and David Fox.
1   Jinbarak.
2   Kalkarindji.
3   Junani.
4   (Overpage)
    Kalkarindji.

2

Wave Hill Walk-off Pavilions

Ground.
Video still, Linda Tegg.

This small project reveals the power of architecture and landscape as an agent of transformation. Formerly a toilet block, it is now a community counselling centre and a hub for local youth. The design is resourceful in the multiple uses it gets out of every element: the wrapped skin is a graffiti-proof cladding, a sunshade, a green wall, habitat, a pergola and a placemaker. The courtyard is a lightwell, a ventilation device, a secure meeting room and a garden. The roof is a large space for meetings, for community gardening and art activities, or for a safe and private retreat. The design attempts to solve difficult problems in a tough and challenging urban environment. An adaption and reuse, it transforms the building, the park, its occupation and the neighbourhood of Waterloo currently undergoing rapid urban renewal and change.

The building was previously a utilitarian toilet block, constructed as a single story brick structure and was decommissioned in the early 1990s, and subsequently utilised by South Sydney Youth Services (now Weave) as a workspace prior to its renovation in 2012. The building sits in Waterloo Oval, a popular public space in this inner city suburb of Sydney, which incorporates an oval, viewing stand, as well as Fernside Skatepark – the only purpose built skatepark in the inner city.

Over and above the reconstruction and reimagining of a dilapidated utilitarian structure in a park, the building is a participant in the repair of lives and communities. The project aims to provide an inviting, safe, light-filled environmentally responsible space for young people to meet staff, and the caseworkers who provide a variety of services to assist with a wide range of social issues. The building repair incorporates the creation of a combination of open plan workspaces and private counselling rooms, focussed around the new light filled courtyard. Existing brickwork walls are refurbished and maintained, and extended with new openings formed. A concrete superstructure supports a flexible column free off-form concrete slab.

Terragram Landscape Architects were central to the success of the vine covered steel trellis. It forms a robust protective overcoat and supports a variety of plants, *Pandorea pandorana* (Wonga Wonga vine) along with *Pyrostegia venusta* (Orange Trumpet vine), that grow around the structure. A new 200 square metre roof terrace is formed in the interstitial space between the high level canopy trellis and slab below. The folded trellis structure sits independently of the building; designed so that either the building or the structure can be removed or relocated in the future, without one affecting the other. Over time, with the growth of the plants, the abstract green form has merged the building visually with its landscape setting, especially the rear feeling like a generous extension of the park rather than something for humans at all.

The building supports the climbing habit of a variety of native plants species that inhabit the lower and upper canopy structures and also provides bird and insect habitat. On the roof terrace, native edible plants are harvested in a small 'bush-tucker' garden, with the ingredients harvested by the young people and used in cooking classes. A roof mounted hive is a home for native bees.

The project forms a focal point for the regeneration of the Redfern, Waterloo, Alexandria and Green Square areas in Sydney's Inner City – one of the biggest and fastest evolving urban regeneration projects in the southern hemisphere. The transformation of the building supports this, essentially an extension of the visual landscape in an act of generosity of the public realm and urban biodiversity.

Roof deck.
Photograph, Richard Glover.

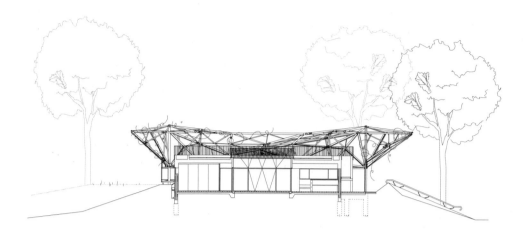

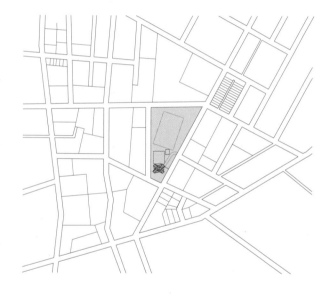

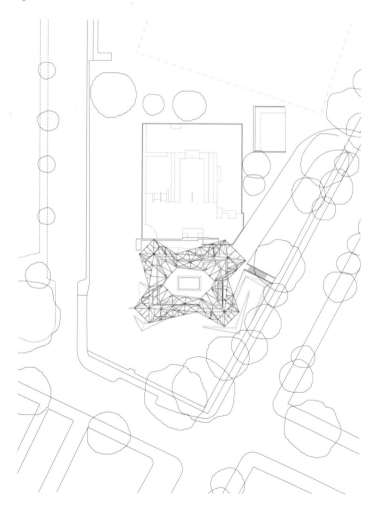

1   Section.
2   Context plan.
3   Site plan.
4   Canopy plan.
5   Roof plan.
6   Floor plan.

Repair

4

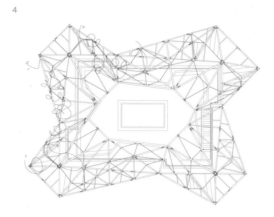

5

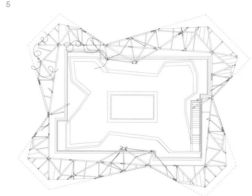

6

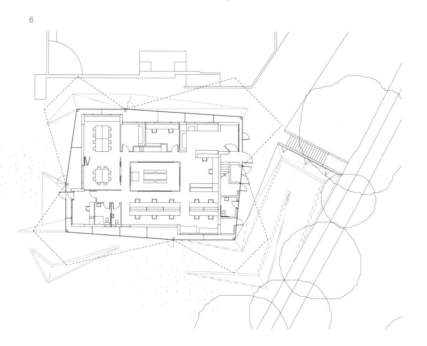

2

3

GRASSLAND COMMON: LINKING ECOLOGY AND ARCHITECTURE

d___LAB., RMIT UNIVERSITY

Ground.
Photograph, Linda Tegg.

Recent examples of urban expansion in Melbourne's northern growth corridor have cleared extensive areas of native grasslands despite that temperate grasslands are the most threatened ecosystem in Australia.(1) The area is characterised by large scale areas of plains grasslands and grassy woodlands, interspersed with agricultural land and volcanic hills from the top of Craigieburn to the south edge of Wallan, along Merri Creek north catchment area. This unbuilt project proposes a visionary alternative to low dense housing estates that are laid across the landscape of this area specifically,(2) and generally also found in peri-urban development sites on the fringe of Australian cities. It explores the possibility of development coexisting as part of a healthy ecosystem, integrating the new built spaces to a shared public 'grassland common' that is kept free from new footprint.

Development is often seen as incompatible with the natural environment which is usually cleared, flattened and destroyed during the development process. A policy called 'offsetting' allows for the conservation of another similar area of vegetation as a trade off for the one you want to clear and is often used to justify the clearing of land on our urban fringes of metropolitan areas as well as more remote bushland for agriculture.

Principles explored in the design were: working with the ecological foundations of the site; recognition of natural systems and processes as primary conditioning factors of urban/architectural/landscape/infrastructural design; reduction of urban sprawl and consolidation of the urban footprint within contained areas that are inclusive of all infrastructural and 'hard' urban services to areas along existing main arteries; and cross-programming.

Historical and current vegetation mapping reveals a unique opportunity for the site to enhance ecological connectivity between important areas in the east and west. At a local scale, remnant patches of grasslands and grassy woodlands can be connected through habitat restoration, while more broadly, the site may also provide a green corridor between Kinglake and Mount Macedon, as Merri Creek provides an existing green connection between the established northern suburbs of Melbourne and the Great Dividing Range to the north.

The area is home to numerous native species, including the threatened Growling Grass Frog and iconic River Red Gum (*Eucalyptus camaldulensis*). The ecological values of the site are addressed by applying principles described as Biodiversity Sensitive Urban Design which aim to create urban environments that are a net positive for biodiversity, while also meeting needs of development.(3) Large, connected areas of plains grassland and plains grassy woodland provide important habitat for the Golden Sun Moth and Striped Legless Lizard, which are nationally threatened species. A series of well connected wetlands and large buffer zones between the Merri Creek and built areas will benefit the Growling Grass Frog and other endemic fauna species.

The dispersal of native species is facilitated by mitigating major barriers to movement, such as roads, in natural areas, and connecting high value remnants to the east and west. The minimisation of disturbance is achieved by the concentration of the built form and reduced noise from less reliance on roads. The minimal footprint also reduces the amount of runoff from the site, while the compact design of the built form accommodates the need for fire in the landscape facilitating natural processes.

The urban and architectural resolutions of the approach are based on the following principles: new built volumes as 'filaments' along existing and/or planned infrastructures, benefiting from adjacency to services and circulation, as well as minimising and containing new footprint, with a narrow cross-section and raised from the ground; vegetated berms accommodating services – pipelines, ducts, private carparks – and buffering residential buildings from highway; new built semi-public areas relating to the public 'grassland common' by buffering, and yet embracing it rather than spreading into it, informed by a mix of integrated programs, from residential to work and community areas including spaces for socialisation, entertainment, commercial, educational, sport, institutional activities and green house farming; flexibility in apartment layout to enable space articulation and potential growth in stages within the original footprint – apartments can shift over time from one to two and three bedrooms.

In determining development objectives for the site, guidance was taken from research reports at RMIT, which suggest that infill development in Melbourne's existing suburbs could accommodated 41% of the projected growth area dwelling targets.(4) Approximately 20,000 new dwellings are accommodated in the urban filaments of this proposal – higher yield could be achieved by increasing density at key points along the filaments, such as service and transport hubs.

(1) Australian Government, Department of Sustainability, Environment, Water, Population and Communities 2011, *Nationally Threatened Ecological Communities of the Victorian Volcanic Plains: Natural Temperate Grassland & Grassy Eucalypt Woodland*, viewed 10 November 2015, <www.environment.gov.au/system/files/resources/e97c2d51-08f2-45e0-9d2f-f0d277c836fa/files/grasslands-victoria.pdf>.

(2) A large portion of the area of this project is currently being developed by Stockland, under the name of Cloverton, planning to house 30,000 people (11,000 residences) over 114 hectares. See Stockland, n.d., *Cloverton - Life at Cloverton*, Stockland, viewed 10 January 2018, <www.stockland.com.au/residential/vic/cloverton/life-at-cloverton>.

(3) For a further description of Biodiversity Sensitive Urban Design, see Garrard, G & Bekessy, S 2015, *Biodiversity Sensitive Urban Design: Creating urban environments that are good for people and good for nature*, RMIT University, Centre for Urban Research and The Meyer Foundation, Melbourne, viewed 24 February 2018, <https://ggarrardresearch.files.wordpress.com/2012/11/bsud-final_reduced-size2.pdf>. BSUD is also discussed in the publication *Linking Ecology and Architecture* (November 2015, RMIT University, limited edition) that profiles this speculative project and other works by two collaborating schools from RMIT University: School of Architecture and Urban Design (formerly: School of Architecture and Design) and School of Global Urban and Social Studies.

(4) Buxton M, Phelan K & Hurley J 2015, *Melbourne at 8 Million: Matching Land Supply to Dwelling Demand*, RMIT University, Centre for Urban Research, September, viewed 10 November 2015, <http://cur.org.au/project/melbourne-8-million-matching-land-supply-dwelling-demand/>.

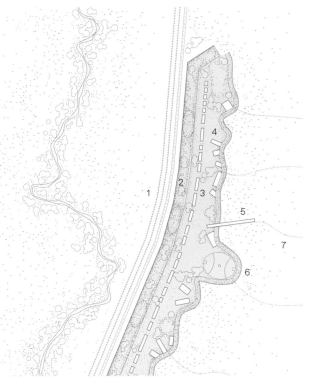

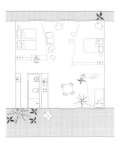

2

Territorial Plan Key

1. Merri Creek.
2. Kalkallo grassland remnant.
3. Donnybrook north rail reserve.
4. Red Gum forest.
5. Bald Hill and grassland.
6. Spring Street Swamp.
7. Beveridge rail reserve.
8. Hernes Swamp.
9. Wallan.
10. Beveridge.
11. Kalkallo.
12. Craigieburn.

⬡ Volcanic mound

🌿 Plains Grassy Woodland
Plains Grassland

Riparian Scrub

Existing wetland

Historical wetland

Site Plan Key

1. Rail/road.
2. Landscape berm.
3. Housing.
4. Community buildings.
5. Greenhouse.
6. Landscape berm.
7. Grassland.

Image Captions

1. Site plan of filament housing.
2. Floor plan of filament housing development showing internal modifications.
3. Existing territorial plan showing sites ecology.
4. Proposed.
5. Imagined inhabitation.

```
0        5
```

3

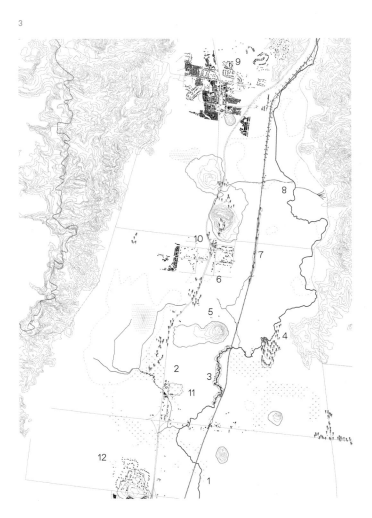

4

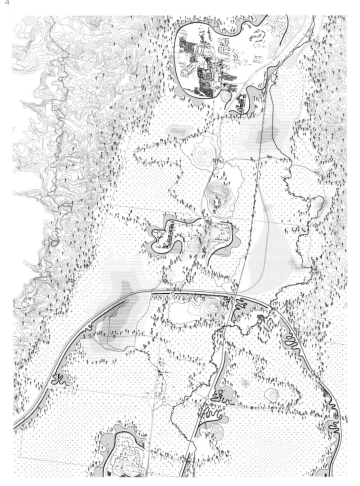

Grassland Common: Linking Ecology and Architecture

1

1   Kangaroos in northern
    Melbourne grassland
    bordered by development,
    Ngarri-djarrang.
    Ground. Photograph, Linda Tegg.
2   Section drawing of filament
    development backing onto the
    road and facing open space.
3   Bald Hill from the North.
    Photograph, Brian Bainbridge.

2

Grassland Common: Linking Ecology and Architecture

TRIABUNNA GATEHOUSE

GILBY + BREWIN ARCHITECTURE

Photograph, Anna Gilby.

The Triabunna Gatehouse is a small public building and garden located at the highway turn-off to a small regional township on the east coast of Tasmania. For many years Triabunna was the service town for a nearby wood chip mill but with the recent downturn of the forestry industry, the mill has closed and the town has suffered economically, with many businesses in decline and people being forced to leave in search of work elsewhere. The Glamorgan Spring Bay Council is now aiming to refocus the township, in particular by addressing the quality of the town's long neglected public realm and actively tapping into the growing tourism industry on the east coast of the state to create new economic opportunities. The Gatehouse project is the first built outcome of an ongoing urban revitalisation strategy for the town commissioned by the council and curated by Gilby + Brewin Architecture called Triabunna Tomorrow. Over the past three years, originating as design research with Architecture students at Monash University and the Regional Urban Studies Laboratory (RUSL) within the School of Architecture & Design at the University of Tasmania, the engagement has involved a careful process of observation, research and community consultation towards conceiving, proposing and now implementing a series of architectural projects that will contribute to the long term social, environmental and economic revitalisation of the town.

The economic and sometimes social decline as an outcome of changing economic activity is widespread across smaller Australian regional towns. Interestingly, the economic activities that were once usually the very reason for the town, were often exploitative of the natural environment (for example, logging, mining, fishing, unsustainable farming) and have been exhausted or become unviable. The repair of the environment is less clear in this project, an argument could be made for the shift of the town's activities away from environmentally destructive ones and the architecture's role in strategically supporting this. Many of these towns are at moments of extreme change. Outside our urbanised centres, these towns are less visible than our large scale urban renewal projects, but the need is pervasive. The almost 'acupunctural' approach affords careful layered and responsive architecture that works with the town and their particular characteristics.

The 'site' for the project is considered across a range of urban scales: the specific location of the project at the western entrance to Triabunna from the Tasman Highway (that currently bypasses the town); the tired urban setting of the township; and the wider, largely hidden cultural and environmental context of the place. In regards to the specific location of the project, the Gatehouse aims to address the effect of the highway bypass that had created a poorly defined entrance to the town with little to entice travellers to pull-in off the highway.

Collected underneath a roof profile that borrows its proportions from an opposite existing community building are a series of primary geometric elements that contain the

various programs; a rectangular enclosure for the public toilets, a cylindrical water tank and a U-shaped seat that define a wi-fi enabled gathering space (that includes a town map), and a small triangular display room positioned at the apex of the plan. The garden around the building incorporates exclusively Tasmanian native, local and endemic plants – the seeds and cuttings for which were saved from a recently closed bush garden nursery. Convict-cut sandstones pulled out from the nearby estuary during the recent wharf redevelopment are dotted throughout the garden forming a row of stepping stones in front of the Display Room. The Display Space showcases a full-size photograph of a rare Indigenous bark and reed canoe that is held at the local museum as well as a video of the canoe being made by a group of young Aboriginal men which communicates the importance of passing on cultural knowledge. The display acknowledges the significant Indigenous history of the place on which the building, and indeed the town, is squatting.

This physical intervention is complemented by integrating programmatic connections to other parts of the town, namely, a satellite exhibition space to be used on rotation by different community groups, a produce stand for students to sell fruit and vegetables grown in the local school garden, and a display area for local tourism business pamphlets.

The Gatehouse project is stage one of a longer term streetscape plan for the town that incorporates water sensitive urban design strategies to reduce the amount of hard surfaces currently straining the stormwater system. It forms part of an ongoing urban revitalisation strategy for the town of Triabunna which aims to incrementally repair the town's public realm via short term, immediately achievable architectural interventions that are embedded in longer term urban design strategies. At a perhaps less tangible macro scale, the project also attempts to help repair a lost connection to the rich culture and environment of the place.

Photograph, Anna Gilby.

Plan Key

1   Display space.
2   Open gathering space and seat.
3   School production stand and signage.
4   Public toilets.
5   Water tank.

Image Captions

1   Territorial plan.
2   Site plan.
3   Territorial section.
4   Section.
5   Floor plan.

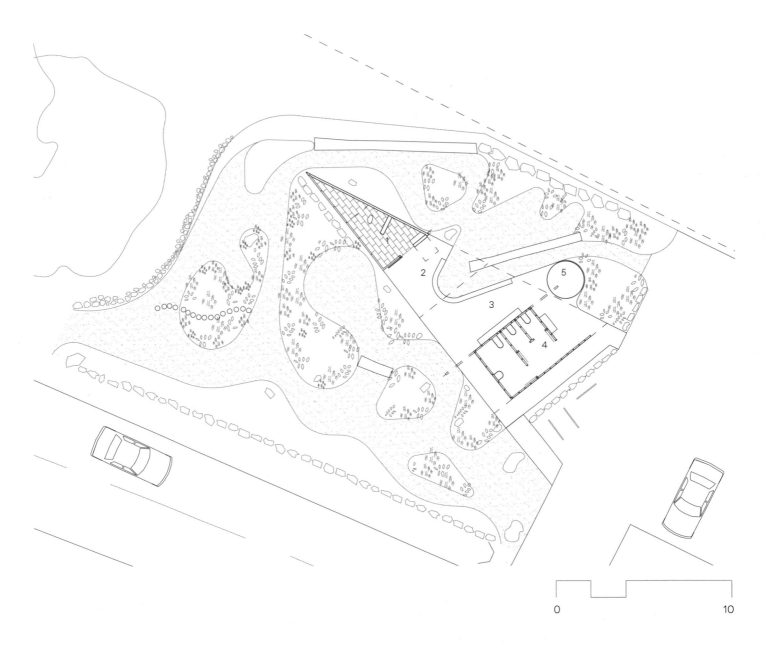

0

10

3

1   View from open space and seating
    area to main road. *Ground*.
    Photograph, Linda Tegg.
2   View towards gatehouse showing
    roof references. *Ground*.
    Photograph, Linda Tegg.
3   Local saltmarsh landscape. *Ground*.
    Photograph, Linda Tegg.

Ground. Video still,
Linda Tegg and David Fox.

Repair

Ground. Video still,
Linda Tegg and David Fox.

WALUMBA
ELDERS CENTRE

IREDALE PEDERSEN HOOK

Photograph, Peter Bennetts.

On the 13 March 2011 the remote Aboriginal Community of Warrmarn, Gija Country East Kimberley in Western Australia, was struck by devastating floods that overwhelmed much of the town and damaged or destroyed most buildings. Some 350 Gija People were forced off their homelands for two years. The Walumba Aged Care Centre was born out of this disaster. The site, within the Turkey Creek river valley at Warmun, the core township for the Gija People, was selected by the Community Elders as it was adjacent to the school and close to the community centre. This location ensured that the Elders in residence could be easily accessed by the young members of the community to provide cultural and emotional support between the generations. Most of Warmun is within the 2011 flood zone (a 1:350 year event) and is adjacent to the old aged care hostel site. The former hostel was destroyed by the flood, but it was seen as important to the community to locate the new Elders Centre near this zone. The location in the flood zone generated the form of the building, with the prosaic raising of the building off the ground which allows for flood waters to flow below it, while ramps and stairs provide access for people and cars even during a flood event.

The new building was sited adjacent to the community school – to act as a focal point for bringing the community back together. To avoid potential future flooding the centre is built 2.4 metres above the natural ground level and is conceptually linked with the idea of a bridge. The concept relates to a bridge not only as physical infrastructure but also as passage of knowledge between generations and as a place of care and respite before the possibility of passing from this existence to the next. The facility seeks to address and manage complex and critical factors inherent in Aboriginal culture such as gender separation, access to outdoor spaces both public and private, supporting Lore and Culture activities including ceremonies that may involve fire and smoke, avoidance relationships including son-in-law/mother-in-law relationships, inter-family conflict issues and mortuary practices called 'sorry business'.

The flood caused both a physical and spiritual trauma to the community. Buildings with long histories were totally destroyed and artefacts washed down the creek. The subsequent relocation of the community members to Kununurra, and the moving of the old Aged Hostel residents was a very traumatic event. Within twelve months many of the Aged Care residents had died. For the Gija people this is not just a 'natural disaster' but a deeper spiritual event, as previously described by deceased Elder Rover Thomas in Girrirr Girrirr dance ceremony which expressed the Spiritual event that Europeans called Cyclone Tracey. The design and construction of the Elders Centre – driven solely by the remaining Gija Elders and their community – was seen as bringing the Elders home, providing a place for the continued practice and transmission of Gija Lore and Culture and as a final reconstruction of the community both physically and spiritually.

From an individual point of view private needs are met; connections between family members are strengthened and the joy of watching their young grandchildren play around the centre and grow up is supported. The harsh micro-climate is mitigated by shade screening systems, breezeway activity zones, wall fans, shade plantings and dust reduction plantings.

The macro scale can be seen as the broader community and Gija Cultural obligations, such as Smoking Ceremonies, Lore Time Practices and Celebrations. Kinship obligations are supported by providing a variety of public places, as well as gender specific zones for more sensitive Gija practices. The building frames views into the wider landscape – to the ceremonial tree to key Creation sites around the river valley. Landscaping plantings have been selected to support Cultural practices – including plantings of Snappy Gums, used in smoking ceremonies, to bush medicine and bush tucker plants.

Funding was provided by the Commonwealth and State governments to rebuild the Community after the flood, however recurrent funding to operate the facility was not included in the recovery grant.

This narrative is consistent with the many problems faced by remote communities that are trying to build and replace critical infrastructure and provide employment on their communities. In Warmun the situation was compounded by external parties who took advantage of it, stealing community funds and forcing the community into receivership. This placed further pressure on their ability to run the Elders Centre as a fully functioning Aged Care Centre.

Community members are now gaining qualifications as aged care workers, and the community is seeking support and funding to operate the centre to the full extent for which it was designed. These and many other challenges persist throughout remote Australia.

Photograph, Peter Bennetts.

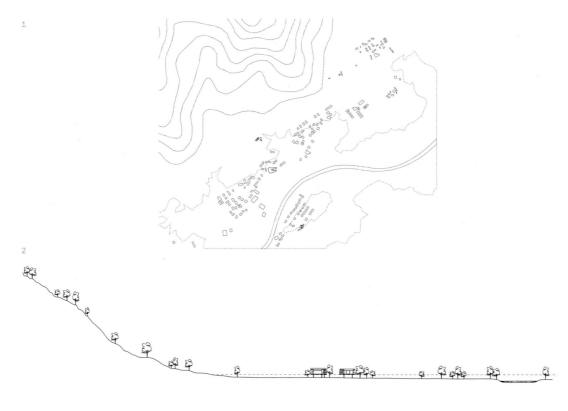

1   Territorial plan.
2   Territorial section.
3   Site plan.
4   Diagrams, view corridor,
      views, ground plane.
5   Section.
6   Floor plan.

Repair

4

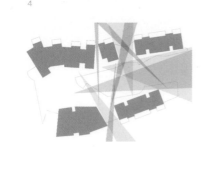
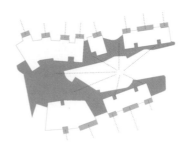
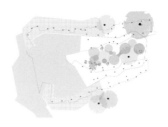

5

6

0   10

1   Photograph, Peter Bennetts.
2   Photograph, Peter Bennetts.
3   View to cultural landscape.
     Photograph, iredale pedersen hook.
4   (Overpage)
     Photograph, Peter Bennetts.

2

Walumba Elders Centre

GLEBE4: THE FORESHORE WALK

JAMES MATHER DELANEY DESIGN

Ground.
Video still, Linda Tegg.

The Glebe4 project includes four elements of a regenerated site in inner west Sydney – The Foreshore Walk, Jubilee Park, The Crescent and the new open space at Harold Park with heritage adaptation of the Grandstand and Bellevue Villa. This project has repaired industrial land and reclaimed harbour areas since 2007 in a highly urbanised precinct that was locked away from public access for more than a century. Combined, these form the western most segment of the City of Sydney's planned harbour foreshore walk from Woolloomooloo to Rozelle.

The four interconnected projects delivered for the client City of Sydney over thirteen years, have returned the foreshore of Glebe to the public, achieving recreational, environmental, urban and heritage outcomes by knitting together disparate open spaces, by restoring existing parkland, and by providing a significant new park. The projects have repaired the precinct in multiple ways: regenerating foreshore brownfield areas and archeological sites; introducing a clear circulation network for pedestrian and cyclists; inserting mangroves and intertidal habitats on an area of reclaimed land; building a new beach, water stairs for access and small boat launching; creating a generous foreshore walk that preserves existing fabric and anticipates sea level rise; providing terrestrial habitat; building on-site stormwater treatment; restoring and adapting a foreshore heritage villa and a nineteenth century grandstand. It has also provided passive recreation, a skate park, playgrounds, barbecue facilities and picnic shelters.

The presentation of a coastal edge is a reflection of a repair project required in many of the urban and post industrial sites in Australia. Sydney Harbour foreshore has suffered privatisation, industrialisation and reclamation for over 200 years. This new and dynamic edge mitigates the negative effects of this history, to reconnect to a broader landscape and systems.

Through The Forsehore Walk in particular, many sites are regenerated, ranging from the micro scale of sites such as small areas of tidal inundation that have allowed salt marsh to flourish, to the macro scale of the precinct with its streets, buildings and infrastructure. Various ecosystems, stormwater infrastructure and circulation networks were patched, repaired, infilled and reconnected – largely through built fabric of the extended area. Flooding issues were contained and turned into habitat opportunity, soils were remediated, walls were repaired, cliffs stabilised, contamination capped and contained.

Water stairs were introduced where sand naturally accumulates, walls deflect to make way for existing trees, resting spots and material variations are located where the sea wall changes direction, construction technique or form. The existing site materiality that has built up over time is kept with new layers added allowing the historical stratification to remain. Paths' orientations, junctions and changes in direction are designed to draw attention to the rich variety of micro detail, whether sandstone rock shelves below the high tide mark, remnants of industrial concrete,

or the cliff and its repair. Where a new seawall was required and there was no option but to use a vertical wall, the precast units were designed with shelves and recesses to trap water between tides to encourage colonisation. Providing the only artificial mangrove environment in Sydney Harbour, the project builds and restores marine intertidal and terrestrial habitat to connect with larger systems including harbour and foreshore areas, riparian zones and sea level change. Plants are grown from local seeds in the community nursery connecting at the social scale and at the Sydney Basin Flora scale ensuring genetic diversity. Stormwater at the catchment level was addressed through a variety of measures to clean water and control flood paths whilst generating public space.

Mature fig trees were lifted from toxic soils and replanted, site excavated sandstone made soils for autochthonous species grown by the community nursery, shallow gradients were reintroduced to the intertidal zones to build habitats. New sea stairs provide access to previously inaccessible small beaches. A new beach was built that allows small boat and canoe launching bringing back a diversity of craft to a harbour dominated by large motorboats. Industrial heritage was repaired and valued, storm water was cleaned by the use of rain gardens, and terrestrial habitats were repaired by the introduction of shrub layers to allow for small birds, animals and plants.

The project connects physically to the broad scale site outside the boundary including various areas and ecosystems: Sydney Harbour and its ecology, tidal range, mud flats, mangroves and foreshore; the freshwater system of Johnstons Creek and the urban stormwater infrastructure with its nineteenth century canalisation; the terrestrial ecology of sandstone and clay with its endemic species and small birds; the nineteenth century industrial landscape and urban form of Glebe and Annandale suburbs; and the surrounding open space network of recreational demand and social interaction.

The project provides paths, cycle routes and hitherto missing connections to streets encouraging walking to promote health and well-being, creating a diversity of transport options and allowing the system to operate more legibly. At an urban scale this project responds to the increased need for connectivity between open space and the urban fabric.

1

2

1   Section A-H, left to right.
2   Territorial plan.
3   Site plan.
4   Detail plan, mangrove.

3

A

B

D E

C

F

G

H

4

0   10

Glebe4: The Foreshore Walk

1

2

Repair

Photograph, Peter Casamento.

Ngarara Place is a significant addition to the cultural and campus life of RMIT University in Melbourne, Victoria. In recognition of the oldest continuing culture in the world, a newly conceived landscape/urban design/public art intervention has been incorporated adjacent to the key cross access (of Chemistry Lane) within the heart of RMIT's city campus, onto existing ground and facades.

This project by Greenaway Architects (Jefa Greenaway, Wailwan | Gamilaraay) stemmed from the University's Indigenous Unit, the Ngarara Willim Centre,[1] to build a visible presence and recognition of Aboriginal and Torres Strait Islander peoples, cultures and histories as connected among the lands of the Kulin Nation in which RMIT stands, with particular deference to the cultural continuity of the custodians of the land especially the Wurundjeri and the Boon Wurrung.

The project draws on four key pillars, which anchor the design narrative embedded in the scheme, being: Connection to Country,[2] Cultural Motifs, Contemporary Aboriginal Art and Knowledge Exchange.

Connection to Country, the initial starting point, reinforces the importance of Aboriginal people's connection to Country. This notion was woven through as exploration of the six/seven seasons of the Kulin Nation, drawing on deep history, Aboriginal knowledge systems and sense of cultural continuity. Consequently this aspect saw the division of the design into seven sections, being six on the ground plane and one in the vertical dimension (to an adjacent glazed facade). The demarcation of the ground plane enabled distinct zones for tiered planting, an area for traditional dance/ceremonial practice, amphitheatre seating and a primary focal point being a smoke pit.

These spaces aim to repair through cultural reclamation, Indigenous pride and building visibility of Indigenous art and culture within our cities. The landscape reinforces and reveals layers of history and meaning, while infusing Indigenous sensibilities within the heart of the city of Melbourne and begins to broaden the frame of reference in which people can connect to place.

A pivotal element, Cultural Motifs, was to infuse cultural motifs which pick up on Indigenous cultural and artistic practices specific to the South East of Australia, namely traditional carving practices (references to Dendroglyphs – carved trees) as well as body paint, through an etched paving graphic which doubles as the primary access points in the courtyard space, as well a considered strategy to engage Indigenous practitioners/creatives throughout the design process (led by an Aboriginal architect, along with an artist and landscape designer).

Knowledge Exchange involved the use of endemic planting design by Charles Solomon (Gubbi Gubbi and Monero/Ngarigo) to communicate the importance of landscape in sustaining life and cultural practice, including specimens traditionally used for edible, medicinal and practical purposes (such as for weaving). Pedagogical panels engage the public by providing a cultural context of interpretation as a means for cultural exchange.

The space importantly acts as a place of pause or contemplation within a busy University, counteracted by an intimately scaled landscape setting. An existing staircase connected to the adjacent Alumni Courtyard (within the Old Melbourne Gaol precinct) provided an opportunity to amplify a sense of enclosure through the completion of an amphitheatre, designed to observe culture rituals (such as traditional smoking ceremony at the start of the academic year) – elders are privileged with custom designed seating.

The most visible gesture signifies the power of art in the public realm, being a contemporary and specifically curated piece of artwork by Aboriginal digital artist Aroha Groves (Weiwan | Gomeroi). The piece evokes nature, place, time and connections to Country and acts as a backdrop that reinforces the landscape setting in which it is located. One is encouraged to understand the significance/deep history that the seasons have played in Indigenous culture for millennia. The communication design reinforces Indigenous knowledge's value, validated by Western scientific knowledge which demonstrates the level of sophistication, understanding, and land stewardship that has sustained Aboriginal peoples on this hostile continent for thousands of generations.

(1) "Ngarara Willim means 'gathering place' in the language of the Wurundjeri". See RMIT University, n.d., *Aboriginal and Torres Strait Islander students*, RMIT University, viewed 20 February 2018, <https://www.rmit.edu.au/students/support-and-facilities/student-support/aboriginal-and-torres-strait-islander-students>.
(2) "In Aboriginal English, a person's land, sea, sky, rivers, sites, seasons, plants and animals; place of heritage, belonging and spirituality; is called 'Country'." See Australian Museum, 2017, *Glossary of Indigenous Australia terms*, Australian Museum, viewed 24 February 2018, <https://australianmuseum.net.au/glossary-indigenous-australia-terms>.

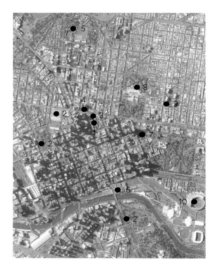

Melbourne centre,
1. Ngarara Place, RMIT University 2. Aboriginal remains
3. Tunnerminnerwait/Maulboyheener marker 4. Barak building
5. Pre-colonial landscape 6. Koorie Heritage Trust
7. Pastor Doug + Lady Nichols Memorial 8. Bunjilaka
9. The Black Mile 10. Kulin Nation gathering place.
Source, Jefa Greenaway Architects.

1

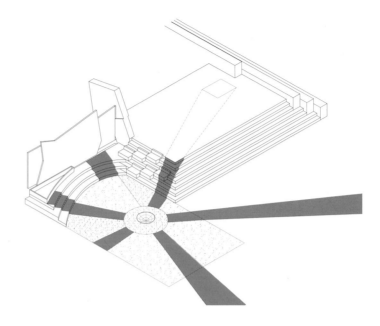

2

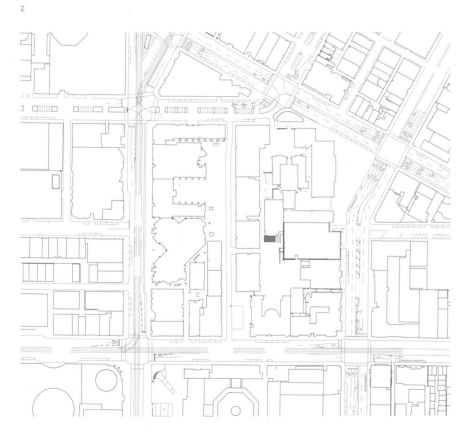

3

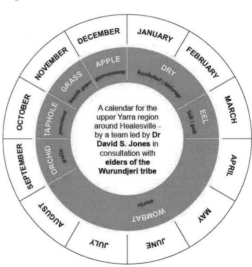

A calendar for the upper Yarra region around Healesville - by a team led by **Dr David S. Jones** in consultation with **elders of the Wurundjeri tribe**

4

5

1   Axonometric view.
2   Territorial plan.
3   Seasons of the Kulin Nation,
     as displayed on site.
4   Elevation.
5   Plan.

0   10

1   Photograph, Jefa Greenaway
    Architects.
2   *Ground*. Photograph, Linda Tegg.
3   Photograph, Peter Casamento.
4   (Overpage)
    Photograph, RMIT University.

1

2

Ngarara Place, RMIT University

Flooded ground plane.
Image, Kerstin Thompson
Architects.

The aim of this competition proposal for Shepparton Art Museum (SAM), a regional art gallery, was to create a cultural, civic and environmental heart for the township of Shepparton, as a means to forge links within an extremely diverse and multicultural community. Situated within a park setting, subject to flooding, in what would have once been a natural floodplain, the design of the building and landscape celebrate and integrate with the broader riverland ecosystem of the Goulburn River, allowing the flooding to occur as part of the site response.

Rather than stack the various functions over several levels, the proposal consolidated the bulk of the program (galleries, administration and auditorium) to the first floor – spreading it across the site to create a substantial canopy. The shelter protects from extremes of local weather, particularly in summer months – yielding a greater area of high-quality civic space. A small ground footprint was required to minimise impeding the flow of the floodwater. A suite of mini buildings incorporate functional spaces. More broadly, the ground plane is figured as a free democratic and accessible space for everyday enjoyment – both day and night – considering incidental use, pedestrian crossover and bicycle flow, connected to the larger urban fabric.

There are two aspects to a theme of continuous context that are central to the design response. The first relates to buildings as part of their greater composite; the second refers to ecosystem integrity. Both acknowledge the interconnectivity and interdependence of architecture and landscape within context and site. This particularly relates to flood sensitive landscapes, which are dynamic and know no boundaries. SAM begins with extending the concept of site, thus its sphere of influence is not limited to the site boundary. Within Victoria Park, it is part of a much greater continuum, embedded within Goulburn Valley basin – one of the largest irrigation systems in Australia. Therefore, the ground plane, landscape and building are imagined as being integral to, and part of, the river ecosystem.

By undertaking a transdisciplinary approach with architects, landscape architects, structural and environmental engineers at the generative stages, an integrated design concept was developed that accounted for all aspects of the facility to work together in productive ways. Driven by the overarching intent to 'go with the flow', indigenous native plantings, ground-plane spatial arrangement (considering climatic and seasonal variation), and water collection/filtration, work with the natural dynamics of the broader riverland ecosystem. A degraded parkland setting is thus transformed for ecological and civic repair – a process which can then permeate outwards beyond the boundaries of the site.

The decision to build in certain places or not, is one we need to make as a society. The opportunity on this site adjacent a waterway was to actually repair the site, rather than a case of working on a sensitive site that had not been degraded.

At the smallest scale, the proposal encompasses the use of planting endemic to the region to meet the performative and experiential design intents. The distinctive textures, colours and resilience of these local plantings foster an appreciation of how each individual species is somehow instrumental within the giant riverland ecology of the Goulburn. The edge of the upper building forms a curved envelope to define adjacent territories, each celebrating particular aspects of the site. These include: the north play area parkland; the west river/lake landscape; the south entry forecourt and the east highway landscape. In this way, the building envelope is less about object-making and more about public realm formation, definition and quality.

By conceptualising SAM's site from an ecological perspective, the extent of the site is necessarily expanded and unable to be quarantined by the Goulburn River ecology. This expands the project's sphere of spatial and ecological consequence, and therefore, its responsibility. At the macro scale, the building and its immediate landscape feed into adjacent wetlands of Victoria Park which turn into the natural system of Goulburn River. All scales are thus interconnected and mutually dependent for their health and resilience.

1   Site section.
2   Territorial plan.
3   Site plan.
4   First floor plan.
5   Roof plan.
6   Ground plan.

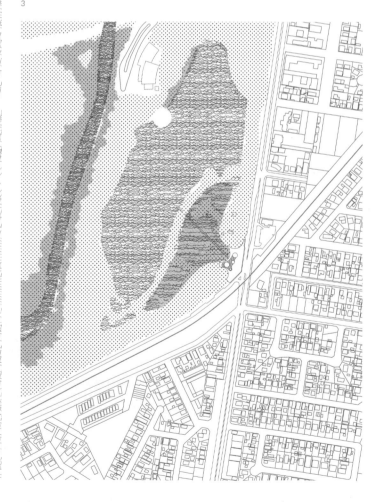

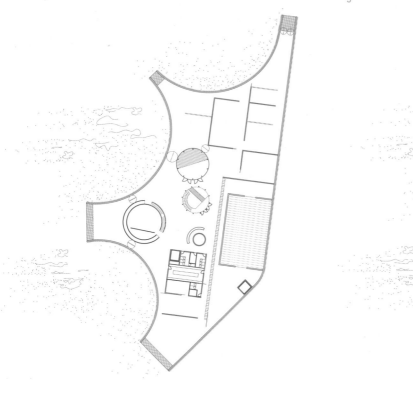
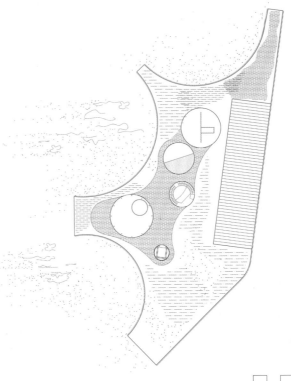

0   10

Shepparton Art Museum

1   Approach from river.
    Image, Kerstin Thompson
    Architects.
2   Unflooded ground plane.
    Image, Kerstin Thompson
    Architects.
3   Aerial photograph of
    Shepparton and the Goulburn
    River. Imagery ©2018 CNES /
    Airbus, DigitalGlobe, Landsat
    / Copernicus, Map data ©2018
    Google.

2

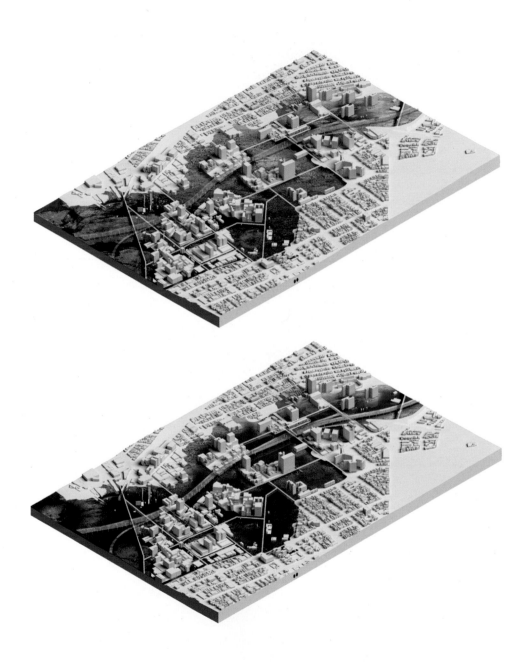

Unflooded, flooded.
Image, Monash University Urban Laboratory.

This architectural/landscape vision is for the regeneration of the low-lying, post-industrial Arden Macaulay precinct in Melbourne. Referencing the hybridity of other altered lowlands, this vision imagines a future where dynamic natural and human-made environments coexist in a dense urban setting. Along the widened floodplain of Moonee Ponds Creek, braided watercourses and wetlands spread between artificially raised islands. New live-work buildings cluster around twentieth century remnants of walled gardens and deep flood-retention ponds, created from fill that raised the islands and that now collect and store water. The islands are connected by various modes of transit and knitted into the larger CBD precinct by high and low bridges that sit above the old road networks. Further upstream, the natural chain of ponds formation is nurtured back into existence, with the channelised drain broken down and meanders reinstated to slow down the velocity of floodwaters.

Downstream, towards the swampy lagoon, a series of dams separate the saltwater from fresh, allowing saltmarsh to establish itself in brackish ponds, with freshwater marshes overflowing into them in times of flood. Around these ponds, residents and workers thrive in an urban setting, centred on the creek valley, where previously the levee-banked waterway was excluded as a boundary limit.

The greater site of this project is the Victorian Southern Lowlands, a physiographic region south of the Great Dividing Range, which includes significant previously swampy sites, in both urbanised and rural areas. The specific sites of regional landscape intervention and repair documented and collected to inform the Arden Macaulay design are Lake Condah, Winton Wetlands, Macleod Morass and Gooseneck Swamp, all of which are small 'acupuncture-like' infrastructural modifications. The specific foci of urban intervention and repair designed for Arden Macaulay is at the edge of West Melbourne Swamp and its extension into the 'Melbourne Lowlands', a region of previous marshy, estuarine intermittently wet space at the mouth of the Yarra/Maribyrnong delta. This area is prone to intensified flooding and is threatened by sea level rise, as the 'deep structure' of the underlying city reasserts itself through pressures of climate dynamics and urbanisation of the upper Moonee Ponds Creek Catchment. All reference sites were visited and examined by the project research team together with Architecture students at Monash University, an important shift in Architectural education that is seeking to more genuinely learn about and from the natural environment.

The period of modernity (c1850-1960) coincided with the growth of colonial settlement, and oversaw the systematic re-engineering and eradication of naturally intermittent waterscapes across Victoria. Substantial areas of low-lying land were either drained to become dry, or flooded to become more satisfactorily wet, through extensive and ambitious engineering schemes such as the drainage of the 'great' Koo-Wee-Rup Swamp and the Wimmera-Mallee irrigation channel system. In this process, innumerable swamps, bogs, marshes and morasses were eradicated, creeks channelised or piped, drains dug and wetlands filled in or flooded to create space and water supply services for agriculture and urbanisation. The natural cycles of intermittently wet and dry ground so vital for native habitat were coerced into a more acceptably stable and 'productive' state. Fear and mistrust of swamps runs deep in western culture but for Indigenous people these same spaces served as important socio-cultural gathering places and sources of abundant food.

Learning from the repair of other reclaimed wetlands, this project puts in place a series of strategies to regenerate Arden Macaulay, a site that was once a swamp and chain of ponds. Its longer-term Indigenous history was a place of meeting, of exchange, of abundance. Its shorter-term history is one of western industrialisation, where polluted swamps and broken waterways were eradicated or channelised for economic gain. This proposal restores some of the inherent ecological and cultural values of Arden Macaulay, while also celebrating its industrial heritage in a form that is relevant to today. By allowing water to again flow through the site and creating a flourishing wetland habitat with islands that growing numbers of people can occupy, Arden Macaulay's natural and built environments become resilient and adaptable to future climate change dynamics and aim to also support the health of less modified other environments over large scales.

This project would provide new (re-established) habitat for migratory birds, plant species and increased biodiversity, grasslands, saltmarsh, freshwater marsh plants, animals and insects, native fish, worms and eels. It would also enable gradation and separation of water environments from salty to fresh, allowing subtly different micro ecologies and plant communities to establish.

Through this approach, new urban frameworks and building typologies can evolve over time to work more consciously in tandem with underlying natural structures while also, through a novel ecosystem, support those less modified further afield.

Site visit, Condah, Victoria.
Photograph, Monash University Urban Laboratory.

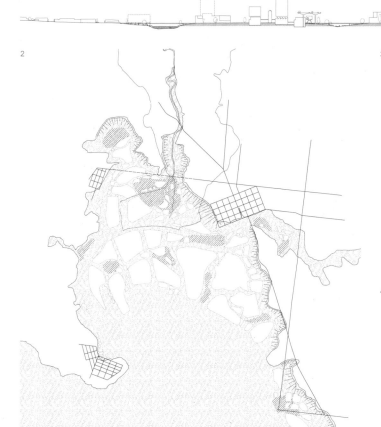

1

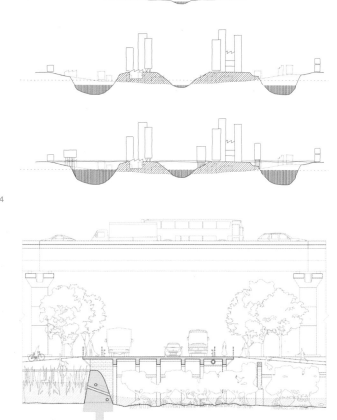

2

3

4

1 Section through valley
  with islands.
2 Territorial plan, Melbourne
  lowlands: island city.
3 Top, valley at risk of
  flooding; middle, cut + fill;
  bottom, connecting dense
  islands.
4 Detail of dam.
5 9-12m rise, 1/100 year
  flood. Water and the damage
  caused by flooding will
  eventually impact most of
  Arden Macaulay. Its low lying
  nature places both existing
  and future properties
  at risk.

6 Islands prioritise existing
  ownership. By raising up
  existing areas of dense land
  ownership, property value
  will be preserved. Whilst not
  all properties will be placed
  on islands, existing and new
  buildings will be adapted to
  inhabit the wetland land.
7 Braided water catchment.
8 Five minute island cities.
9 Plan of Arden Macaulay
  Island City.

0   10

5

6

7

8

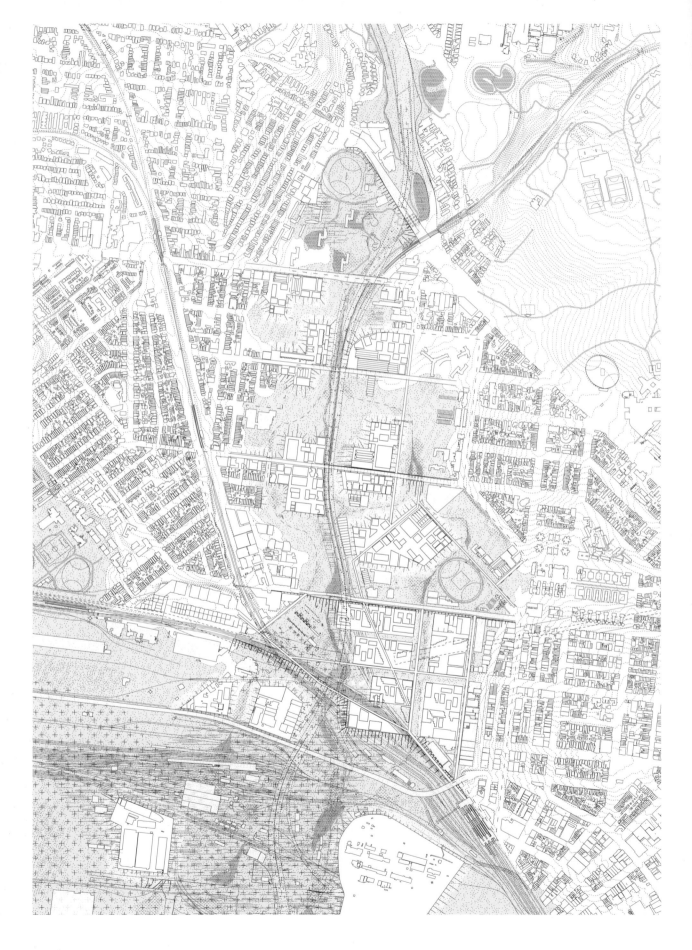

Arden Macaulay Island City

1   View from chain of ponds/new
    public realm to high density
    island.
2   View within the valley.
3   Clockwise, site research at
    Kooweerup, Kooweerup, Arden,
    Terangpom, Mokoan and
    Deep Creek. Images, Monash
    University Urban Laboratory.

1

2

Repair

Photograph, Christopher Frederick Jones.

With the death of the nationally heritage listed Tree of Knowledge,(1) Barcaldine sought advice on reparations for the site and a memorial. Prior to considering any built form, the architects encouraged the local council to rethink the project as an opportunity to strengthen the character of the place and connect this idea to the repair, retention of, and connections to, the town's broader historical assets.

Barcaldine, central to its region, also sits close to the geographical centre of Queensland. Built adjacent to the railway line which precedes it, the town is unique in that its main street is one sided while the other side is a loose collection of buildings within a rail reserve. The region, originally reliant on the wool industry for its livelihood, now relies on tourism.

Where nearby outback towns like Longreach have lost much of their heritage buildings, the town's character and significant (heritage) places are being repaired, protected, and reinstated through this project.

A masterplan was developed connecting the town's unique streetscape with the tree and the restoration and adaptive reuse of the old Globe Hotel. The initial project re-established the original plaza around the Tree of Knowledge as a public space and gateway. The proposed masterplan relocated the information centre and removed carparking immediately adjacent the Tree. The Globe, a building located for more than 100 years at the major crossroads of national highways both south-north and east-west, was saved from demolition. Its expressed timber frame, single skin timber infill, its floors and ceilings have been renovated and the verandahs replaced. The verandah space, which creates a shared threshold of private and public, are part of the street quality, deconstructing the building object in the streetscape into occupied and activated space.

The effect of these small urban interventions ensure that visitors interact with commercial businesses and the towns heritage walk in ways that the previous planning did not enable. The second major project, resulting from this overarching thinking, consists in the arrangement of the information centre, local heritage room, bank tenancy and art gallery into the old Globe Hotel. The relocation of all these programs, and related spaces, into the existing historical building has not only 'repaired' it, but also enhanced the town's unique character.

The treatment of the new thresholds and facades create a new layer in this town, where this building becomes a generous lantern, spilling light through its polycarbonate facade into the public realm.

At the scale of the town these projects take on important civic roles as gateways, public plazas, signposts and public scaled lanterns (The Globe). They are pragmatic community focussed buildings as well as ones of national and local heritage. The effect of the work also includes an improved economy based on tourism that has also seen the broader repair of the streetscape by private owners. The project strengthens the relationship and connections between the town and its people, its visitors, and the Tree.

(1) "The Tree of Knowledge site, located in the centre of Barcaldine in central west Queensland, marks the first significant labour struggle in Australia's history. The 10 metre tall Ghost Gum was used as the meeting place for shearers during their unsuccessful 1981 strike…In April 2006 the Tree of Knowledge was poisoned and did not recover. It was felled on 29 July 2007, and a memorial was opened at the site in 2009". See Australian Government, Department of the Environment and Energy n.d., *National Heritage Places - The Tree of Knowledge*, Australian Government, Department of the Environment and Energy, viewed 23 February 2018, <http://www.environment.gov.au/heritage/places/national/tree>.

Ground.
Photograph, Linda Tegg.

1

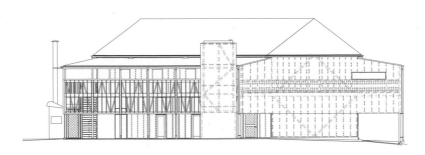

2

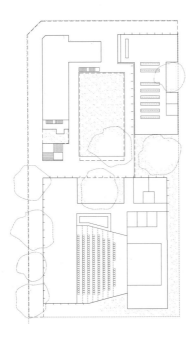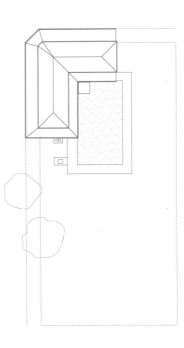

3

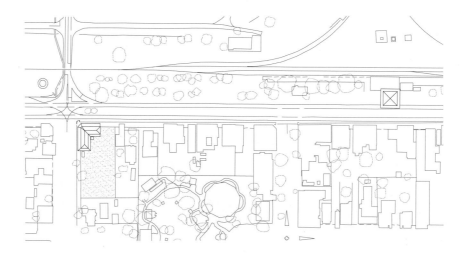

1   East elevation.
2   Master plan,
    site and roof plan.
3   Context plan.
4   Clockwise elevations south,
    north, west, and section.
5   Ground and first floor plan.

4

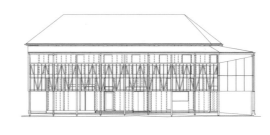

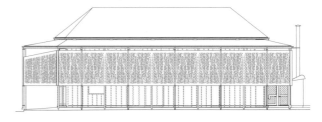

5

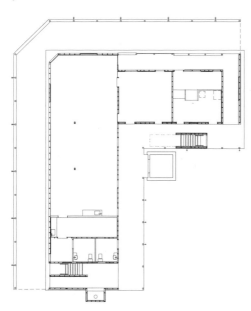

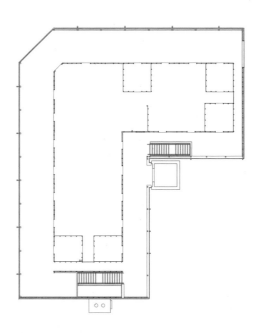

0   10

1-3 *Ground.*
    Photographs, Linda Tegg.
4   (Overpage) View from Globe
    first floor verandah with the
    Tree of Knowledge memorial
    in the distance. Photograph,
    Christopher Frederick Jones.

1

2

3

PRINCE ALFRED PARK AND POOL UPGRADE

NEESON MURCUTT ARCHITECTS WITH SUE BARNSLEY DESIGN LANDSCAPE ARCHITECTURE

Ground.
Video still, Linda Tegg.

Located at the edge of central Sydney, the project was part of the reinvigoration plan of an underutilised area of 7.5 hectares in Prince Alfred Park – it contributed to this by upgrading the public pool and addressing its relationship to the park and street. The overriding design principle preferences landscape over built form to activate and make public open space in all its interfaces, rather than to produce a building 'in' a park.

The old 1950s pool building was removed from the middle of the park, and the existing pool was renovated. This visually and physically opens up the park creating a new spatial quality and enabling a more vital ecology that connects the pool curtilage to the wider park, bounding streets, and local waterways. The site belongs to a series of urban systems – a collection of public open spaces, public pools and different recreational typologies including playgrounds, pedestrian and cycle pathways, and sport infrastructures. It sits within a greater water catchment that extends up to Surry Hills and Redfern, and down to Blackwattle Bay – the site of The Foreshore Walk project in Glebe included in this catalogue/book. Site-wide stormwater management was redefined with capture from the upper catchment for irrigation of the adjacent playing field and pool lawns, while bio-retention swales filter and cleanse the reduced flows to the harbour. New trees and an extensive understorey landscape have recalibrated the experience and sustainability of the park, the layered strata protecting mature trees from compaction and providing habitat. It is a sectional site – with canopy, ground plane and an important subterranean dimension.

The new 1,000 square metre pool building is conceived as a 'folded ground plane' with a green roof of native 'meadow'(1) grasses that connect to the surrounding park and the memory of both the former landscape and Cleveland Paddocks. In the spatial urban realm, the green roof is more a street infrastructure, or an extension of the ground plane and park, than a roof, and it is only once one enters the pool that its role as a roof is revealed: a 2,320 square metre biotic surface topped with 35,917 plants, continually transpiring, oxygenating, cooling and humidifying the site, sequestering carbon and insulating the rooms below, as well as an urban habitat for birds and insects.

The roof 'meadow' creates biodiversity with five varieties of indigenous wildflowers and grasses including kidney weed (*Dichondra repens*), short-hair plume grass (*Dichelachne micrantha*), lavender grass (*Eragrostis elongata*), common tussock grass (*Poa labillardieri*), and bluebells (*Wahlenbergia spp*) – a small grassland herb first seen when the lawn was left unmown around the old pool. To ensure the long-term viability of this constructed landscape a soil scientist designed a lightweight growing mix for these conditions and a grassland specialist supervised installation of the plants.(2)

The building, 6 metre deep x 120 metre long, is intimate yet monumental, scaled to both the swimmer and the city.

Two shaped landscape mounds made from contaminated fill, define the outdoor pool enclosure, simultaneously connecting and separating park and pool, while a ribbon-like fence secures the site, slipping across the topography to come in and out of view.

The landscape roof conceals the presence of Chalmers Street with its busy traffic from the actual pool, while also creating a generous streetscape to the pedestrian. The roof and grassy mounds soundproof the pool from the road, park and railway, and buffer winds, giving it an otherworldly atmosphere.

This project has positively impacted on social sustainability, local community and well-being. Prince Alfred Park was underutilised and perceived as dangerous, with a degree of criminal activity – a place to be avoided. It is now a popular, accessible, and safe year-round destination that also improves access to Central Station not only from the surrounding suburbs but also from the growth areas south of the city.

(1)   For a discussion on the use of the term 'meadow' in relation to this project see Whitworth, D 2017, 'Do Not Mow: planting a subtle argument', *Landscape Australia*, 12 October, viewed 15 October 2017, <https://landscapeaustralia.com/articles/do-not-mow-planting-a-subtle-argument/>.
(2)   The soil scientist was SESL and the grassland specialist was Australian Wetlands Consulting.

The pool prior to the upgrade.
Photograph, Brett Boardman.

1

2

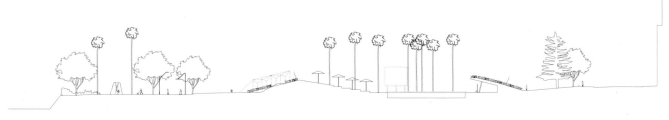

3

4

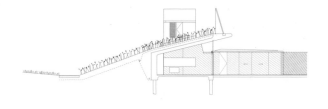

5

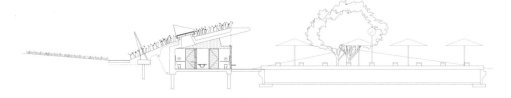

6

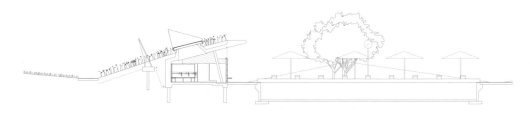

7

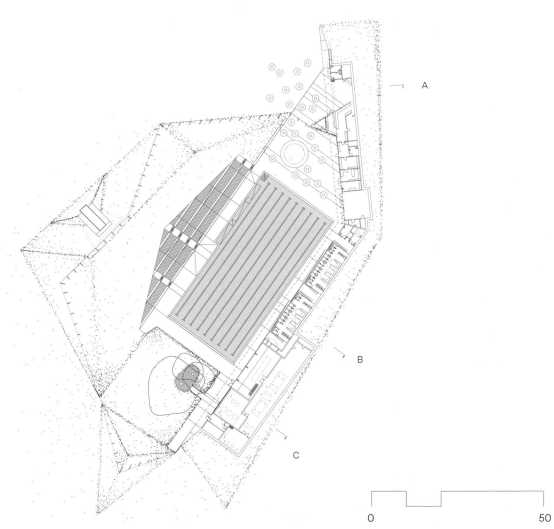

A

B

C

0   50

1   Photograph, Brett Boardman.
2   View from street.
     Photograph, © Erieta Attali.
3   *Ground*.
     Photograph, Linda Tegg.
4   (Overpage)
     Photograph, Brett Boardman.

1

2

Repair

KULLURK/COOLART: SOMERS FARM AND WETLANDS

NMBW ARCHITECTURE STUDIO WITH WILLIAM GOODSIR AND RMIT ARCHITECTURE

Outbuilding. Photograph, Lucinda McLean.

The various built and open spaces constitutive of this project – an existing house, a new outbuilding containing an external room and sleeping areas, new wetlands and bird hide – sit within the area of Kullurk,(1) which was the local Indigenous Bunurong peoples' own choice in 1840 for a reserve of land for their imagined future. A permanent water source is located there and early maps show that aboriginal routes cross through the area. Unfortunately, this wish was not granted. The various project's interventions are spread out through a property of 100 acres that faces the Westernport coastal reserve and is connected to the Coolart Wetlands and Homestead as a result of a subdivision of the larger Coolart estate on the south eastern coast of Victoria just outside metropolitan Melbourne.

The project is an ongoing making of architecture, wetlands and regenerative farming, a nexus of natural systems and human movement adjacent to an intermittently closed and open lake lagoon.

Initially, when the project commenced, the property was a grazed farm and house paddocks with two dams. Now, seventeen acres of regenerating wetland is working in conjunction with the farmland and larger environment. In the standard sense of the architect's commission, the project started as a conventional house addition, however, from the beginning it was understood that the project was more: the outdoor room which makes up half of the footprint of the new outbuilding is a space along a landscape path. Ten years later, a separate 2x2 metre bird hide structure was built in the regenerating wetlands, a 'design-make' project with RMIT Architecture students in collaboration with William Goodsir. This is a process that broadens the reach of this project to an educational setting and the knowledge base of future practitioners.

The project reinstates the changing and temporal qualities of swampland, an in-between condition, not solid, not liquid. Like a lot of the low-lying land around Westernport this land was channelised and drained to increase the extent of solid land that could be farmed. The pre-colonial conditions are not really known and even to attempt to replace them to its previous exact condition is to misunderstand this dynamic landscape as only one point in time. Instead, the landscape is 'repaired' by catalysing the context for repair through the stewardship of the site, and physically patching certain conditions to invite life in: by altering the ground contours from the narrow channel to broaden the movement and temporality of water and by 'not doing' as much as 'doing'. For example, by allowing certain areas to retain water and connect to wetlands, dormant and translocated seed could germinate. After some years the owners noticed many 'self-sown' plants including Coastal Beard Heath (*Leucopogon parviflorus*) – this plant is extremely difficult to propagate as it needs to pass through the digestive system of birds.

There is now a chain of temporal water bodies linked to the permanent water body that supports this landscape to function as a part of and connected to, the wider, less disturbed one.

The physical repair on this site is landscape based, where the architecture creates an occupation of the site that enables a close stewardship and points to the role of the private landowner. This strategy could also be described as catalytic. At the same time there has been consideration of this landscape and system repair in the decisions made around the outbuilding and bird hide. The new architectural structures work to create conditions for movement and intimacy through the siting of structure, seats, and shelves.

The bird hide embodies much of the project's intentions. Designing a bird hide is a negotiation between human movement and bird systems. The siting of the hide is considered in relation to the macro scale of the bird and wind systems, with strong consideration to the flyways of migrating birds that arrive at this site. It is constructed using a minimal structure, so that noise and disruption are reduced while being built. Landscape here is not a broad panorama to be consumed as experienced in much contemporary coastal architecture. Rather, it is an intimate experience of being embedded within, with the rare experience of one's existence being minimised in deference to what is being observed. The siting of a structure separate from the house creates a path of movement. The bird hide is a platform for stillness along the path, a place to be still, to be quiet, waiting to hear, to observe. The seats of the bird hide are configured to allow for people to face outwards, or face inwards together.

How we engage with the natural environment changes how we value it.

(1) "Kullurk/Kulluck/Kulluk/Kullurt/Callert/Colourt/Collert/Coollourt/ Coolurt/Coolart", shortened to "Kullurk/Coolart", is a collection of names from Hansel Fels, M 2011, 'I succeeded Once': The Aboriginal Protectorate on the Mornington Peninsula, 1839-1840, ANU Press, Canberra, ACT, Australia, p. 223.

Historic map of extent of wetlands pre European settlement Dashed red line: Indigenous Boonwurrung routes, dashed black line: indicative migratory bird flyways. Gaughwin, D & Sullivan, H, 1984, 'Aboriginal Boundaries and Movement in Western Port, Victoria', *Aboriginal History*, vol. 8, pp. 80-98 (Map p. 90), <https://search.informit.com.au/ documentSummary;dn=055016885148495;res=IELIND>.

1

2

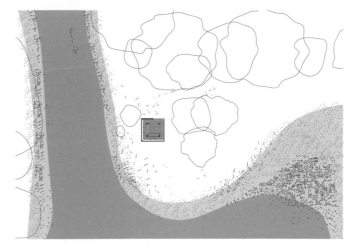

5

bay   primary dune   intermittent closed and open lake lagoon   secondary dune

6

<u>Image Captions</u>
1   Bird hide section.
2   Bird hide plan.
3   Outbuilding section.
4   Outbuilding plan.
5   Coastal edge and farm
     section.
6   Context plan, original
     Coolart estate (outer
     red line), property
     boundary (inner red line).
7   Site plan.

<u>Plan Key</u>
1   Outbuilding.
2   Bird hide.
3   Coolart Wetlands and
     Homestead.
4   Permanent water body.
5   Wetlands.
6   Ways.

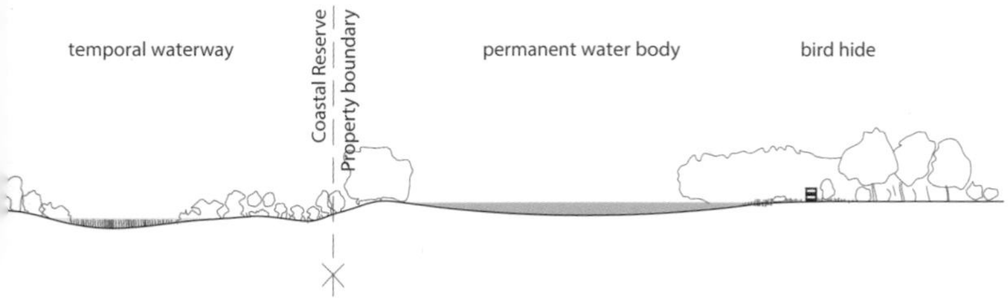

temporal waterway   Coastal Reserve   Property boundary   permanent water body   bird hide   wetland   dam   outbuilding

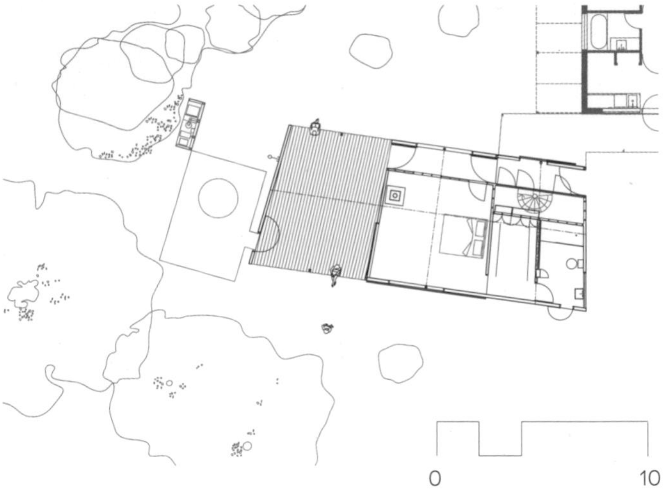

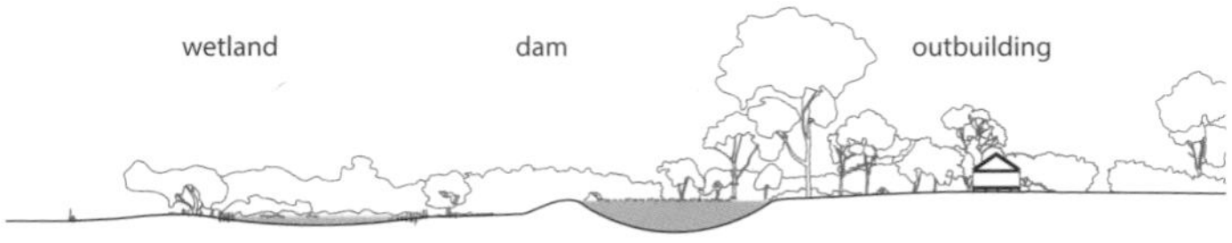

0   10

7

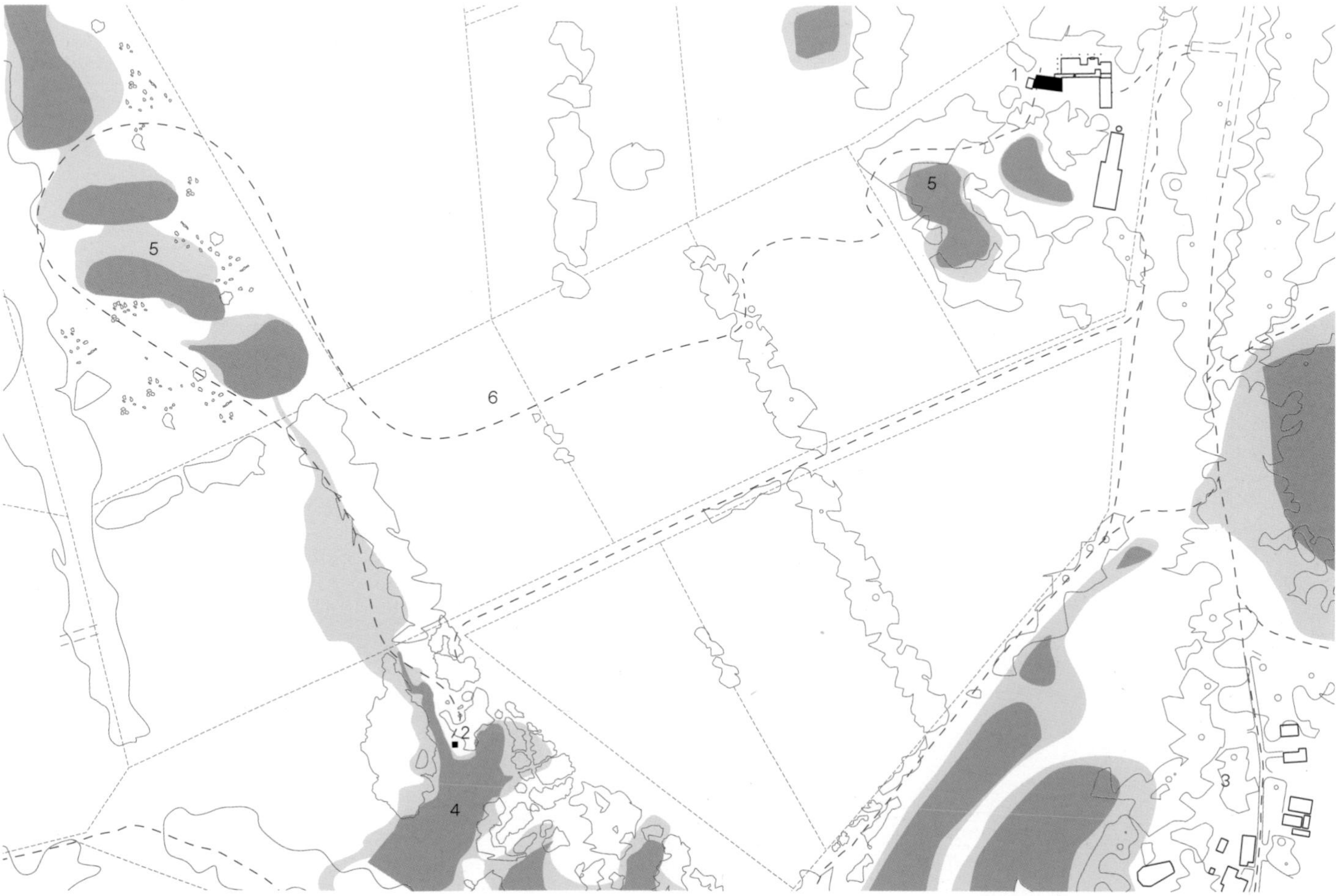

1

2

Ground.
Video still, Linda Tegg.

Designed in 1967-69 for Mary and Grant Featherston, two industrial designers, in an inner suburb north-east of Melbourne, this house is located on the threshold between the built suburban fabric and an open area of a park reserve, a creek and the green fields of a school.

This project has been included as an historical project that nonetheless is strongly contemporary in character and approach. Boyd's legacy continues in the work of contemporary Australian architects and also prompts a way forward for architecture, particularly in relationship to the landscapes they inhabit through a quality of continuous space found in his work where the buildings are spatially reliant and sympathetic to the places they occupy.(1)

The response to Mary and Grant's dream to live in 'the open' was to design a house with no individual and separate rooms. Provided, instead, with areas of inhabitation of spatial continuity, the openness of this house carries at once the character of two different conditions – that of the big industrial shed and that of the covered outdoor space. Potentially interchangeable programs are located through platforms for the studio, dining, living and bedroom areas underneath a translucent roof (originally fibreglass, now polycarbonate).

The sense of openness of covered outdoor areas, is here visibly reflected in the retention of the sloping and exposed ground plane that carries through the building. The retaining of the ground plane – both its slope and the actual soil itself – inside the house is a radical shift in how a building is conceived as part of its site. This work confidently demonstrates an approach and relationship to a site that includes it as part of the response, removing another layer of separation and moving towards a building conceived as part of a continuum rather than a discrete object.

The exposed ground inside the house connects spatially to the exterior, through the large glazed south facade, which is not a frame for 'possessing' the view, but rather a medium through which indoor and outdoor landscapes join. Platforms float above and in between the internal garden, contributing to create an unseparated space which erases any hierarchy between architectural components; ground, mezzanine, upper floors, but also architectural and landscape presences and all facades on the perimeter, including the translucent roof, coexist as interrelated parts and yet in a continuum.

The shift towards a more integrated built and open vegetated space, as well as more careful approach to siting buildings in the Australian landscape (which consists of many very diverse conditions) could be also discussed in the work of the Griffins among others and later, around the same time as the Featherston house, through the moment/generation of architects that was particularly enlightened in the seventies. This latter group were motivated by ethical and environmental considerations of the time and made careful buildings that responded to their contexts: Merchant Builders, Glenn Murcutt, Gabriel Poole, Troppo Architects and others. Internationally this trajectory was being pursued by the Smithsons, De Carlo and arguably, in their own way, through the utopian provocations of Superstudio, Archigram, Buckminster Fuller and Cedric Price among others.

Alison and Peter Smithson, empathetic references to Boyd who reviewed some of their work, suggest qualities for buildings of the 'Conglomerate Order' – qualities that not surprisingly can precisely describe this house:
"A building of the Conglomerate Order…has a capacity to absorb spontaneous additions, subtractions, technical modifications without disturbing its sense of order, indeed such changes enhance it;…has faces which are all equally considered…no back, no front, all faces are equally engaged with what lies before them; the roof is 'another face'; is an inextricable part of a larger fabric; is dominated by one material, the conglomerate's matrix;…is lumpish and has weight."(2)

(1) Boyd's inclination to 'spatial continuity' and forms of integration between built and open spaces is the focus of a book by Mauro Baracco and Louise Wright: Baracco, M & Wright, L 2017, *Robin Boyd: Spatial Continuity*, Routledge, London, UK and New York, USA.
(2) These observations were published by Alison and Peter Smithson more than twenty years after Boyd's death; see Smithson, A & P 1993, *Italian Thoughts*, Alison & Peter Smithson, London, UK (printed in Sweden), p. 62.

Circa 2005.
Photograph, Aaron Pocock.

1

2

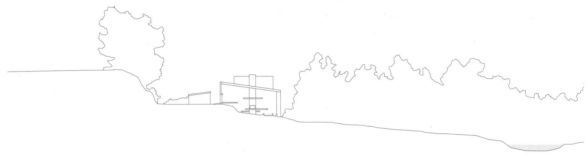

3   4

1   View from south.
2   Site section.
3   Territorial plan.
4   Site plan.
5   Section.
6   Ground floor plan.
7   Upper levels plan.

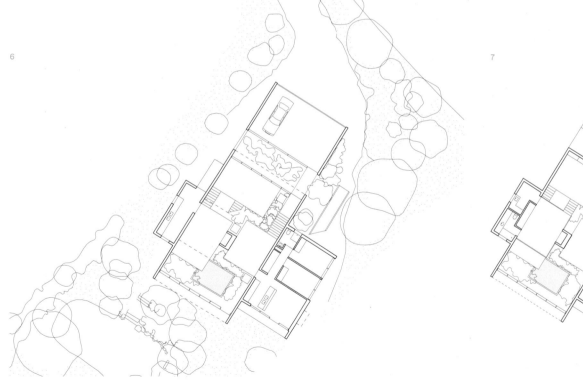

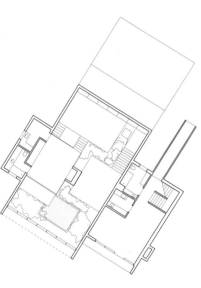

1

2

MAIN ASSEMBLING BUILDING, TONSLEY INNOVATION DISTRICT

WOODS BAGOT WITH TRIDENTE ARCHITECTS AND OXIGEN

Photograph, Sam Noonan.

The decline of the manufacturing industry in Australia could be described as an economic and social injury requiring repair.

In 1964 Chrysler opened its Australian vehicle manufacturing plant in the suburb of Tonsley (a former farm and market garden). It was the largest assembly plant in Australia, operating under one roof. In the 1980s Mitsubishi Motors purchased the site and continued to manufacture cars there until 2008. The facility became a centre for the development of manufacturing skills in South Australia.

In 2010 the site was recommissioned as an innovation district by the South Australian State Government. It was originally assumed the main assembly building would be demolished, however Woods Bagot, engaged to undertake the masterplan, identified benefits to retaining the existing structure, resulting in a compelling adaptive reuse. By retaining the existing structure the project has saved approximately 90,000 tons of carbon which is equivalent to taking 25,000 average cars off the road for one year.

Following the masterplan, Woods Bagot was the lead consultant for the MAB and Pods project in collaboration with Tridente Architects and sub consultant Oxigen for the Tonsley Park Landscape and Public Realm Design.

The main assembly building, an area of eight hectares, was stripped back to the steel structure and saw tooth roof. The extensive concrete slab, which itself reveals the history of manufacturing on the site through its many scars and markings, and the roof, unite the space. Under this roof (which also supports a 4 megawatt solar array) which is at times open to the sky above internal gardens, there are various small buildings housing a mix of programs related to clean technology development, advanced manufacturing, education and research: Sustainable Industries Education Centre (TAFE South Australia); School of Computer Science, Engineering and Mathematics of Flinders University; Siemens offices and the State Drill Core Reference Library among others.

The adaptive reuse of an old building significantly lessens waste and the consumption of new materials and land that won't need to be developed. The retention of the main assembly building allows for the social history of the car manufacturing industry of this site to be acknowledged, reinvented for new industries.

A total of 19 million tonnes of construction and demolition waste was generated in Australia in 2008-09. Of this total waste stream, 8.5 million tonnes was disposed to landfill while 10.5 million tonnes, or 55%, was recovered and recycled.(1) 8.5 million tonnes is equivalent to just under half of all household waste. Landfills dominate the waste infrastructure stock and receive some 40% of Australia's waste. They are the favoured destination for mixed waste, essentially due to the availability and capacity of existing facilities, and the moderate cost of landfilling in comparison with options to recover more resources. Australia's 1,168 operational (licensed and unlicensed) landfills receive around 20 million tonnes of waste each year,(2)

meaning that construction and demolition waste accounts for nearly half of this.

Using what we already have so as to spare land from further destruction is a critical strategy of repair.

(1) Australian Government, Department of the Environment and Energy 2011, *Construction and demolition waste status report - management of construction and demolition waste in Australia*, introduction to 2 related report documents, viewed 24 February 2018, <http://www.environment.gov.au/protection/national-waste-policy/publications/construction-and-demolition-waste-status-report>.

(2) Australian Government, Department of the Environment and Energy 2013, *Australia's waste and resource recovery infrastructure, National waste report*, introduction to the related report, viewed 24 February 2018, <http://www.environment.gov.au/protection/national-waste-policy/national-waste-reports/national-waste-report-2013/infrastructure>.

Photograph, Sam Noonan.

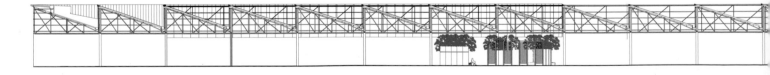

1   Territorial plan.
2   Site concept sketch.
3   Long section.
4   Detail section.

4

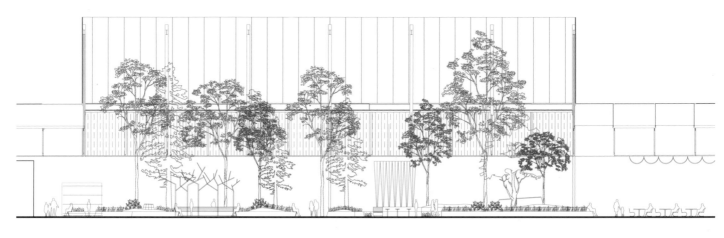

0   10

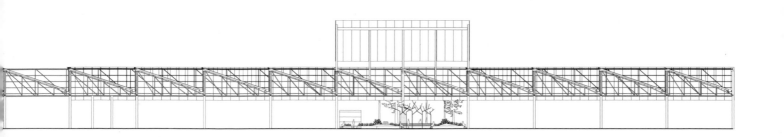

1

2

Main Assembling Building, Tonsley Innovation District

BIOGRAPHIES
AND
CREDITS

REPAIR

Australian Institute of Architects
Australian Pavilion
16th International Architecture Exhibition
of La Biennale di Venezia
Biennale Architettura 2018

Commissioner:
Janet Holmes à Court AC

Creative Directors:
Baracco+Wright Architects in
collaboration with Linda Tegg
Theme: *Repair*

Repair aims to expand the point of view
from the object of architecture, to the way
it operates in its context, advocating a role
for architecture that catalyses or actively
engages with the environmental, social and
cultural repair of the places it is a part of.

Repair is a critical strategy of
architectural culture. It is particularly
relevant to Australian architects who work
in one of the most diverse and ecologically
sensitive landscapes in the world. Our
cities are interspersed and bordered by
remnant vegetation, connected to large
natural systems as well as built over the
traditional cultural landscapes of our First
Nations peoples. They are also the scenes
of developing ecosystems at which humans
are the centre of.

The aim to present architecture from
a different point of view is behind the
decision to collaborate with artist Linda
Tegg, whose practice often presents us
with a different way of looking. Together,
Baracco+Wright Architects and Linda Tegg
have collaborated to create and install a
grassland in the pavilion, *Grasslands Repair*,
the life-sustaining light installation *Skylight*,
and the work *Ground* through which
architecture is presented through video
rather than in singular images.

CREATIVE DIRECTORS

Baracco+Wright

Mauro Baracco is a practising architect and a director of
Baracco+Wright Architects. He has a PhD in Architecture
from and is also an Associate Professor at RMIT University
in the School of Architecture and Urban Design, Melbourne,
Australia where he was the Deputy Dean of Landscape
Architecture (2013-15). Louise Wright is a practising
architect and a director of Baracco+Wright Architects.
She has a PhD in Architecture from and also is a sessional
lecturer in design at RMIT University, Melbourne, Australia.

Baracco+Wright Architects, founded in 2004, combine
the academic and practice world and are shifting more and
more towards landscape based approaches that effect and
catalyse environmental repair through decisions of siting,
ground plane, hydrology and other ecological conditions.
They have been published and awarded nationally and
internationally. Their work has been described as
quietly radical.

COLLABORATOR

Linda Tegg

Linda Tegg works with photography, performance, video,
and installation to investigate the contingent viewing
conditions through which we orient ourselves in the world.
Her work has been extensively exhibited in Australia, Mexico,
The United States, and Europe. Tegg was the Samstag
Scholar of 2014 and The Georges Mora Foundation Fellow
of 2012. Linda is currently a Lecturer in Creative Practice at
Deakin University, and the inaugural Artist In Residence at
the School of Geography at the University of Melbourne.

L-R Linda Tegg, Mauro Baracco and Louise Wright.
Photograph, Sharyn Cairns.

David Freudenberger

David has a diverse research career as an ecologist. He joined CSIRO Wildlife and Ecology in 1991 to conduct grazing management research in the rangelands of eastern Australia. By 2000, CSIRO shifted research focus from eastern rangelands to agricultural landscapes dominated by woodlands. This led him to research on the impact of landscape fragmentation on woodland bird assemblages and other taxa. In such highly cleared landscapes restoration is a priority, so he led a number of research projects on the ecosystem services derived from government supported native plantings in southern NSW. This research put him in contact with the NGO, Greening Australia, which he joined in 2007 as Chief Scientist. There his collaborative research projects included effectiveness and cost of revegetation technologies, carbon sequestration measurement and modelling, biofuels from native species, and the benefits of biochar application for improving restoration effectiveness. He joined the Fenner School at the Australian National University in Canberra in 2012 to continue his current research in applied restoration practice and lecture in management of forested landscapes.

Paul Memmott

Professor Paul Memmott is a trans-disciplinary researcher (architect/anthropologist) and the Director of the Aboriginal Environments Research Centre (AERC) and the Indigenous Design Place Initiative at the University of Queensland where he is affiliated with the School of Architecture and the Institute of Social Science Research. The AERC field of research encompasses the cross-cultural study of the people-environment relations of Indigenous peoples with their natural and built environments. Research interests encompass Aboriginal housing and settlement design, Aboriginal access to institutional architecture, Indigenous constructs of place, cultural landscapes and cultural heritage, vernacular architecture and Native Title, social planning in Indigenous communities and sustainable remote-area buildings and villages.

Catherine Murphy

Catherine Murphy is an academic in the Department of Architecture at Monash University, where she teaches in the Masters of Urban Planning and Design course. Her current research is exploring how alternative design and planning processes could address climate change impacts on cities, as part of a project for the Cooperative Research Centre for Water Sensitive Cities. She has a background in urban and cultural planning, and has worked as a program manager, curator and writer/editor.

Tim O'Loan

Tim O'Loan is an urban designer and landscape architect. Having worked for a leading practice in the United Kingdom and a large, highly innovative global architectural group, he now leads the Design Practice across Australia and New Zealand for AECOM. Tim has spent most of the past decade building a team focussed on developing forward-thinking urban policy and development strategies that underpin world-class infrastructure to enhance the environment, equity, and economy of our cities. He sees that there is an increasing need for landscape architects and urban designers to engage with social equity, access to employment, housing, food and water; this is the next frontier for city makers of all types.

Chris Sawyer and Susie Kumar

Chris Sawyer together with Susie Kumar are landscape architects and the founding directors of Site Office. Chris is an Adjunct Professor of Landscape Architecture at RMIT University. Site Office is a Melbourne based landscape architectural and urban design practice that works primarily with local government and state government organisations with the goal of crafting beautiful places for animals, plants and people to thrive. They have created and developed a number of projects that hover over and through special terrain, of traditional owners, fragmented ecologies and disturbed landscapes to aid humans' connection with nature as well as the preservation and restoration of nature.

Lance Van Maanen

Lance van Maanen is a practising architect based in Melbourne with experience across a wide range of project types in Australia. With a focus on modes of architectural representation, Lance embraces a range of three dimensional techniques to enhance an understanding of the built form and environment with a particular interest in immersive technologies that bridge the physical and immaterial worlds. Lance contributes to architectural education through teaching and critiquing as a sessional tutor at RMIT university, and has been published in various industry journals.

Jonathan Ware

Jonathan Ware is a practising architect based in Melbourne. He is also a design studio leader in the Masters programs of Landscape Architecture and Architecture at RMIT University. His work and research integrates architecture and landscape spaces which seek to heighten our experience of place, by learning from and contributing to the local ecology and built typologies of site.

CONTRIBUTORS

Giovanni Aloi

Giovanni Aloi is an art historian in modern and contemporary art. He studied History of Art and Art Practice in Milan and then moved to London in 1997 to study at Goldsmiths University where he obtained a Doctorate on the subject of natural history in contemporary art. Aloi currently teaches at the School of the Art Institute of Chicago, Sotheby's Institute of Art New York and London, and Tate Galleries. In 2007, Aloi launched *Antennae: The Journal of Nature in Visual Culture* (www.antennae.org.uk). *Speculative Taxidermy: Natural History, Animal Surfaces, and Art in the Anthropocene* was published in early 2018 by Columbia University Press. His forthcoming book titled *Why Look at Plants: The Vegetal World in Contemporary Art*, co-authored with Caroline Picard, is due later in 2018 by Brill Publishers. Aloi is the co-editor of the University of Minnesota Press series Art after Nature.

Carroll Go-Sam

Carroll Go-Sam is an Indigenous graduate in architecture and researcher in the School of Architecture, University of Queensland. She is closely affiliated with the Aboriginal Environments Research Centre (AERC, UQ) and is currently a research fellow within Indigenous Design Place (IDP), a cross-faculty strategic research initiative. Carroll was previously a recipient of an ARC Indigenous Discovery Award (2014-2016). Her research interests lay at the intersection of Indigenous themes in architecture and related fields leading to diverse works, including book chapters, conference papers, encyclopaedia entries, professional journals, online media, architectural design and written creative works.

Caroline Picard

Caroline Picard is a writer, publisher, and curator. Her writing has appeared in *Artslant*, *ArtForum* (critics picks), *Flash Art International*, and *Paper Monument*, among others. She is the Executive Director of The Green Lantern Press – a not-for-profit publishing house and art producer in operation since 2005 – and the Co-Director of Sector 2337, a hybrid artspace/bar/bookstore in Chicago. Curating exhibitions since 2005, Picard has worked with artists like Ellen Rothenberg, Edra Soto, Xaviera Simmons, and others, presenting exhibitions at La Box ENSA Bourges, Gallery 400, Vox Populi, The Hyde Park Art Center, and more. In 2014, she was the Curatorial Fellow at La Box, ENSA in France, and became a member of the SYNAPSE International Curators' Network of the Haus der Kulturen der Welt in Berlin in 2015. A recent series of exhibitions, *Ghost Nature*, *The New [New] Corpse*, and *Imperceptibly and Slowly Opening* investigate inter-species borders, how the human relates to its environment and what possibilities might emerge from upturning an anthropocentric view. Publications regularly accompany these shows, instrumentalising the book format as an alternative method to disseminate and refract ephemeral exhibitions. During her tenure as Publisher and Editor of The GLP she has released over forty books featuring writing by Magalie Guérin, Graham Harman, Roberto Harrison, Hannah B Higgins, Timothy Morton, Jamila Woods, and others.

Carolyn Young

Carolyn Young is an artist who lives in New South Wales, Australia. She uses photography to rethink and reimagine the human place in nature. Through her art practice, Carolyn aims to build connections between culture and nature by drawing on the knowledge of nature stewards, and sharing these stories with the public. Carolyn has a PhD in visual arts, an Honours degree in Natural Resources, and previously worked in the environmental sciences. Her art practice often involves collaborating with ecologists. Carolyn is currently the Creative Arts Fellow at the National Library of Australia. She is researching the work of nineteenth century naturalists, including John Gould's *The Mammals of Australia*, to make new art focussing on endangered mammals in Australian grassy woodlands.

INTERVIEWEES

Ryan Moroney

Ryan Moroney is a practising architect, senior consultant at CoDesign Studio and project coordinator at Architects Without Frontiers Australia. He works across neighbourhood and international development projects that aim to make social cohesion, connection to place and local craftsmanship a priority for policy, planning and the design of buildings and neighbourhoods.

Ricky Ray Ricardo

Ricky Ray Ricardo is a writer and communications manager at T.C.L.-Taylor Cullity Lethlean in Melbourne. He is a former editor of *Landscape Architecture Australia* magazine and former editorial assistant at *Topos* (Germany). In 2015 he was a co-creative director of *This Public Life*, the Festival of the Australian Institute of Landscape Architects, with Claire Martin and Cameron Bruhn.

Sarah Lynn Rees

Sarah Lynn Rees is a Palawa woman descending from the Plangermaireener people of north east Tasmania. She is a Charlie Perkins scholar with a MPhil in Architecture and Urban Design from the University of Cambridge where she produced a thesis on Indigenous housing in remote Australian communities. Sarah also holds a Bachelor of Environments (Architecture) from the University of Melbourne. Sarah has recently returned from London where she worked with Stirling Prize Winner, Will Alsop OBE RA and is currently working as a Graduate Architect at Jackson Clements Burrows Architects; Director Indigenous Architecture and Design Victoria (IADV); Associate Consultant at Greenshoot Consulting; Research Assistant at the University of Melbourne; and Regional Project Manager for MPavilion. Sarah also sits on various boards and committees including EmAGN, National Trust Landscape Reference Group and National Trust Aboriginal Advisory Committee.

COLLABORATORS ON *GROUND*

David Fox

David Fox is a designer who works across a broad range of fields. His open approach and dedication to craft makes him a valuable collaborator. Most recently he has been working with Linda Tegg and Baracco+Wright Architects on *Ground*, a series of videos that aim to rethink how architecture is seen and understood.

**GARDEN HOUSE,
WESTERNPORT,
VICTORIA, 2013.**

**BARACCO+WRIGHT
ARCHITECTS.**

Project team:
Mauro Baracco, Louise
Wright, Catherine Horwill.

–

**WAVE HILL
WALK-OFF PAVILIONS,
JINBARAK, JUNANI AND
KALKARINDJI, NORTHERN
TERRITORY, 2016.**

**BOWER STUDIO,
UNIVERSITY OF
MELBOURNE.**

Project team:
Studio leaders David
O'Brien, George Stavrias,
James Neil, Ilari Lehtonen,
Mia Hutson, Jack Hinkson.

Students:
James Connor, Sarah
Fraraccio, Jinwoo Jung,
Olof Klintmalm, Justin
Milesi, Xeying Ng, Camilla
Paradice, Dan Smith, Nina
Tory-Henderson, Toby
Woolley, Esther Ziebell.

Community Partners:
Gurindji Aboriginal
Corporation,
Karungkarni Arts,
Gurindji Language Centre.

**WEAVE YOUTH AND
COMMUNITY SERVICES,
SYDNEY, NEW SOUTH
WALES, 2013.**

COLLINS AND TURNER.

Project team:
Penny Collins, Huw Turner,
Terragram (landscape).

–

**GRASSLAND COMMON:
LINKING ECOLOGY
AND ARCHITECTURE,
MELBOURNE, VICTORIA,
2015 (UNBUILT).**

**D___LAB., RMIT
UNIVERSITY.**

Project team:
Mauro Baracco, Pia Ednie-
Brown, Catherine Horwill,
Jonathan Ware (School of
Architecture and Urban
Design, formerly School of
Architecture and Design,
d___Lab., Centre of Design
Practice Research); Georgia
Garrard, Sarah Bekessy,
Marco Amati, Simon van
Wijnen (School of Global
Urban and Social Studies,
Centre for Urban Research).
Project supported by
the former Global Cities
Research Institute,
RMIT University, 2015.

–

**TRIABUNNA GATEHOUSE,
TRIABUNNA, TASMANIA,
2016.**

**GILBY + BREWIN
ARCHITECTURE.**

Project team:
Anna Gilby, Ross Brewin,
Andrew Power,
Nina Tory-Henderson.

**WALUMBA ELDERS
CENTRE, WARMUN,
GIJA COUNTRY,
EAST KIMBERLEY,
WESTERN AUSTRALIA,
2014.**

**IREDALE PEDERSEN
HOOK.**

Project team:
Finn Pedersen, Adrian
Iredale, Martyn Hook, Joel
Fuller, Rebecca Angus,
Jason Lenard, Nikki Ross,
Caroline Di Costa, Khairani
Khalifah, Drew Penhale,
Mary Mcaree, Layla Cluer,
Jonathan Alach, Matt
Fletcher, Jonathan Ware.

–

**GLEBE 4,
THE FORESHORE WALK,
SYDNEY, NEW SOUTH
WALES, 2006.**

**JAMES MATHER
DELANEY DESIGN.**

Project Team:
James Mather Delaney
design (lead), Lacoste
Stevenson Architects
(heritage adaptation
Grandstand and Bellevue
Villa), TZG-Tonkin Zulaikha
Greer Architects (shelters).

NGARARA PLACE,
RMIT UNIVERSITY,
MELBOURNE, VICTORIA,
2016.

GREENAWAY
ARCHITECTS.

Project team:
Jefa Greenaway (Wailwan
| Gamilaraay), Soft
Landscaping by Charles
Solomon (Gubbi Gubbi and
Monero/Ngarigo), Artwork
by Aroha Groves (Weiwan
| Gomeroi), Documentation
by Maya Wong.

–

SHEPPARTON ART
MUSEUM, SHEPPARTON,
VICTORIA, 2017 (UNBUILT,
COMPETITION ENTRY).

KERSTIN THOMPSON
ARCHITECTS.

Project Team:
Kerstin Thompson, Kelley
Mackay, Tamsin O'Reilly,
Ben Pakulsky, Hillary
Sleigh, Lloyd McCathie.

ARDEN MACAULAY
ISLAND CITY,
MELBOURNE, VICTORIA,
2017 (UNBUILT).

MONASH UNIVERSITY
URBAN LABORATORY.

Project Team:
Nigel Bertram, Catherine
Murphy, Rutger Pasman,
Jesse Oehm, Alexander
Williams, David Mason,
Leonor Gausachs.

–

THE GLOBE,
BARCALDINE,
QUEENSLAND, 2016.

M3ARCHITECTURE
IN ASSOCIATION
WITH BRIAN HOOPER
ARCHITECT.

Project team:
Michael Lavery, Michael
Christensen, Michael
Banney, Ben Vielle,
Brain Hooper.

–

PRINCE ALFRED PARK
AND POOL UPGRADE,
SYDNEY, NEW SOUTH
WALES, 2013.

NEESON MURCUTT
ARCHITECTS WITH
SUE BARNSLEY
DESIGN LANDSCAPE
ARCHITECTURE.

Project Team:
Rachel Neeson, Nick
Murcutt, Tamas Jones,
Jenny Hien, Louise Holst,
Joseph Grech, Isabelle
Toland, Amelia Holliday,
David Coleborne, Sean
Choo, Anne Kristin Risnes,
Sue Barnsley.

KULLURK/COOLART:
SOMERS FARM
AND WETLANDS,
MORNINGTON
PENINSULA, VICTORIA,
2002-CONTINUING
(OUTBUILDING, 2002;
BIRD HIDE, 2012).

NMBW ARCHITECTURE
STUDIO, WITH WILLIAM
GOODSIR (PLAIN
ARCHITECTURE) AND
RMIT ARCHITECTURE
(FOR THE DESIGN AND
CONSTRUCTION OF THE
BIRD HIDE).

Project Team:
Lucinda McLean,
Nigel Bertram, Marika
Neustupny, William Goodsir
and RMIT Architecture
students: Ilai Bavati, Anh
Duc Bui, Ben Eddie, Imogen
Fry, Samka Kit, David Smith,
Renee Soulibe, Paul Viselka,
James Woodman, Guillaume
Delauney.

–

FEATHERSTON HOUSE,
MELBOURNE, VICTORIA,
1967-69.

ROBIN BOYD
(1919 - 1971).

Project Team:
Robin Boyd (in constant
conversation with Grant
and Mary Featherston).

MAIN ASSEMBLY
BUILDING, TONSLEY
INNOVATION DISTRICT,
ADELAIDE, SOUTH
AUSTRALIA, 2016.

WOODS BAGOT WITH
TRIDENTE ARCHITECTS
AND OXIGEN LANDSCAPE
ARCHITECTS.

Project Team:
Woods Bagot with Tridente
Architects and Oxigen
Landscape Architects,
Renewal South Australia.

EXHIBITORS

Baracco+Wright Architects
See under Creative Directors.

Bower Studio, University of Melbourne

Bower Studio sits within the Melbourne School of Design at the University of Melbourne. Initiated in 2008 and led by David O'Brien the program links the aspirations and capacities of marginalised communities with the consultation, design and construction expertise of students and Faculty. Bower Studio has partnered with fifteen communities in remote locations in Australia and Papua New Guinea and has led teams designing and building a variety of infrastructure types. It focusses on housing, health hardware and generating spaces to make art and preserve culture. The program values engagement, confidence building and research in addition to hard outcomes.

Collins and Turner

Collins and Turner is a multidisciplinary architecture and design studio based in Sydney, founded in 2002 by Penny Collins and Huw Turner. The practice is driven by a strong focus on design, with a dynamic approach to innovation in the construction of environments for living, working, learning and recreation. The diverse work of the studio is guided by a consistent philosophical approach, rather than a predetermined architectural style. Collins and Turner aims to create unique, beautiful, sustainable, considered buildings and spaces that work to integrate the needs and desires of the clients, as well as the individual pragmatic requirements of context and function.

d___Lab., RMIT University

d___Lab. is located within the School of Architecture and Urban Design at RMIT University. It undertakes practice-based research projects engaging constructed and material environments, working with industry partners, through collaborative team investigations focussed on technological, urban and the cultural and poetic dimensions of lived environments. Grassland Common: Linking Ecology and Architecture, is part of 'd___Lab. Cities' for the investigation of systems and services that sustain cities for future urban and regional scenarios. It is a collaboration between the School of Architecture and Urban Design, and the School of Global, Urban and Social Studies.

Gilby + Brewin Architecture

Gilby + Brewin Architecture is a design focussed architecture studio based in Melbourne, Australia with projects located in Victoria, Tasmania and Western Australia. The practice undertakes culturally, socially and environmentally responsible projects across a range of urban scales and settings. With each project, Gilby + Brewin have a commitment to producing deeply contextualised architecture that whilst positively framing the activity and comfort of the inhabitants, also resonates with the surrounding built and landscape context. At the core of the practice is the belief that architecture is a fundamentally civic endeavor, whether it be for a private dwelling or a broader public use.

Greenaway Architects

Greenaway Architects (GA) is an Australian architectural practice, of twenty years, which fuses Indigenous sensibilities into architectural, interior, landscape and urban design projects. Founded by Catherine and Jefa Greenaway, this boutique practice advocates a holistic approach to design thinking which seeks to move beyond design silos, as a means of placing people at the centre of all decisions. The team actively seeks out collaborations with artists, creatives and partners to develop a participatory process of creative problem solving. With a speciality in residential and educational projects GA seeks to infuse narratives that reveal layers of history and memory, while celebrating and giving visibility to cultural dimensions that showcase connections to the oldest continuing culture in the world. GA Director, Jefa Greenaway champions design leadership at the University of Melbourne, as Regional Ambassador (Oceania) for the International Indigenous Design Alliance (INDIGO) and as founding chair of the not-for-profit organisation Indigenous Architecture + Design Victoria (IADV).

iredale pedersen hook

iredale pedersen hook is a progressive architecture practice with studios in Perth and Melbourne and a rapidly expanding diverse body of work throughout Australia. The projects are as individual and eclectic as the landscape they occupy. Each piece of architecture seeks to embody a unique design response of innovation and delight. The studio is dedicated to the pursuit of appropriate design of effective sustainable buildings with a responsible environmental and social agenda. Their projects have won over 130 awards including many prestigious international awards. They continue to publish, teach and exhibit throughout the world.

m3architecture and Brian Hooper Architects

The directors of m3architecture and Brian Hooper Architect have known each other for more than 30 years. Collaboration between the practices (The Tree of Knowledge 2009 and The Globe 2015) has yielded Australian architecture awards in both Heritage and Public Buildings, as well as an Australian Timber Design award. m3architecture was established in 1997 and is based in

Brisbane, Queensland. The practice is run by Directors Michael Banney, Michael Christensen, Michael Lavery and Ben Vielle. Ideas lead the practice's work. m3architecture has a focus on the public realm. The practice has been published globally and has been awarded extensively. This includes being honoured with the highest prize for Public Buildings, Heritage and Small Projects in Australian Architecture. Established in 1998, Brian Hooper Architect is based in Yeppoon, Queensland. Brian Hooper's work is spread across the vast Western and North Queensland regions. In addition to his awards for the work in Barcaldine, Brian has been awarded the Australian Institute of Architects Robin Dods Award for Residential Architecture and the J.W. Wilson Building of the Year Award.

James Mather Delaney design

JMD design is a Sydney based practice working primarily in the public realm with a commitment to achieving both site specific and environmentally responsible design solutions that restore, enhance and amplify the usability, diversity, connectivity and legibility of the civic and the natural systems on site. The practice works across a range of scales in order to engage with the urban, hydrological, geomorphological and ecological processes whilst celebrating the particular, the quotidian and the small scale. JMD design collaborates across disciplines on sites with complex fabric that require adaptation, remediation and reinterpretation. Projects include streets, public squares, regional parklands, former industrial sites and disused infrastructure

Kerstin Thompson Architects

Kerstin Thompson Architects (KTA) was founded in Melbourne, Australia in 1994. The practice creates immersive, restorative, innovative and meaningful places in which landscape, interior and architecture are uniquely integrated. KTA's work is defined by its clarity of approach and sensitivity to place. KTA's expertise is drawn from a portfolio of varied work that ranges in scale and program, with a civic, commercial, cultural and residential focus. Current significant projects include; Victorian College of the Arts (former Mounted Police stables) for the University of Melbourne; Arthur and Yvonne Boyd Riversdale creative learning centre, accommodation and gallery for Bundanon Trust; and 100 Queen Street, Melbourne tower redevelopment for GPT Group.

Monash University Urban Laboratory

Monash University Urban Laboratory is a research unit within the Faculty of Art, Design & Architecture (MADA). It has the ambition of making a significant contribution to some of the most pressing urban issues facing cities and regions – through propositional plans, designs and speculations, through academic and other publications, and through broader commentary. The spatial scope and scale of the research moves from the urban and suburban, to the regional and global. Arden Macaulay Island City is part of a larger research project produced in partnership with the multi-disciplinary Co-operative Research Centre for Water Sensitive Cities and students from the Master of Architecture program.

Neeson Murcutt Architects

Neeson Murcutt Architects is an energetic, studio-based architectural practice recognised for innovation and delivery of award-winning architecture and urban design. Project types range from single houses to multi-unit housing, public and community projects, sports facilities, and schools. The practice has a broad understanding of 'site' that incorporates community, context, microclimate, topography, landscape, ecology, history and collective memory. Projects morph, becoming almost inseparable from their setting. The practice's work is strategic always, and at every scale. Prince Alfred Park and Pool is a sustainability exemplar, having the biggest green roof in Sydney and is the first City of Sydney project to be trigeneration ready.

NMBW Architecture Studio

NMBW Architecture Studio was established in Melbourne in 1997 by Marika Neustupny, Lucinda McLean and Nigel Bertram. All three directors work across practice and teaching, combining ongoing research with built outcomes. The practice has established an analytical, research-based approach, linking site-specific actions to larger community and environmental concerns. The work has an emphasis on social engagement and cultural specificity realised through collaborations with a diverse range of other practitioners. Each project is a study of the practices of local tradition, the everyday and the way in which spaces, structure and materials are put together.

Oxigen

Oxigen is one of Adelaide's, and Australia's, most awarded landscape architecture, architecture and urban design practices. Oxigen's everyday work affects the quality of life in cities and regional areas by the simple act of designing in ways that improve the health and liveability of environments. Oxigen's approach is always specific to the site, drawing on the principles for design from the site context, climate, ecology and people's use. A portfolio of completed environmental and cultural projects defines the practice and gives it a strong reputation within the extended field of landscape architecture and urban design.

sue barnsley design landscape architecture is a studio practice in Sydney, working across a range of landscapes from private gardens, to Olympic infrastructure, parks and urban ecological restoration. Projects are acknowledged as artful and regenerative. Restoring the Waters at Clear Paddock Creek, Commonwealth Place in Canberra, the Brickpit Ring Walk in Sydney Olympic Park and Barcom Park in Darlinghurst, established the reputation of the office. The more recent completion of One Bligh Street, Prince Alfred Park and Jubilee Playground acknowledge the contribution of the practice to the city's design culture.

Tridente Architects

Tridente Architects has comprehensive experience in Architecture, Interior Design, Master-planning and Urban Design. Their focus is on the delivery of exemplary outcomes for their clients through design as demonstrated by numerous peer awards. Pivotal to their approach is the investigative process which questions every aspect of each project to find the most applicable but not necessarily the most obvious solution. Tridente Architects has successfully delivered projects in education, institutional, residential, commercial, retail, health, and industrial sectors delivering solutions for their clients within strict parameters and in complex environments.

Woods Bagot

Woods Bagot place human experience at the centre of their design process in order to deliver engaging, future-oriented projects that are underpinned by three main tenets: limitless curiosity, computational design based on the analysis of user behavior, and super typologies. They do this as a global design and consulting studio with a team of over 1,000 experts working across 17 studios in Australia, Asia, the Middle East, Europe, and North America. Their global studio model allows them to work collaboratively across time zones and borders, using the latest technology to share design intelligence and strengthen their knowledge base around the world.

SPECIAL THANKS

The Australian Institute of Architects and Venice Biennale Committee.

RMIT University Architecture, Aboriginal Environments Research Centre at the University of Queensland, Monash University, University of Melbourne, Deakin University, and Australia Council for the Arts.

Thank you to all the architects and associated teams who submitted projects for repair.

Thank you to the owners and occupiers of the works we filmed, and the architects who facilitated access and took care of us. A special thank you to the ever gracious Mary Featherston who gave us access to the Featherston house in the middle of moving house, and to Deanne Butterworth with Sarah Aitken, Shian Law and Luke Fryer who made the house come alive.

We are particularly grateful to the Gurindji Aboriginal Corporation and the Karungkarni Art Centre for hosting us in Kalkarindji. Thank you to elders Timmy Vincent, Kathleen Sambo, Rosemary Johnson, Violet Wadrill, Biddy Wavehill and Jimmy Wavehill for sharing their stories with us, and participating in the filming at Jinbarak.

Weave Youth and Community Services were accommodating of our crew on a very lively day in the centre. Thank you Shiobhan Bryson for working with us and to Bree Webb, Sena Rabuatoka, Carol Rabuatoka, Katie Vellins and Isaiah Te-Rangi for your participation in the film.

We have been very fortunate to have an excellent ground crew. In Melbourne thank you to Hannah Gatland, Vanessa Cox, Ros and Mike Tegg, Charmaine Kuhn, and Chris and Davor at Flying Dragon. In Sydney thank you to Amber Todd, Cate Hartman, Tim Walsh, Michael Fairbain and Skymedia.

Thank you to all the contributors to the catalogue and all the copyright owners of images who generously allowed us to use them. David Fox quietly worked with Linda Tegg to provide invaluable technical and conceptual collaboration, particularly on the video work *Ground*.

Thank you to Diego Carpentiero who was always ready to help.

Without the expertise and generosity of Sue Murphy and John Delpratt we would never have been able to create a grassland. We enjoyed their company immensely.

Giampiero Cane and Marina, Giovanna, Carlo, Michele, Concetta, Sandrina and Carmen at the Istituto Professionale di Stato per l'Agricoltura e l'Ambiente 'D. Aicardi' in Sanremo, and their wonderful students who enthusiastically took on the huge task of growing the Grassland and we are forever in their debt. Thank you to Luca Zunino of Zunino Cactus for assistance and transporting the plants, and Claudio Bruno from Vigor Plant.

Thank you to the time and knowledge shared with us from Flora Victoria, Brian Bainbridge, the Victorian Indigenous Nursery team, Reuben Berg and Indigenous Architecture Design Victoria (IADV) and Julia at Exportcerts. Nic Burnham from NDYLIGHT Lighting Design was very clever and generous assisting us with his expertise to find a light spectrum that would keep the plants alive – plants that had never been artificially lit before.

Thank you to the Wurundjeri Land and Compensation Cultural Heritage Council Aboriginal Corporation for meeting with us and sharing their language.

Many people shared precious grassland seeds with us: Greening Australia, Flora Victoria, Western Goldfields Indigenous Nursery, Victorian Indigenous Nursery, Fair Dinkum Seeds, Nindethana, The Seed Shed, John Delpratt, and Neville Walsh and the Royal Botanic Gardens who opened their seedbank to us to provide rare species.

Thanks to Shauna Toohey and Misha Hollenbach of P.A.M. Perks and Mini who 'got it', and designed the workwear and garments for *Repair*.

Studio Round were extremely supportive and caring with our material to create our graphic language. Thank you to Sharyn Cairns who captured our image.

We are very grateful to the staff of the Australian Institute of Architects. Especially Jennifer Cunich for her encouragement and support; Lauren Craddock for her calm and attentive assistance; and a big thank you to Miranda Grace for placing enormous faith in us, being extremely helpful and generally going above and beyond to make sure it all happened.

Mauro Baracco,
Louise Wright and
Linda Tegg

Ground.
Photograph, Linda Tegg.
Robin Boyd, Featherston House.

AIATSIS 1996, *The AIATSIS map of Indigenous Australia*, AIATSIS, <https://aiatsis.gov.au/explore articles/aiatsis-map-indigenous australia>.

Attwood, B 2000, 'The Articulation of "Land Rights" in Australia: The Case of Wave Hill', *Social Analysis: The International Journal of Social and Cultural Practice*, vol. 44, no. 1, April.

Australian Association of Bush Regenerators (AABR) n.d., *Working with natural processes: the Bradley method*, Australian Association of Bush Regenerators, <http://www.aabr.org.au/learn what-i-bush-regeneration/general principles/the-bradley-method/>.

Australian Government 2006, *White Box - Yellow Box - Blakely's Red Gum Grassy Woodlands and Derived Native Grasslands listing advice and conservation advice*, <http://www.environment.gov.au system/files/pages/dcad3aa6 2230-44cb-9a2f-5e1dca33db6b files/box-gum.pdf>.

Australian Government, Department of Sustainability, Environment, Water, Population and Communities 2011, *Nationally Threatened Ecological Communities of the Victorian Volcanic Plain: Natural Temperate Grassland & Grassy Eucalypt Woodland*, Commonwealth of Australia, Barton, ACT, Australia, <http://www environment.gov.au/system/files resources/e97c2d51-08f2-45e0 9d2f-f0d277c836fa/files grasslands-victoria.pdf>.

Australian Government, Department of the Environment and Energy 2011, *Construction and demolition waste status report - management of construction and demolition waste in Australia*, introduction to two related report documents, <http://www.environment.gov au/protection/national-waste policy/publications/construction and-demolition-waste-status report>.

Australian Government, Department of the Environment and Energy 2013, *Australia's waste and resource recovery infrastructure, National waste report*, introduction to the related report, <http:/ www.environment.gov.au protection/national-waste-policy/ national-waste-reports/ national-waste-report-2013/ infrastructure>.

Australian Government, Australian Institute of Health and Welfare 2015, *The health and welfare of Australia's Aboriginal and Torres Strait Islander peoples: 2015*, <https://www.aihw.gov.au reports/indigenous-health welfare/indigenous-health welfare-2015/contents/table-of contents>.

Australian Government, Department of the Environment and Energy n.d., *National Heritage Places - The Tree of Knowledge*, Australian Government, Department of the Environment and Energy, <http://www.environment.gov.au heritage/places/national/tree>.

Australian Government, Department of Environment and Energy n.d., *Outback Australia - the rangelands*, <http://www environment.gov.au/rangelands>.

Australian Institute of Architects 2017 (May), *Indigenous Housing Policy*, Australian Institute of Architects, <http://sitefinity architecture.com.au/docs default-source/national-policy indigenous-housing-policy-2017 pdf?sfvrsn=2>.

Australian Museum, 2017, *Glossary of Indigenous Australia terms*, Australian Museum, <https:/ australianmuseum.net.au/glossary indigenous-australia-terms>.

Baracco, M 2011 (ed.), *Tree Sprawl*, School of Architecture and Design, RMIT University, Melbourne, Australia.

Baracco, M with Ware, J 2015, *Regenerated Towns in Regenerated Nature*, architecture and landscape architecture design research laboratory for the urban, social and economic rehabilitation of rural towns in the West Wimmera, Victoria, d___Lab., School of Architecture and Urban Design, RMIT University; West Wimmera Shire Council; Horsham Rural City Council; Habitat 141, Greening Australia; Parks Victoria; Kowree Farm Tree Group, <http://www townsandnature.com/>.

Baracco, M, Bekessy, S, Garrard, G, Ednie-Brown, P & Amati, M 2015 *Linking Ecology and Architecture*, RMIT University, Melbourne, Victoria, Australia.

Baracco, M & Ware, J 2016, *Officina Imperia*, architecture and landscape architecture design research laboratory, d___Lab, School of Architecture and Urban Design, RMIT University; Imperia Confindustria; Imperia Council; Polimi-Milan Polytechnic, Dipartimento di Architettura e Studi Urbani, <http: officinaimperia.com/>.

Baracco, M & Wright, L 2017, *Robin Boyd: Spatial Continuity*, Routledge, London, UK and New York, USA.

Barwick, DE 1984, 'Mapping the past: An atlas of Victorian clans 1835-1904' in *Aboriginal History Part 1*, vol. 8.

Barwick, DE 1998, 'Rebellion at Coranderrk' in LE Barwick & RE Barwick (eds), *Aboriginal History Monograph 5*, Australian National University, Canberra, Australia.

Berger, J 1980, 'Why Look at Animals?', in *About Looking*, Vintage, London, UK (1993).

Berndt, RM (ed.) 1970, *Australian Aboriginal Anthropology: modern studies in the social anthropology of the Australian Aborigines*, University of Western Australia Press for the Australian Institute of Aboriginal Studies AIAS, Canberra, ACT, Australia.

Blake, BJ (ed.) 1998, *Wathawurrung and the Colac language of southern Victoria*, Pacific Linguistics, The Australian National University, Canberra, ACT, Australia, <https:// victoriancolle5 2f0758a9821f40464 f742c1/items/56c69086400d0c3 518d14bdb/item- media/56d6732d2162f11 c380e1440/original.pdf>.

Blake, BJ 2011, *Dialects of Western Kulin, Western Victoria, Yartwatjali, Tjapwurrung, Djadjawurrung*, La Trobe University, Melbourne, Victoria, Australia, <http://www.vcaa. vic.edu.au/documents/alcv/ dialectsofwesternkulin- westernvictoria.pdf>.

Bonyhady, T 2004, 'Woodchipping the Spirit of Tasmania', *Art Monthly Australia*, no. 173, September.

Boyce, J 2011, *1835: The Founding of Melbourne & the Conquest of Australia*, Black Inc., Collingwood, Victoria, Australia.

Boyd, R 1960, *The Australian Ugliness*, F W Cheshire, Melbourne, Victoria, Australia.

Boyd, R 1970, *Living in Australia*, Pergamon Press, Sydney, NSW, Australia.

Brooks, D 1991, *The Arrernte landscape of Alice Springs*, Institute for Aboriginal Development, Alice Springs, Northern Territory, Australia.

Brown, PL (ed.) 1941, *Clyde Company papers - 1 Prologue 1821- 1835*, Oxford University Press, London, UK (1956).

Builth, H 2014, *Ancient Aboriginal Aquaculture Rediscovered - The Archaeology of an Australian Cultural Landscape*, LAP Lambert Academic Publishing, Saarbrucken, Germany.

Burgess, CP, Johnston, FH, Bowman, DMJS & Whitehead, PJ 2005, 'Healthy Country: Healthy People? Exploring the health benefits for Indigenous natural resource management', *Australian and New Zealand Journal of Public Health*, vol. 29, no. 2.

Burgess, CP, Johnston, FH, Berry, HL, McDonnell, J, Yibarbuk, D, Gunabarra, C, Mileran, A & Bailie, RS 2009, 'Healthy country, healthy people: the relationship between Indigenous health status and 'caring for country' ', *The Medical Journal of Australia*, vol. 190, no. 10.

Buxton M, Phelan K & Hurley J 2015, *Melbourne at 8 Million: Matching Land Supply to Dwelling Demand*, RMIT University, Centre for Urban Research, September, <http://cur.org.au/project/melbourne-8-million-matching-land-supply-dwelling-demand/>.

City of Melbourne n.d., *Unleashing the Potential of Nature, Discussion Paper on City Ecology, Ecosystems and Biodiversity*, City of Melbourne, <https://participate.melbourne.vic.gov.au/application/files/2214/2369/1370/Urban_Ecology_Discussion_Paper.pdf>.

Clark, ID 1990, *Aboriginal languages and Clans: An Historical Atlas of Western and Central Victoria, 1800-1900*, Department of Geography and Environmental Science, Monash University, Melbourne, Victoria, Australia.

Cribb, AB & Cribb, JW 1981, *Wild medicine in Australia*. Intl Specialized Book Service Inc.

Dawson, J 1881, *Australian Aborigines: the languages and customs of several tribes of Aborigines in the western district of Victoria*, George Robertson, Melbourne, Victoria, Australia.

De Angelis, D 2005, *Aboriginal Use Plants of the Greater Melbourne Area*, La Trobe University Environment Collective, Melbourne, Victoria, Australia, <http://www.latrobe.edu.au/wildlife/downloads/Aboriginal-plant-use-list.pdf>.

Delpratt, CJ 1999, 'Investigations of seed production potential of indigenous grassland forbs', Masters thesis, The University of Melbourne, Australia.

Dodd, M 2015, 'Garden House', *Architecture Australia*, vol. 104, no. 5, September/October.

Douglas, J 2015 'Kin and knowledge: The meaning and acquisition of Indigenous ecological knowledge in the lives of young people in Central Australia', PhD thesis, Charles Darwin University, Northern Territory, Australia.

Duxbury, L 2010, 'A Change in the Climate: New Interpretations and Perceptions of Climate Change through Artistic Interventions and Representations', *Weather, Climate and Society*, no. 2.

ERA-Energy Resources of Australia Ltd. n.d., *Sustainability: Ranger Mine Site*, ERA-Energy Resources of Australia Ltd., <http://www.energyres.com.au/sustainability/progressive-rehabilitation/ranger/>.

Everingham, S 2017, 'Kakadu National Park: Jabiru residents in limbo as governments, mining company contemplate town's future', *ABC News*, 20 July, <http://www.abc.net.au/news/2017-07-18/jabiru-residents-in-limbo-as-uranium-mining-draws-to-a-close/8718432>.

Flora Victoria: The Grassland Experts n.d., *Products*, Flora Victoria: The Grassland Experts, <https://chris-findlay.squarespace.com/species-and-prices/>.

Foucault, M 1966, *The Order of Things: An Archaeology of The Human Science*, Routledge, London, UK and New York, USA (1970, 2003).

Foucault, M 1973, 'The force of flight', in JW Crampton & S Elden (eds) 2007, *Space, Knowledge and Power: Foucault and Geography*, Ashgate, New York, USA.

Foucault, M 1975, *Discipline and Punish: The Birth of the Prison*, Penguin, London, UK (1991).

Foucault, M 1976, 'Questions of Geography', in C Gordon (ed.) 1980, *Power/Knowledge: Selected Interviews and Other Writings, 1972-1977*, Harvester Press, Brighton, UK.

Gammage, B 2011, *The Biggest Estate on Earth: How Aborigines made Australia*, Allen & Unwin, Crows Nest, NSW, Australia.

Gaughwin, D & Sullivan, H 1984, 'Aboriginal Boundaries and Movement in Western Port, Victoria', *Aboriginal History*, vol. 8.

Gibbons, P & Lindenmayer, D 2002, *Tree Hollows and Wildlife Conservation in Australia*, CSIRO Publishing, Collingwood, Victoria, Australia.

Gibson-Roy, P 2015, 'When is a Yam Daisy more than a Yam Daisy? When is a grassland more than a grassland?', *Australasian Plant Conservation*, vol. 24, no. 1.

Gilbert, J 2018, 'Call of the Reed Warbler: A manifesto for regeneration', *Landscape Australia*, 19 January, <https://landscapeaustralia.com articles/call-of-the-reed warbler-charles-massys-call-to action/>.

Girardet, H 2013, 'Sustainability is unhelpful: we need to think about regeneration', *The Guardian*, 10 June, <https://www.theguardian.com/sustainable-business/blog/sustainability-unhelpful-think-regeneration>.

Girardet, H 2015, *Creating Regenerative Cities*, Routledge, Abingdon, Oxon, UK, and New York, USA.

Go-Sam, C & Memmott, P 2016, 'Dossier: Remote Indigenous Settlements – more than tiny dots on a map', *Architecture Australia*, vol. 105, no. 5, September/October.

Gott, B 1999, *The Great Plains Crash. Proceedings of a conference on the grasslands and grassy woodlands of Victoria*, Indigenous Flora and Fauna Association, Melbourne, Victoria, Australia.

Government of Western Australia, Department of Housing and Warmun Taskforce 2013, *Warrambany of Warrmarn: the flood of Warmun, 13 March 2011*, <http://www.housing.wa.gov.au/HousingDocuments/Warrambany_of_Warrmarn_The_Flood_Of_Warmun.pdf>.

Grace, R 2013, 'Finding Country', *ArchitectureAU*, 28 October, <https://architectureau.com/articles/finding-country/>.

Grant, E, Greenop, K, Refiti, A & Glenn, D (eds) 2018, *The Handbook of Contemporary Indigenous Architecture*, Springer Nature, Singapore.

Greening Australia n.d., *Great Southern Landscapes: Victorian Volcanic Plains*, Greening Australia, <greeningaustralia.org.au/project/Victorian-volcanic-plains>.

Gundjeihmi Aboriginal Corporation n.d., *Uranium Mining*, Gundjeihmi Aboriginal Corporation, <http://www.mirarr.net/uranium-mining>.

Gunn, M et al. n.d., *Barwon River Guide*, <http://geelongbeekeepersclub.org/wp-content/uploads/2014/12/Barwon-River-Plant-Guide.pdf>.

Hahs, AK 2017, 'Soft cities: Making room for nature in our urban future', *Foreground*, 20 April 2017, <https://www.foreground.com.au/environment/biodiversity-in-our-urban-future/>.

Hansel Fels, M 2011, *'I succeeded Once': The Aboriginal Protectorate on the Mornington Peninsula, 1839-1840*, ANU Press, Canberra, ACT, Australia.

Hansen, W 2017, *The Book of Greek & Roman Folktales, Legends & Myths*, Princeton University Press, Princeton, New Jersey, USA.

Hardy, F 1968, *The Unlucky Australians*, Nelson, Melbourne, Victoria, Australia.

Harlan, B 2015, 'Digging Deep Reveals the Intricate World of Roots', *National Geographic*, 15 October, <https://www.nationalgeographic.com/photography/proof/2015/10/15/digging-deep-reveals-the-intricate-world-of-roots/>.

Hercus, LA 1969, *The languages of Victoria: a late survey*, no. 6, Australian Institute of Aboriginal Studies-AIAS, Canberra, ACT, Australia.

Hicks, LE & King, RJH 2007, 'Confronting Environmental Collapse: Visual Culture, Art Education, and Environmental Responsibility', *Studies in Art Education*, vol. 48, no. 4.

Hyde, R 2013, *Future Practice: Conversations from the Edge of Architecture*, Routledge, London, UK and New York, USA.

Ho, G, Mathew, K & Anda, M (eds) 2009, *Sustainability of indigenous communities in Australia: Selected papers from the National Conference (12-14 July 2006)*, Murdoch University, Perth, Western Australia, Australia.

Hollier, N 2006, 'The Unlucky Australians. When Frank Hardy went bush he made some alarming discoveries', *The Age Book Reviews*, 8 September, <https://www.theage.com.au/news/book-reviews/the-unlucky australians/2006/09/08/1157222319244.html>.

Howitt, AW 1904, *The Native Tribes of South-east Australia*, Macmillan and Co., London, UK.

Jackson, T 2009, *Prosperity without Growth: Economics for a Finite Planet*, Earthscan, London, UK.

Johnston, C 2016, ' 'Into the Aboriginal world'- Victoria's secret emerges from lake and creek ' *The Age*, 31 December, <http://www.theage.com.au/victoria/into-the-aboriginal-world---victorias-secret-emerges-from-lake-and-creek-20161229-gtjok8.html>.

Keeffe, K 1988, 'Aboriginality: Resistance and Persistence', *Australian Aboriginal Studies*, no. 1.

La Biennale di Venezia 2016, *Reporting From the Front: Biennale Architettura 2016. Volume 1: Exhibition, Volume 2: Participating Countries, Collateral Events*, catalogue of 15ᵗʰ Mostra Internazionale di Architettura, La Biennale di Venezia, Marsilio, Venice, Italy.

Lakoff, G 2010, 'Why It Matters How We Frame the Environment', *Environmental Communication: A Journal of Nature and Culture* 4, no. 1.

Latz, PK 2007, *The Flaming Desert*, IAD Press, Alice Springs, Northern Territory, Australia.

Lindenmayer, D, Michael, D, Crane, M, Okada, S, Florance, D, Barton, P & Ikin, K 2016, *Wildlife Conservation in Farm Landscapes*, CSIRO Publishing, Clayton South, Victoria, Australia.

Lotus, 2012, monographic issue on *Landscape Urbanism*, no. 150.

Lotus, 2014, monographic issue on *Geography in motion*, no. 155.

Lotus, 2015, monographic issue on *City as nature*, no. 157.

Lourandos, H 1997, *Continent of Hunter Gatherers: New Perspectives in Australian Prehistory*, Cambridge University Press, Cambridge, UK.

Low, T 2002, *The New Nature: Winners and Losers in Wild Australia*, Viking Books, Melbourne, Victoria, Australia.

Macaffer, J & Watts, G 2008, *Mornington Peninsula Reconciliation Background Paper*, Mornington Peninsula Shire, 26 May.

MacKay, R, Pendrell, L & Trafford, J (eds) 2014, *Speculative Aesthetics*, Lulu Press, Morrisville, North Carolina, USA.

Maiden, JH 1889, *The useful native plants of Australia:(including Tasmania)*, Turner and Henderson, Sydney, NSW, Australia.

Mainar, JM and Vodvarka, F 2013, *New Architecture Indigenous Lands*, University of Minneapolis Press, Minneapolis, USA.

Marder, M 2013, 'What is Plant Thinking?' in *Klesis - Revue Philosophique, Philosophies de la Nature*, vol. 25.

Marsh, D 2017, 'An ecological approach to grazing', *Landscape Australia*, 9 November, <https://landscapeaustralia.com/articles/an-ecological-approach-to-grazing/>.

Massy, C 2017, *Call of the Reed Warbler: A New Agriculture - a New Earth*, University of Queensland Press, St Lucia, Queensland, Australia.

Mathews, S 2007, *From Agit-Prop to Free Space: The Architecture of Cedric Price*, Black Dog Publishing, London, UK.

McDonald, A, Besser, L & Russell, A n.d., 'Warmun: A tale of two disasters', a *Four Corners* investigation, *ABC News*, <http://www.abc.net.au/news/2016-06-06/warmun-a-tale-of-two-disasters/7462544>.

McGaw, J and Pieris, A 2015 *Assembling the Centre: Architecture for Indigenous Cultures - Australia and Beyond*, Routledge, London, UK and New York, USA.

Meakins, F 2016, 'Friday essay: the untold story behind the 1966 Wave Hill Walk-Off', *The Conversation*, 19 August, <https://theconversation.com/friday-essay-the-untold-story-behind-the-1966-wave-hill-walk-off-62890>.

Memmott, P & Chambers, C (eds) 2003, *TAKE 2: Housing Design in Indigenous Australia*, Royal Institute of Architects, Canberra, ACT, Australia.

Memmott, P 2007, *Gunyah, Goondie and Wurley: The Aboriginal Architecture of Australia*, University of Queensland Press, St Lucia, Queensland, Australia.

Memmott, P et al. 2013, *Aboriginal responses to climate change in arid zone Australia: regional understandings and capacity building for adaptation: Final Report*, National Climate Change Adaptation Research Facility, Gold Coast, Queensland, Australia.

Memmott, P & Keys, C 2015, 'Redefining architecture to accommodate cultural difference: designing for cultural sustainability', *Architectural Science Review*, vol. 58, no. 4.

Mitchell, N, Rossler, M & Tricaud, P 2009, *World Heritage Cultural Landscapes. A Handbook for Conservation and Management. World Heritage paper No 26*, UNESCO World Heritage Centre, Paris, France.

MoMALearning, n.d., *Trio A, Yvonne Rainer*, MoMALearning, <https://www.moma.org/learn/moma_learning/yvonne-rainer-trio-a-1978>.

Montgomery, DR 2008, *Dirt: The Erosion of Civilisations*, University of California Press, Berkeley, USA.

Morton, S, Sheppard, A & Lonsdale, M (eds) 2014, *Biodiversity: Science and Solutions for Australia*, CSIRO Publishing, Collingwood, Victoria, Australia.

Mostafavi, M with Doherty, G (eds) 2010, *Ecological Urbanism*, Lars Müller Publishers, Zürich, Switzerland.

Nash, D 2003, *Aboriginal Plant Use: NSW Southern Tablelands*, online database, <http://www.anbg.gov.au/apu/index.html>.

Newton, PW (ed.) 2008, *Transitions: Pathways Towards Sustainable Urban Developments in Australia*, CSIRO Publishing, Collingwood, Victoria, Australia.

Nicolin, P 2014, 'The Properties of Resilience', *Lotus*, no. 155, monographic issue on *Geography in motion*.

Northern Territory Government, Department of the Chief Minister 2018, *Information update 2 - A strong future for Jabiru*, 6 February, <https://dcm.nt.gov.au/news/2018/february-2018/a-strong-future-for-jabiru-information-update-2>.

OECD (Organisation for Economic Co-operation and Development) 2001, *Sustainable Development: Critical Issues*, OECD, Paris, France.

Ossola, A, Hahs, AK & Livesley, SJ 2015, 'Habitat complexity influences fine scale hydrological processes and the incidence of stormwater runoff in managed urban ecosystems', *Journal of Environmental Management*, vol. 159, 15 August, ScienceDirect, <https://www.sciencedirect.com/science/article/pii/S03014797153 0058X?via%3Dihub>.

Pascoe, B 2014, *Dark Emu: Black Seeds Agriculture Or Accident?*, Magabala Books, Broome, Western Australia, Australia.

Presland, G 2008, *The Place for a Village: how nature has shaped the city of Melbourne*, Museum Victoria Publishing, Melbourne, Victoria, Australia.

Prime Minister's Urban Design Taskforce 1994, *Urban Design in Australia: Report*, Commonwealth of Australia, Australian Government Publishing Service, Canberra, ACT, Australia, <https://urbandesign.org.au/content/uploads/2015/08/PMs_Taskforce_on_UD_1994.pdf>.

Pullin, R 2011, *Eugene von Guérard: Nature Revealed*, with essays by Michael Varcoe-Cocks and Tim Bonyhady, National Gallery of Victoria, Melbourne, Victoria, Australia.

Reed, C & Lister, NM 2014, *Projective Ecologies*, Harvard University GSD and Actar Publishers, New York, USA.

Ricardo, RR 2015, 'Regenerated Towns in Regenerated Nature: an interview with Mauro Baracco', *Landscape Architecture Australia*, no. 146, May.

Ricardo, RR 2017, 'Editorial: Tracking Australian Urban Design', *Landscape Architecture Australia*, no. 156, November.

Ricardo RR 2017, 'Grassland: A provocation', *Landscape Architecture Australia*, no. 156, November.

Rigby, M 2018, 'Yam Island homes destroyed as king tide raises calls for better flood protection', *ABC News*, 6 February, <http://www.abc.net.au/news/2018-02-06/yam-island-locals-lose-everything-as-king-tide-causes-floods/9397794>.

Robertson, J 2017, ' 'Alarming' rise in Queensland tree clearing as 400,000 hectares stripped', *The Guardian*, 5 October, <https://www.theguardian.com/environment/2017/oct/05/alarming-rise-in-queensland-tree-clearing-as-400000-hectares-stripped>.

Romensky, L 2016, 'Boort's significant Indigenous history on a global scale', *ABC Central Victoria*, 12 February, <http://www.abc.net.au/news/2016-02-12/boorts-indigenous-history-on-a-global-scale/7164258>.

Rowland, MJ & Ulm, S 2011, 'Indigenous Fish Traps and Weirs of Queensland', *Queensland Archaeological Review*, vol. 14.

Sanders, W (ed.) 2016, *Engaging Indigenous Economies: Debating Diverse Approaches*, Research Monograph, no. 35, ANU Press, Canberra, ACT, Australia.

Schetzer, A 2016, 'Fighting for survival, some animals and plants are thriving in the heart of Melbourne', *The Age*, 30 April, <https://www.theage.com.au/national/victoria/fighting-for-survival-some-animals-and-plants-are-thriving-in-the-heart-of-melbourne-20160428-gogzle.html>.

Schultz, R & Cairney, S 2017, 'Caring for country and the health of Aboriginal and Torres Strait Islander Australians', *The Medical Journal of Australia*, vol. 207, no. 1.

Schwägerl, C 2011, 'Living in the Anthropocene: Toward a New Global Ethos', *Yale Environment 360*, 24 January, <http://e360.yale.edu/features/living_in_the_anthropocene_toward_a_new_global_ethos>.

Shiell, A & Stephen, A (eds), *The Lie of the Land*, National Centre for Australian Studies, Monash University, Clayton, Victoria, Australia.

Smallacombe, S, Davis, M, Quiggin R et al. 2007, *Scoping project on Aboriginal Traditional Knowledge*, Report 22, Desert Knowledge CRC, Alice Springs, Northern Territory, Australia.

Smithson, A & P 1993, *Italian Thoughts*, Alison & Peter Smithson, London, UK (printed in Sweden).

Smyth, RB 1878, *The aborigines of Victoria: with notes relating to the habits of the natives of other parts of Australia and Tasmania*, J. Ferres, Government Printer, Melbourne, Victoria, Australia.

Till, J 2009, *Architecture Depends*, MIT Press, Cambridge, Massachusetts, USA, and London, UK.

The Holy Bible, New International Version, Grand Rapids: Zondervan Publishing House, 1984.

Topos, 2015, monographic issue on *Resilient Cities and Landscapes*, no. 90.

Tschumi B, 1996, *Architecture and Disjunction*, MIT Press, Cambridge, Massachusetts, USA, and London, UK.

Threlfall, CG, Mata, L, Mackie JA, Hahs AK, Stork, NE, Williams NSG & Livesley, SJ 2017, 'Increasing biodiversity in urban green spaces through simple vegetation interventions', *Journal of Applied Ecology*, vol. 54, no. 6, Wiley Online Library, <http://onlinelibrary.wiley.com/doi/10.1111/1365-2664.12876full?platform=hootsuite>.

U.N. General Assembly 2002, *Report of the World Summit on Sustainable Development Johannesburg, South Africa*, 26 August-4 September, United Nations, New York, USA.

Vanderbilt, T 2002, 'A Thousand Words: Simon Starling Talks about Kakteenhaus', *Magazine Article ArtForum International, Questia: Trusted online research*, <https://www.questia.com/magazine/1G1-101779189/a-thousand-words-simon-starling-talks-about-kakteenhaus>.

VCAA (Victorian Curriculum and Assessment Authority) n.d., *Victorian Aboriginal Languages: History* <http://www.vcaa.vic.edu.au/documents/alcv/history.pdf>.

Victorian Heritage Database. 2017, *Aboriginal Canoe Tree, Mount Mary Vineyard*, <http://vhd.heritagecouncil.vic.gov.au/places/115085/download-report>.

Vincent, E & Neale, T 2017, 'Unstable relations: a critical appraisal of indigeneity and environmentalism in contemporary Australia', *Australian Journal of Anthropology*, vol. 28.

von Uexküll, J 1940, *A Foray Into the Worlds of Animals and Humans*, Minnesota University Press, Minneapolis, USA (2010).

Wainwright, O 2017, 'Plant power: why greenery is more than just a fig leaf for urban development', *The Guardian*, 21 February <https://www.theguardian.com/cities/2017/feb/20/power-plants-reen-finger-good-for-development>.

Walliss, J 2017, 'A failed manifesto: OMA and the Australian countryside', *ArchitectureAU*, 12 October, <https://architectureau.com/articles/the-antipodean-limits-of-a-manifesto-oma-and-the-australian-countryside-1/?utm source=ArchitectureAU&utm campaign=516ee136b0->.

Walliss, J 2017, 'The Antipodean limits of a manifesto: OMA and the Australian countryside', *Landscape Australia*, 10 October, <https://landscapeaustralia.com/articles/the-antipodean-limits-of-a-manifesto-oma-and-the-australian-countryside/>.

Ward, C 2016, 'An historic handful of dirt: Whitlam and the legacy of the Wave Hill Walk-Off', *The Conversation*, 21 August, <https://theconversation.com/an-historic-handful-of-dirt-whitlam-and-the-legacy-of-the-wave-hill-walk-off-63700>.

Washington, H 2015, *Demystifying Sustainability: Towards Real Solutions*, Routledge, London, UK and New York, USA.

Whitworth, D 2017, 'Do Not Mow: planting a subtle argument', *Landscape Australia*, 12 October, <https://landscapeaustralia.com/articles/do-not-mow-planting-a-subtle-argument/>.

Williams, N, Marshall, A & Morgan JW (eds) 2015, *Land of Sweeping Plains: Managing and Restoring the Native Grasslands of South-Eastern Australia*, CSIRO Publishing, Clayton South, Victoria, Australia.

Wilsen, EN (ed.), *We Are Here. Politics of Aboriginal Land Tenure*, University of California Press, Berkeley, USA.

Winton, T 2015, *Island Home: A Landscape Memoir*, Penguin, Melbourne, Victoria, Australia.

Wohlleben, P 2016, *The Hidden Life of Trees: What They Feel, How They Communicate – Discoveries from a Secret World*, Blanc Inc., Carlton, Victoria, Australia.

Wright, L 2016, 'Iredale Pedersen Hook wins international prize', *ArchitectureAU*, 20 June, <https://architectureau.com/articles/iredale-pedersen-hook-wins-international-prize/>.

Zardini, M 2009, 'Different Ways of Becoming Green, Environmentally Friendly and Sustainable', *Lotus*, no. 140, monographic issue on *Sustainability*.

Zardini, M 2015, 'Toward a Sensorial Urbanism', *Lotus*, no. 157, monographic issue on *City as nature*.

Zillman, S & and O'Brien, K 2016, 'Wave Hill 50th anniversary: Stockmen who walked off station pause to remember', *ABC News*, 19 August, <http://www.abc.net.au/news/2016-08-18/wave-hill-stockman-remember-50th-anniversary/7760708>.

Zola, N & Gott, B 1992, *Koorie Plants, Koorie People: traditional Aboriginal food, fibre and healing plants of Victoria*. Koorie Heritage Trust, Melbourne, Victoria, Australia.

Principal Partner

Austral Bricks

As the 2018 Australian Pavilion Principal Partner, Austral Bricks have been closely involved with the Venice Architecture Biennale since 2008. Once more, we are immensely proud to play our part in the 2018 exhibition and look forward to continuing our association into the future. By helping to support the Australian Exhibition at the Venice Architecture Biennale, we also demonstrate our long-standing relationship with the architecture community in Australia.

As Australia's largest manufacturer of a wide range of building products, our organisation collaborates with architects in many different ways. This includes bespoke product development, providing expert advice on designing with building materials and facilitating thought-provoking educational programs.

Recent developments in Australian architecture are a particular source of pride for us. This year's Biennale is another step forward in the evolution of design excellence and recognition of Australian architecture on the international stage. As both manufacturer and supplier we are attuned to the needs of those who are helping to shape the modern built environment. What better place to celebrate this collaboration than at the 2018 Venice Architecture Biennale with a record contingent of Australia's architectural community.

Associate Partner

Smeg Australia

Smeg Australia has proudly supported Australia's exhibition at the Venice Architecture Biennale since 2012. Recognising the importance of this international event, Smeg Australia is honoured to be a part of Australia's role in this global conversation on architecture. Through the hard work and dedication of the creative directors, Australia has produced outstanding exhibitions, contributing to the international architectural industry and proudly representing the nation at the Biennale.

Smeg Australia values the importance of quality design, technology and sustainability, supporting the significant role architects play by shaping the spaces our communities live, work and play in. Through its involvement in the Venice Architecture Biennale program, Smeg has developed a significant understanding of architect's needs, challenges and opportunities, which are evident in its close collaborations with Italy's and some of the world's leading architects.

Taking the opportunity to enrich the experience of the Australian architects who attend the Venice Architecture Biennale Vernissage, Smeg host a bespoke tour of the Emilia Romagna region, the location for its international headquarters, immersing the guests in Italian culture, history, architecture, food and wine.

Smeg Australia look forward to seeing Repair come to life for the 2018 Venice Architecture Biennale. Sparking conversation around the future of our environments and the role architects play in that, we have no doubt that Australia's success at the Venice Architecture Biennale will continue to grow.

Wood Solutions

A dialogue with Associate Professor Jacki Schirmer,
University of Canberra Health Research Institute, on Workplace:
Wellness + Wood = Productivity
Biophilic design stems from biophilia, meaning the love of nature,
a term made popular by American psychologist Edward O. Wilson in
the 1980s, when he noted how urbanisation led to a detachment from
the natural world.

In Harmony with the natural world
Biophilia is actually a pretty simple concept, this idea that
humans need to be connected to nature for our wellbeing.

Current research on workplace biophilic design.
Until recently, we've really not had a whole lot of evidence to support
that common hypothesis that having things like wooden surfaces in
the office would be good for your wellbeing. What I found and got really
excited about was that there's a really strong association between the
presence of wood and wellbeing. I've rarely seen a data* set or a study
which has shown such a clear link.

If you're a worker and you could see no wooden surfaces at all from
your workplace, 53% of that type of worker was satisfied with what was
going on in their workplace. When you move that up to having eight or
more wooden surfaces -we're talking things here like wooden chairs,
wooden panelling on the walls, wooden floorboards, even quite small
wooden items- but if you get to eight or more, then 82% of people were
satisfied with their work.

Benefits of biophilic design
Having wooden surfaces in your workplace is strongly associated with:
improved worker wellbeing, workplace satisfaction, and with all the
positive things that can flow from that like improved productivity.

*The survey results were based on the results
of an online survey of 1000 'typical' Australians working
in indoor environments.

Associate Partner

bespoke
careers

Bespoke Careers

Bespoke Careers are excited to be a part of the 2018 Australian
Pavilion exhibition at the Venice Architecture Biennale for the first time.
As a global team of knowledgeable, empathetic and well connected
individuals supporting the profession, we wanted to extend this
relationship to the world stage of architecture, at the Architecture
Biennale. We are a team that is passionate about design and the
profession we work with, but what really drives us is making the right
connections. It's no accident that we have offices located in world's
most creative cities. This is where the talent is and that's what we thrive
on. Helping individuals find their dream job and working with design
studios to secure exceptional talent is our thing.

Network Venice – Platinum Partner

HASSELL

Network Venice – Gold Partners

TERROIR  SILVESTER⅃⅃Uꟻ

 ANITA LUCA
BELGIORNO
NETTIS
FOUNDATION

Network Venice – Silver Partners

A J+C
ALLEN JACK+COTTIER

architectus™

DENTON
CORKER
MARSHALL
architecture + urban design

KENNEDY
NOLAN

Jackson
Clements
Burrows
Architects

HILLAM
ARCHITECTS

MIRVAC
DESIGN

Clarke
Hopkins
Clarke

NHArchitecture

TKDArchitects
Tanner Kibble Denton

SCCI

Network Venice – Bronze Partners

Monash University
Bijl Architecture
Collins and Turner

SJB Architects
University of Adelaide

University of Queensland
School of Architecture
University of Sydney

Government Support

Catalogue Partner

Australian Cultural Fund Donors

Janet Holmes à Court
Penelope Seidler

Media Partner

architecturemedia

In Kind Partners

Philips
Aesop
NDYLIGHT
Perks and Mini
Planned Cover

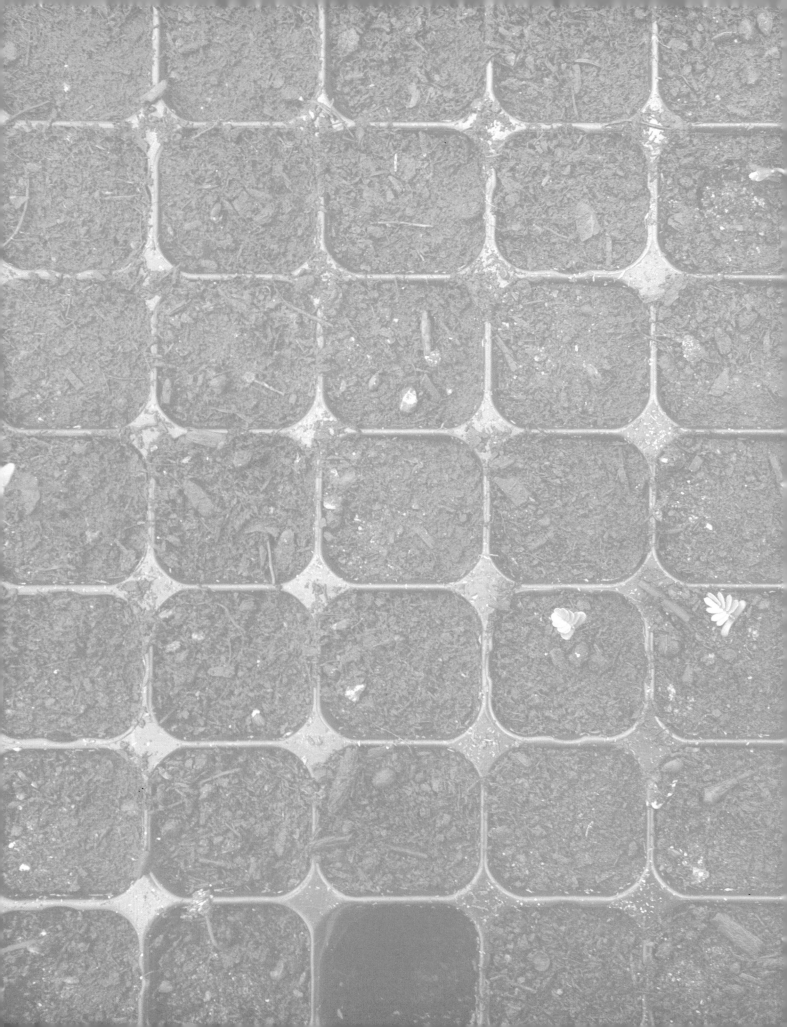